SOCIAL CONSTRUCTION

A READER

SOCIAL CONSTRUCTION

A READER

EDITED BY
MARY GERGEN AND KENNETH J. GERGEN

SAGE Publications
Los Angeles • London • New Delhi • Singapore

First published 2003
Reprinted 2005, 2007, 2008

SAGE Publications Ltd
1 Oliver's Yard 55 City Road
London EC1Y 1SP

SAGE Publications Inc
2455 Teller Road
Thousands Oaks, California 91320

SAGE Publications India Pvt Ltd
B1/I1 Mohan Cooperative Industrial Area
Mathura Road, New Delhi 110 044
India

SAGE Publications Asia-Pacific Pte Ltd
33 Pekin Street #02-01
Far East Square
Singapore 048763

British Library Cataloguing in Publication data

A catalogue record for this book is available
from the British Library

ISBN: 978-0-7619-7229-7

Library of Congress Control Number: 2002111615

contents

ACKNOWLEDGEMENTS

The authors and publishers wish to thank the following for permission to use copyright material. Every effort has been made to trace all of copyright holders but if any have been inadvertently overlooked, the publishers will be pleased to make the necessary arrangements at the first opportunity.

Reading 1: The University of Chicago Press for excerpts from Kuhn, T. (1970) *The Structure of Scientific Revolutions*, Chicago: The University of Chicago Press pp. 4,5, 10–11, 37–39, 84–85, 94.

Reading 2: Pearson Education for excerpts from Garfinkel, H. (1965) *Studies in Ethnomethodology*, New Jersey: Prentice Hall. pp. 35–38, 42–44.

Reading 3: American Psychological Association for 'The Social Constructionist Movement in Modern Psychology', *American Psychologist*, 40, pp. 266–275.

Reading 4: Blackwell Publishers for Wittgenstein, L. (1963) *Philosophical Investigations*, Oxford: Blackwell Publishers Ltd., pp. 8–15.

Reading 5: University of Wisconsin Press for McCloskey, D. N. (1998) *The Rhetoric of Economics*, Madison: University of Wisconsin Press, pp. 21–27.

Reading 6: Gudmund Iversen for Iversen, G. R. (2000) *Knowledge as a Numbers Game* (Not yet published).

Reading 7: The University of Chicago Press for Martin, E. (1996) 'The egg and the sperm: How science has constructed a romance based on stereotypical male-female roles', From Keller, E. and Longino (eds) *Feminism and Science*, Oxford: Oxford University Press, pp. 103–117. Originally published in *Signs: Journal of Women in Culture and Society*, Vol. 16, No. 3 (1991), Chicago: The University of Chicago Press.

Reading 8: The University of Chicago Press for Lutz, C. A. (1988) *Unnatural Emotions*, Chicago: The University of Chicago Press, pp. 53–76.

Reading 9: Regents of the University of California and the University of California Press for Morris, D. B. (1991) *The Culture of Pain*, Berkeley: University of California Press, pp. 31–37.

Reading 10: Reproduced by permission of Georges Borchardt, Inc. for the Editions Gallimard, Foucault, M. (1980) *The History of Sexuality*, Vol. 1 New York: Random House, Inc., pp. 58–70. Originally published in French as *La Volonte du Savior*, France: Editions Gallimard.

Reading 11: Columbia University Press for excerpts from Willis, P. (1977) *Learning to Labour: How Working Class Kids get Working Class Jobs*, New York: Columbia University Press, pp. 1–4, 11–16, 22–24.

Reading 12: Routledge for Gergen, M. (1997) 'Life Stories: Pieces of a Dream', In Gergen, M. and Davis, S. N. (eds) *Toward a New Psychology of Gender*, New York: Routledge, pp. 203–215.

Reading 13: AltaMira Press for Tillmann-Healy, L. M. (1996) 'A Secret Life in a Culture of Thinness', in Ellis, C. and Bochner, A. (eds) *Composing Ethnography*, CA: AltaMira Press, pp. 76–105.

Reading14: Reprinted by permission of Westview Press, a member of Perseus Books, L.L.C. Lather, P. and Smithies, C. (1997) *Troubling the Angels: Women living with HIV/AIDS*, New York: Westview Press, pp. 128–131.

Reading 15: AltaMira Press for Fox, K.V. (1996) 'Silent Voices: A subversive Reading of Child Sexual Abuse', in Ellis, C. and Bochner, A. (eds) *Composing Ethnography*, CA: AltaMira Press, pp. 330–356.

Reading 16: The Apex Press for De Roux, G. (1991) 'Together against the Computer: PAR and the Struggle of Afro-Columbians for Public Service', in Fals-Borda, O. & Rahman, M. (eds) *Action and Knowledge: Breaking the Monopoly with Participatory Action Research*, New York: The Apex Press, pp. 37–53.

Reading 17: Sage Publications Inc. and Marcelo Diversi for Diversi, M. (1998) 'Glimpses of Street life: Representing Lived Experience Through Short Stories', *Qualitative Inquiry*, Vol. 4, pp. 131–147.

Reading 18: Westview Press for Sampson, E. F. (1993) *Celebrating the Other: A Dialogic Account of Human Nature*, CO: Westview Press, pp. 42–65.

Reading 19: Reproduced by permission of Routledge, Inc., part of the Taylor & Francis Group. Butler, J. (1990) *Gender Trouble*, New York: Routledge, pp. 142–149.

Reading 20: Sage Publications Inc and John Shotter for Shotter, J. (1990) 'The Social Construction of Remembering & Forgetting', in Middleton, D. and Edwards, D. (eds) *Collective Remembering*, Thousand Oaks: Sage Publications, pp. 20–138.

Reading 21: Cambridge University Press for Billig, M. (1999) *Freudian Repression: Conversation Creating the Unconscious*, Cambridge: Cambridge University Press, pp. 42–57.

Reading 22: Blackwell Publishing Ltd for Harre, R. (1986) *The Social Construction of Emotions*, Oxford: Blackwell, pp. 4–7.

Reading 23: Lawrence Erlbaum Associates Ltd. for Gergen, K.J. (1994) 'The Communal Creation of Meaning', in Overton, W.F. and Palermo, D.S. (eds) *The Nature and Ontogenesis of Meaning*, NJ: Erlbaum, pp. 17–40.

Reading 24: White, M. (1990) 'Narrative Therapy and Externalizing the Problem' In White, M. and Epston, D. (1990) *Narrative Means to Therapeutic Ends*. With permission from W.W. Norton and Company Ltd.

Reading 25: Reproduced by permission of Harvard University Press from Bruner, J. (2000) *The Culture of Education*, Cambridge, Mas.: Harvard University Press, pp. 19–25, Copyright 1996 by the President and Fellows of Harvard College.

Reading 26: Stipes Publishing L.L.C. for Cooperrider, D. and Whitney, D. (2000) 'A Positive Revolution in Change: Appreciative Inquiry', in Cooperrider, D., Sorensen, P., Whitney, D. and Yaeger, T. (eds) *Appreciative Inquiry*, Champaign, Illinios; Stipes Publishing L.L.C. pp. 4–7 and 17–24.

Reading 27: The Haworth Press, Inc. Becker, C., Chasin, L., Chasin, R., Herzig, M. Roth, S. (1995) 'From Stuck Debate to New Conversation on Controversial Issues; A Report from the Public Conversations Project', *Journal of Feminist Family Therapy*, Vol. 7. New York: The Haworth Press, pp. 143–163.

Reading 28: Paladin and Grafton Books for Barthes, R. (1973) *Mythologies*, London: Paladin and Grafton Books, pp. 15–26.

Reading 29: Wylie Agency for Dorfman, A. (1983) *The Empire's Old Clothes: What the Lone Ranger, Barbar, and Other Innocent Heroes do to Our Minds*', New York: Pantheon Books, pp. 3–63.

Reading 30: Taylor & Francis for Hebdige, D. (1979) 'Style in Revolt: Revolting Style', in *Subculture: The Meaning of Style*, London: Routledge, pp. 106–117.

Reading 31: Palgrave Publishers Ltd. for Odeh, A.L. (1997) 'Post-Colonial Feminism and the Veil', *Feminist Review*, Vol. 43, pp. 26–37, Hampshire: Palgrave Publishers Ltd.

Reading 32: Derek Edwards, Malcolm Ashmore and Jonathan Potter for Edwards, D., Ashmore, M. and Potter, J. (1995) 'Death and Furniture: The Rhetoric, Politics and Theology of Bottom Line Arguments against Relativism', *History of the Human Sciences*, Vol. 8, pp. 26–35.

Reading 33: Sage Publications Ltd. for Hepburn, A. (2000) On the Alleged Incompatibility Between Relatavism and Feminist Psychology, *Feminism and Psychology*, Vol. 10, pp. 91–106.

Reading 34: New York University Press for Bohan, J. and Russel, G. (1999) *Conversations About Psychology and Sexual Orientation*, New York: New York University Press, pp. 19–29.

**the social construction of the real
and the good**

part one

Contemporary constructionism has multiple roots. They grow from a variety of different dialogues that span the humanities and the sciences. In this sense, social constructionism is not a singular and unified position. Rather, it is better seen as an unfolding dialogue among participants who vary considerably in their logics, values, and visions. To be sure, there is substantial sharing, but there is no single slate of assumptions to which all would adhere. And the dialogues remain in motion. To articulate a final truth, a foundational logic, or a code of values would indeed be antithetical to the flow of the dialogue itself.

This initial group of readings gives voice to a number of important contributions to contemporary constructionism. Although there are seven contributions comprising this section, in an important sense they represent three major lines of argument central to a constructionist sensibility.

THE COMMUNAL ORIGINS OF KNOWLEDGE

Perhaps the pivotal assumption around which the constructionist dialogues revolve is that what we take to be knowledge of the world and self finds its origins in communal interchange. What we take to be true as opposed to false, objective as opposed to subjective, scientific as opposed to mythological is brought into being by historically and culturally located groups of people. This view stands in dramatic contrast to two of the most important intellectual and cultural traditions of the West. First the tradition of the individual knower, the rational, self-directing and knowledgeable agent of action is thrown into question. We shall have much to say about this conception as the volume unfolds, but for now it is important to recognize that the constructionist dialogues will challenge the individualist tradition, and increasingly invite an appreciation of relationship as central to knowledge and human well-being. Second, the communal view of knowledge also represents a major challenge to the view of Truth, or the possibility that any one arrangement of words is necessarily more objective or accurate in its depiction of reality than any other. To be sure, accuracy may be achieved within a given community (not Truth but 'truth'), but any attempt to determine the superior account would itself be the outcome of a given community of agreement. All authorities of truth are thus both legitimated and relativized.

Without doubt, the most influential opening to the communal view of knowledge is located in the pages of Thomas Kuhn's 1962 volume, *The Structure of Scientific Revolutions*. At one point this book was the most frequently cited book in the English language. In Reading I we include several excerpts from this work, which together demonstrate perhaps the central thesis of the volume. As Kuhn proposed, knowledge within any discipline depends on a communally shared commitment to a *paradigm*. Roughly speaking, a paradigm consists of (1) an array of assumptions about what exists (ontology), how it may be known (epistemology), and how scientific work 'ought' to proceed (ethics), and (2) a pattern of activities held to be consistent with these assumptions. The importance of Kuhn's proposal is twofold: first, a commitment to a paradigm must *precede* the generation of knowledge. Thus it is the commitment to an *a priori* set of assumptions and practices that makes knowledge possible. In effect, different paradigms will create different scientific realities, and there is no means of standing outside a paradigm of some kind to adjudicate among them. Truth exists only within a paradigm. The second significant point is that individual minds are not the source of knowledge, but communities – people in relationship. Individual knowledge, on this account, is not a private achievement but owes its origins to community participation.

While Kuhn's work grew from the soil of historical study, highly congenial ideas had also been brewing for many years within sociology. Mannheim's *Ideology and Utopia*, Fleck's *Genesis and Development of a Scientific Fact*, and Berger and Luckmann's *The Social Construction of Reality*, among others, had all been concerned with the social processes giving rise to scientific truth claims. Such work also contained important implications that went far beyond the realm of science. Rather, one could begin to see that everyday knowledge – indeed the grounds for all our daily activity – were also lodged in community negotiations. These implications were made most fully apparent by the work of sociologist, Harold Garfinkel (Reading 2) and his colleagues. As Garfinkel reasoned, built into the conventions of ongoing conversation are 'methods' for *creating* various events, objects, institutions, and the like as 'real.' These reality-generating practices are termed 'ethnomethods'. For example, to classify a particular event as a 'suicide' requires that people come to an agreement that, from the enormous and complex flux of everyday life events, a certain configuration counts as suicide. Depending on the ethnomethods in operation, however, what one group might call suicide could be interpreted as 'an act of honor,' or an 'accident' or, given a certain kind of conversation we might come to see all cigarette smokers as engaged in suicidal behavior. As Garfinkel also reasoned, these unwritten agreements can be fragile; if participants question them the consequences can be painful (e.g. asking a natural scientist to be clear on what 'material' is). The Garfinkel contribution we include here demonstrates our high degree of dependence on our ethnomethods, and the intense frustration that can result from failures to participate in them. In a broad sense, this reading points to the enormous trust we must place in each other from moment to moment to support the common rules for constructing reality.

Over time the work of historians of science, sociologists of knowledge, and other like-minded scholars leaped across disciplinary boundaries, co-mingled, and concatenated. Slowly it became possible to discern family resemblances within the various forms of argument and to articulate a set of assumptions with application across all disciplines of knowledge. We excerpt here from what became a pivotal demonstration in psychology, Kenneth Gergen's 1985 article, 'The Social Constructionist Movement in Modern Psychology.' We include the excerpt (Reading 3) primarily as a way of bringing clarity to central constructionist ideas as they had developed and to demonstrate the kinds of challenge they pose to more traditional disciplines. This excerpt also brings into focus the significance of language within the constructionist dialogues, a topic addressed by the next set of readings. For more extended accounts the reader might wish to explore Latour's *Science in Action*, McCarthy's *Knowledge as Culture*, Potter's *Representing Reality*, or Abhib and Hesse's *The Construction of Reality*.

THE CENTRALITY OF LANGUAGE

Many scholars believe that Ludwig Wittgenstein (Reading 4) was the most significant philosopher of the 20th century. After reading his later work, in particular, one can never see the aim of philosophy in the same way again. Why? In large measure because Wittgenstein's work challenged the capacity of philosophy to yield true understanding of knowledge, rationality, ethics, the self, and all the other subjects of longstanding concern. As Wittgenstein proposed, our descriptions and explanations of the world are created within linguistic exchange, or what he calls 'language games.' Games of language are essentially constituted in a rule-like fashion; to make sense at all requires that one play by the rules. The rules of grammar present the most obvious case; but there are also myriad rules of content. For example, we cannot say that 'my love is oblong,' not because it is grammatically incorrect, nor because such a statement is empirically falsifiable. Rather, our ways of describing love in the 21st century do not happen to include the adjective, 'oblong.' Expanding on this point, we can see the major questions asked by philosophers as forms of language games. The long-standing epistemological problem of whether the mind truly has access to the world as it is, for example, is a problem only within a given game of language? We must agree to a game in which there is a 'mental world' on the one hand and a 'material world' on the other (an 'in here' and 'out there') for the question of epistemology to be intelligible or important. If you do not agree to play by the rules, there is no 'problem of individual knowledge.'

In the present volume we feature only a brief excerpt from Wittgenstein's major work, *Philosophical Investigations*. It is important to note that Wittgenstein viewed language games as embedded in what he called 'forms of life,' that is, patterns of relationship of humans and the world about them. This broader vision of language games is congenial with the Kuhn and Garfinkel views of knowledge or understanding as communally created. Central to the community is obviously a shared language and that language serves to 'make real' the objects or events within that community. The form of life within the community is quite similar to what Kuhn means by 'paradigms' within various sectors of science.

The constructionist emphasis on language has brought new life to one of the oldest academic disciplines in Western culture, namely rhetoric. For early Romans, rhetorical skill – or essentially the ability to persuade – was held essential for effective participation in civic life. Although rhetoric continued to play an important part in higher education over the centuries, the 20th century prizing of science cast a pall over the discipline. As commonly held, the scientific goal was to describe and explain nature as it is – accurately and objectively. Arts of persuasion were not only irrelevant, from this standpoint, but detrimental to good science. The good scientist should be insulated from the force of pretty words, oratory, or beautiful metaphors – all 'mere rhetoric'. Yet, once we realize that objects of study come to be what they are within communities of language users, the idea of 'an object' or 'a fact' uncontaminated by language ceases to be compelling. Effective science and effective rhetoric are hand in glove. Rhetoric is essentially successful communication by the standards of a particular community. McClosky's 1985 work, *The Rhetoric of Economics*, was a ground breaking demonstration of this view. We select several passages here (Reading 5) that emphasize the literary/aesthetic grounds for what are otherwise taken to be hard-boiled economic concepts. The interested reader might also wish to explore Simons' *The Rhetorical Turn*, or Nelson, Megill and McClosky's *The Rhetoric of the Human Sciences*.

Aren't there means of protecting scientific conclusions from the force of language? In traditional science one major vehicle for ensuring against 'subjective' bias and achieving both accuracy and reliability is the technology of statistics. Statistical formulations are the result of pure logic, it is argued, and statistical outcomes don't depend on the particular values or ideologies of the investigator. In Reading 6, Gudmund Iversen, a Professor of Statistics at Swarthmore College, provides a significant challenge to the traditional assumptions. As his reading demonstrates, when subjected to differing statistical procedures (one might say paradigms), the same data can be used to draw quite diverse – even antithetical – conclusions. In effect, statistics is also a language, and it too can be used to construct the world in a variety of ways.

THE IDEOLOGICAL SATURATION OF KNOWLEDGE

The increased awareness of the communal construction of knowledge, along with its linguistic constraints, do far more than unsettle our traditional beliefs in truth, objectivity and knowledge – beyond history and culture. Thrown into question is also the right of any particular group – scientific or otherwise – to claim ultimate authority of knowledge. Such a conclusion has had enormous repercussions in the academic community and beyond. This is so especially for scholars and practitioners concerned with social injustice, oppression, and the marginalization of minority groups in society. If communities create realities (facts and good reasons) congenial to their own traditions, and these realities are established as true and good for all, then alternative traditions will be obliterated, and the people who represent these traditions will be devalued. Thus, all statements of scientific fact, canons of logic, foundations of law, or spiritual truths will either explicitly or implicitly favor certain ways of life over others. For example, a scientist may use the most rigorous methods of testing intelligence, but the indirect effects of presuming that 'there is intelligence' and that 'people differ in their possession of this capacity' are specific to a given tradition or paradigm. Merely entering the paradigm and moving within the tradition is deeply injurious to those people classified as inferior by its standards. In effect, the longstanding distinction between *facts* and *value* – objective reflections of the world, and subjective desires or feelings of 'ought' – cannot be sustained.

The literature on the political and moral saturation of seemingly 'objective descriptions' of the world is now staggering. Fausto-Sterling's *Myths of Gender: Theories About Women and Men*, Keller's *Reflections on Gender and Science*, and Prilletensky's *The Morals and Politics of Psychology* are all good beginnings to the dialogue. The present offering by Emily Martin (Reading 7) has played a powerful role in the debates on knowledge as ideology. The importance is partly owing to the fact that Martin takes as her target the boastfully non-partisan truth claims of the natural sciences, including medicine. Her specific focus is on the traditional biological account of fertilization, and the common presumption (observable 'fact') that the male sperm penetrates the female egg. As Martin demonstrates, there are many ways of telling this story, and the traditional one not only privileges an androcentric view of male-female relations, but also narrows the potentials of the science.

REFERENCES

Arbib, M.A., and Hesse, M. B. (1986). *The construction of reality*. Cambridge: Cambridge University Press.

Berger, P. & Luckmann, T. (1967). *The social construction, of reality*. London: Allen Lane.

Fausto-Sterling, A. (1985). *Myths of gender: Theories about women and men*. New York: Basic books.

Fleck, L. (1979) *Genesis and development of a scientific fact.* Chicago: University of Chicago Press.

Keller, E. F. (1985). *Reflections on women and science.* New Haven: Yale University Press.

Kuhn, T. S. (1962). *The structure of scientific revolutions.* Chicago: University of Chicago Press.

Latour, B. (1987). *Science in action.* Cambridge, MA: Harvard University Press.

Mannheim, K. (1951). *Ideology and utopia.* New York: Harcourt Brace.

McCarthy, E. D. (1996). *Knowledge as culture.* New York: Routledge.

McCloskey, P.N. (1985). *The rhetoric of economics.* Madison, WI: University of Wisconsin Press.

Nelson, J.S., Megill, A. and McCloskey, D. (Eds) (1987) *The rhetoric of the human sciences.* Madison: University of Wisconsin Press.

Potter, J. (1996). *Representing reality.* London: Sage.

Prilletensky, I. (1994). *The morals and politics of psychology.* Albany, NY: SUNY Press.

Simons, H. W. (Ed.) (1990). *The rhetorical turn.* Chicago: University of Chicago Press.

Wittgenstein, L. (1978). *Philosophical investigations.* Oxford: Blackwell.

1

on scientific paradigms

thomas s. kuhn

Effective research scarcely begins before a scientific community thinks it has acquired firm answers to questions like the following: What are the fundamental entities of which the universe is composed? How do these interact with each other and with the senses? What questions may legitimately be asked about such entities and what techniques employed in seeking solutions? At least in the mature sciences [e.g. physics, chemistry] answers to questions like these are firmly embedded in the educational initiation that prepares and licenses the student for professional practice. Because that education is both rigorous and rigid, these answers come to exert a deep hold on the scientific mind. That they can do so does much to account both for the peculiar efficiency of the normal research activity and for the direction in which it proceeds at any given time.

By choosing (the term, 'paradigm'), I mean to suggest that some accepted examples of actual scientific practice – examples which include law, theory, application, and instrumentation together – provide models from which spring particular coherent traditions of scientific research. These are the traditions which the historian describes under such rubrics as 'Ptolemaic astronomy' (or 'Copernican'), 'Aristotelian dynamics' (or 'Newtonian'), 'corpuscular optics' (or 'wave optics'), and so on. The study of paradigms, including many that are far more specialized than those named illustratively above, is what mainly prepares the student for membership in the particular scientific community with which he will later practice. Because he there joins men who learned the bases of their field from the same concrete models, his subsequent practice will seldom evoke overt disagreement over fundamentals. Men whose research is based on shared paradigms are committed to the same rules and standards for scientific practice. That commitment and the apparent consensus it produces are prerequisites for normal science, i.e., for the genesis and continuation of a particular research tradition.

One of the things a scientific community acquires with a paradigm is a criterion for choosing problems that, while the paradigm is taken for granted, can be assumed to have solutions. To a great extent these are the only problems that the community will admit as scientific or encourage its members to undertake. Other problems, including many that had previously been standard, are rejected as metaphysical, as the concern of another discipline, or sometimes as just too problematic to be worth the time. A paradigm can, for that matter, even insulate the community from those socially important problems that are not reducible to the puzzle form, because they cannot be stated in terms of the conceptual and instrumental tools the paradigm supplies. Such problems can be a distraction, a lesson brilliantly illustrated by several facets of seventeenth-century Baconianism and by some of the contemporary social sciences. One of the reasons why normal science seems to progress so rapidly is that its practitioners concentrate on problems that only their own lack of ingenuity should keep them from solving.

If, however, the problems of normal science are puzzles in this sense, we need no longer ask why scientists attack them with such passion and devotion. A man may be attracted to science for all sorts of reasons. Among them are the desire to be useful, the excitement of exploring new territory, the hope of finding order, and the drive to test established knowledge. These motives and others besides also help to determine the particular problems that will later engage him. Furthermore, though the result is occasional frustration, there is good reason why motives like these should first attract him and then lead him on. The scientific enterprise as a whole does from time to time prove useful, open up new territory, display order, and test long-accepted belief. Nevertheless, *the individual* engaged on a normal research problem *is almost never doing any one of these things*. Once engaged, his motivation is of a rather different sort. What then challenges him is the conviction that, if only he is skilful enough, he will succeed in solving a puzzle that no one before has solved or solved so well. Many of the greatest scientific minds have devoted all of their professional attention to demanding puzzles of this sort. On most occasions any particular field of specialization offers nothing else to do, a fact that makes it no less fascinating to the proper sort of addict.

Turn now to another, more difficult, and more revealing aspect of the parallelism between puzzles and the problems of normal science. If it is to classify as a puzzle, a problem must be characterized by more than an assured solution. There must also be rules that limit both the nature of acceptable solutions and the steps by which they are to be obtained. To solve a jigsaw puzzle is not, for example, merely 'to make a picture.' Either a child or a contemporary artist could do that by scattering selected pieces, as abstract shapes, upon some neutral ground. The picture thus produced might be far better, and would certainly be more original, than the one from which the puzzle had been made. Nevertheless, such a picture would not be a solution. To achieve that, all the pieces must be used, their plain sides must be turned down, and they must be interlocked without forcing until no holes remain. Those are among the rules that govern jigsaw-puzzle solutions. Similar restrictions upon the admissible solutions of crossword puzzles, riddles, chess problems, and so on, are readily discovered.

If we can accept a considerably broadened use of the term 'rule' – one that will occasionally equate it with 'established viewpoint' or with 'preconception' – then the problems accessible within a given research tradition display something much like this set of puzzle characteristics. The man who builds an instrument to determine optical wave lengths must not be satisfied with a piece of equipment that merely attributes particular numbers to particular spectral lines. He is not just an explorer or measurer. On the contrary, he must show, by analyzing his apparatus in terms of the established body of optical theory, that the numbers his instrument produces are the ones that enter theory as wave lengths. If some residual vagueness in the theory or some unanalyzed component of his apparatus prevents his completing that demonstration, his colleagues may well conclude that he has measured nothing at all. For example, the electron-scattering maxima that were later diagnosed as indices of electron wave length had no apparent significance when first observed and recorded. Before they became measures of anything, they had to be related to a theory that predicted the wave-like behavior of matter in motion. And even after that relation was pointed out, the apparatus had to be redesigned so that the experimental results might be correlated unequivocally with theory. Until those conditions had been satisfied, no problem had been solved.

In the development of any science, the first received paradigm is usually felt to account quite successfully for most of the observations and experiments easily accessible to that science's practitioners. Further development, therefore, ordinarily calls for the construction of elaborate equipment, the development of an esoteric vocabulary and skills, and a refinement of concepts that increasingly lessens their resemblance to their usual common-sense prototypes. That professionalization leads, on the one hand, to an immense restriction of the scientist's vision and to a considerable resistance to paradigm change. The science has become increasingly rigid. On the other hand, within those areas to which the paradigm directs the attention of the group, normal science leads to a detail of information and to a precision of the observation-theory match that could be achieved in no other way.

The transition from a paradigm in crisis to a new one from which a new tradition of normal science can emerge is far from a cumulative process, one achieved by an articulation or extension of the old paradigm. Rather it is a reconstruction of the field from new fundamentals, a reconstruction that changes some of the field's most elementary theoretical generalizations as well as many of its paradigm methods and applications. During the transition period there will be a large but never complete overlap between the problems that can be solved by the old and by the new paradigm. But there will also be a decisive difference in the modes of solution. When the transition is complete, the profession will have changed its view of the field, methods, and its goals. One perceptive historian, viewing a classic case of a science's reorientation by paradigm change, recently described it as 'picking up the other end of the stick,' a process that involves 'handling the same bundle of data as before, but placing them in a new system of relations with one another by giving them a different framework.' Others who have noted this aspect of scientific advance have emphasized its similarity to a change in visual gestalt: the marks on paper that were first seen as a bird are now seen as an antelope, or vice versa. That parallel can be misleading. Scientists do not see something *as* something else; instead, they simply see it. We have already examined some of the problems created by saying that Priestley saw oxygen as dephlogisticated air. In addition, the scientist does not preserve the gestalt subject's freedom to switch back and forth between ways of seeing. Nevertheless, the switch of gestalt, particularly because it is today so familiar, is a useful elementary prototype for what occurs in full-scale paradigm shift.

Like the choice between competing political institutions, that between competing paradigms proves to be a choice between incompatible modes of community life. Because it has that character, the choice is not and cannot be determined merely by the evaluative procedures characteristic of normal science, for these depend in part upon a particular paradigm, and that paradigm is at issue. When paradigms enter, as they must, into a debate about paradigm choice, their role is necessarily circular. Each group uses its own paradigm to argue in that paradigm's defense.

The resulting circularity does not, of course, make the arguments wrong or even ineffectual. The man who premises a paradigm when arguing in its defense can nonetheless provide a clear exhibit of what scientific practice will be like for those who adopt the new view of nature. That exhibit can be immensely persuasive, often compellingly so. Yet, whatever its force, the status of the circular argument is only that of persuasion. It cannot be made logically or even probabilistically compelling for those who refuse to step into the circle. The premises and values shared by the two parties to a debate over paradigms are not sufficiently extensive for that. As in political revolutions, so in paradigm choice – there is no standard higher than the assent of the relevant community. To discover how scientific revolutions are effected, we shall therefore have to examine not only the impact of nature and of logic, but also the techniques of persuasive argumentation effective within the quite special groups that constitute the community of scientists.

2

socially negotiating knowledge

harold garfinkel

For Kant the moral order 'within' was an awesome mystery; for sociologists the moral order 'without' is a technical mystery.   Familiar scenes of everyday activities, treated by members as the 'natural facts of life,' are massive facts of the members' daily existence both as a real world and as the product of activities in a real world. They furnish the 'fix,' the 'this is it' to which the waking state returns one, and are the points of departure and return for every modification of the world of daily life that is achieved in play, dreaming, trance, theater, scientific theorizing or high ceremony.

MAKING COMMONPLACE SCENES VISIBLE

In accounting for the stable features of everyday activities sociologists commonly select familiar settings such as familial households or work places and ask for the variables that contribute to their stable features. Just as commonly, one set of considerations are unexamined: the socially standardized and standardizing 'seen but unnoticed,' expected, background features of everyday scenes. The member of the society uses background expectancies as a scheme of interpretation. With their use actual appearances are for him recognizable and intelligible as the appearances-of-familiar-events. Demonstrably he is responsive to this background, while at the same time he is at a loss to tell us specifically of what the expectancies consist. When we ask him about them he has little or nothing to say.

For these background expectancies to come into view one must either be a stranger to the 'life as usual' character of everyday scenes, or become estranged from them. As Alfred Schutz pointed out, a 'special motive' is required to make them problematic. In the sociologists' case this 'special motive' consists in the programmatic task of treating a societal member's practical circumstances, which include from the member's point of view the morally necessary character of many of its background features, as matters of theoretic interest. The seen but unnoticed backgrounds of everyday activities are made visible and are described from a perspective in which persons live out the lives they do, have the children they do, feel the feelings, think the thoughts, enter the relationships they do, all in order to permit the sociologist to solve his theoretical problems.

The study reported in this paper attempts to detect some expectancies that lend commonplace scenes their familiar, life-as-usual character, and to relate these to the stable social structures of everyday activities. Procedurally it is my preference to start with familiar scenes and ask what can be done to make trouble? The operations that one would have to perform in order to multiply the senseless features of perceived environments; to produce and sustain bewilderment, consternation, and confusion; to produce the socially structured affects of anxiety, shame, guilt, and indignation; and to produce disorganized interaction should tell us something about how the structures of everyday activities are ordinarily and routinely produced and maintained.

The anticipation that persons *will* understand, the occasionality of expressions, the specific vagueness of references, the retrospective-prospective sense of a present occurrence, waiting for something later in order to see what was meant before, are sanctioned properties of common discourse. They furnish a background of seen but unnoticed features of common discourse whereby actual utterances are recognized as events of common, reasonable, understandable, plain talk.

Persons require these properties of discourse as conditions under which they are themselves entitled and entitle others to claim that they know what they are talking about, and that what they are saying is understandable and ought to be understood. In short, their seen but unnoticed presence is used to entitle persons to conduct their common conversational affairs without interference. Departures from such usages call forth immediate attempts to restore a right state of affairs.

The sanctioned character of these properties is demonstrable as follows. Students were instructed to engage an acquaintance or a friend in an ordinary conversation and, without indicating that what the experimenter was asking was in any way unusual, to insist that the person clarify the sense of his commonplace remarks. Twenty-three students reported twenty-five instances of such encounters. The following are typical excerpts from their accounts.

CASE 1

The subject was telling the experimenter, a member of the subject's car pool, about having had a flat tire while going to work the previous day.

(S)   I had a flat tire.
(E)   What do you mean, you had a flat tire?

She appeared momentarily stunned. Then she answered in a hostile way: 'What do you mean, "What do you mean?" A flat tire is a flat tire. That is what I meant. Nothing special. What a crazy question!'

CASE 2

(S) Hi, Ray. How is your girl friend feeling?
(E) What do you mean, 'How is she feeling?' Do you mean physical or mental?
(S) I mean how is she feeling? What's the matter with you? (He looked peeved.)
(E) Nothing. Just explain a little clearer what do you mean?
(S) Skip it. How are your Med School applications coming?
(E) What do you mean, 'How are they?'
(S) You know what I mean.
(E) I really don't.
(S) What's the matter with you? Are you sick?

CASE 3

'On Friday night my husband and I were watching television. My husband remarked that he was tired. I asked, "How are you tired? Physically, mentally, or just bored?"'

(S) I don't know, I guess physically, mainly.
(E) You mean that your muscles ache or your bones?
(S) I guess so. Don't be so technical.
     (After more watching)
(S) All these old movies have the same kind of old iron bedstead in them.
(E) What do you mean? Do you mean all old movies, or some of them, or just the ones you have seen?
(S) What's the matter with you? You know what I mean.
(E) I wish you would be more specific.
(S) You know what I mean! Drop dead!

CASE 4

During a conversation (with the E's female fiancee) the E questioned the meaning of various words used by the subject ...

For the first minute and a half the subject responded to the questions as if they were legitimate inquiries. Then she responded with 'Why are you asking me those questions?'

and repeated this two or three times after each question. She became nervous and jittery, her face and hand movements ... uncontrolled. She appeared bewildered and complained that I was making her nervous and demanded that I 'Stop it' ... The subject picked up a magazine and convered her face. She put down the magazine and pretended to be engrossed. When asked why she was looking at the magazine she closed her mouth and refused any further remarks.

CASE 5

My friend said to me, 'Hurry or we will be late.' I asked him what did he mean by late and from what point of view did it have reference? There was a look of perplexity and cynicism on his face. 'Why are you asking me such silly questions? Surely I don't have to explain such a statement. What is wrong with you today? Why should I have to stop to analyze such a statement? Everyone understands my statements and you should be no exception!'

CASE 6

The victim waved his hand cheerily.

(S) How are you?
(E) How am I in regard to what? My health, my finances, my school work, my peace of mind, my ...?
(S) (Red in the face and suddenly out of control.) Look! I was just trying to be polite. Frankly, I don't give a damn how you are.

CASE 7

My friend and I were talking about a man whose overbearing attitude annoyed us. My friend expressed his feeling.

(S) I'm sick of him.
(E) Would you explain what is wrong with you that you are sick?
(S) Are you kidding me? You know what I mean.
(E) Please explain your ailment.
(S) (He listened to me with a puzzled look.) What came over you? We never talk this way, do we?

3

knowledge as socially constructed

kenneth j. gergen

Social constructionist inquiry is principally concerned with explicating the processes by which people come to describe, explain, or otherwise account for the world (including themselves) in which they live. It attempts to articulate common forms of understanding as they now exist, as they have existed in prior historical periods, and as they might exist should creative attention be so directed. At the metatheoretical level most such work manifests one or more of the following assumptions.

What we take to be experience of the world does not in itself dictate the terms by which the world is understood. What we take to be knowledge of the world is not a product of induction, or of the building and testing of general hypotheses. The mounting criticism of the positivist-empiricist conception of knowledge has severely damaged the traditional view that scientific theory serves to reflect or map reality in any direct or decontextualized manner.

The terms in which the world is understood are social artifacts, products of historically situated interchanges among people. From the constructionist position the process of understanding is not automatically driven by the forces of nature, but is the result of an active, cooperative enterprise of persons in relationship. In this light, inquiry is invited into the historical and cultural bases of various forms of world construction. For example, historical investigation has revealed broad historical variations in the concept of the child (Aries, 1962), of romantic love (Averill, 1985), of mother's love (Badinter, 1980), and of self (Verhave & van Hoorne, 1984). In each case constructions of the person or relationships have undergone significant change across time. In certain periods childhood was not considered a specialized phase of development, romantic and maternal love were not components of human makeup, and the self was not viewed as isolated and autonomous. Such changes in conception do not appear to reflect alterations in the objects or entities of concern but seem lodged in historically contingent factors.

The degree to which a given form of understanding prevails or is sustained across time is not fundamentally dependent on the empirical validity of the perspective in question, but on the vicissitudes of social processes (e.g., communication, negotiation, conflict, rhetoric). As proposed in this case, perspectives, views, or descriptions of persons can be retained regardless of variations in their actual conduct. Regardless of the stability or repetition of conduct, perspectives may be abandoned as their intelligibility is questioned within the community of interlocutors. Observation of persons, then, is questionable as a corrective or guide to descriptions of persons. Rather, the rules for 'what counts as what' are inherently ambiguous, continuously evolving, and free to vary with the predilections of those who use them. On these grounds, one is even led to query the concept of truth. Is the major deployment of the term *truth* primarily a means for warranting one's own position and discrediting contenders for intelligibility (Gergen, 1984)?

In this vein, Sabini and Silver (1982) have demonstrated how people manage the definition of morality in relationships. Whether an act is defined as envy, flirtation, or anger floats on a sea of social interchange. Interpretation may be suggested, fastened upon, and abandoned as social relationships unfold across time. In the same way, Mummendey and her colleagues (Mummendey, Bonewasser, Loschper, & Linneweber, 1982) have shown how decisions are reached as to whether an action constitutes aggression. Thus, aggression ceases to exist as a fact in the world and becomes a labeling device for social control.

Forms of negotiated understanding are of critical significance in social life, as they are integrally connected with many other activities in which people engage. Descriptions and explanations of the world themselves constitute forms of social action. As such they are intertwined with the full range of other human activities. The opening, 'Hello, how are you?' is typically accompanied by a range of facial expressions, bodily postures, and movements without which the expression could seem artificial, if not aberrant. In the same way, descriptions and explanations form integral parts of various social patterns. They thus serve to sustain and support certain patterns to the exclusion of others. To alter description and explanation is thus to threaten certain actions and invite others. To construct persons in such a way that they possess inherent sin is to invite certain lines of action and not others. Or to treat depression, anxiety, or fear as emotions from which people involuntarily suffer is to have far different implications than to treat them as chosen, selected, or played out as on a stage.

It is in this vein that many investigators have been concerned with the prevailing images or metaphors of human action employed within the field of psychology. Queries have been raised over the broad social implications of viewing persons as machines (Shotter, 1975), as self-contained individuals (Sampson, 1977, 1983), or as economic bargainers in social relations (Wexler, 1983). Attacks have also been levied against the damaging effects on children of the prevailing constructions of the child's mind (Walkerdine, 1984), the sexism implicit in investigation that assumes the superiority of universal principles in moral decision making (Gilligan, 1982), the effects of theories of cognitive mechanism in their implicit unconcern with material circumstances in society (Sampson, 1981), and the anomic effects of psychological assessment in organizations (Hollway, 1984).

REFERENCES

Aries, P. (1962). *Centuries of childhood: A social history of family life*. New York: Vintage.

Averill, J. (1985). The social construction of emotion: With special reference to love. In K. J. Gergen & K. E. Davis (Eds). *The social construction of the person*. New York: Springer Verlag.

Badinter, E. (1980). *Mother love, myth and reality*. New York: Macmillan.

Gergen, K. J. (1984). Warranting voice and the elaboration of the self. Paper presented at the Wales Conference on Self & Identity, Cardiff, Wales.

Gilligan, C. (1982). *In a different voice*. Cambridge, MA: Harvard University Press.

Hollway, W. (1984). Fitting work: Psychological assessment in organizations. In J. Henriques, W. Hollway, C. Urwin, V. Louze, & V. Walkerdine (Eds). *Changing the subject* (pp. 26–59). London: Metheun.

Mummendey, A., Bonewasser, M., Loschper, G., & Linneweber, V., et al., (1982). It is always somebody else who is aggressive. *Weitschrift fur Sozialpsychologie, 13*, 341–52.

Sabini, J. & Silver, M. (1982). *The moralities of everyday life*. London & New York: Oxford University Press.

Sampson, E. E. (1977). Psychology and the American ideal. *Journal of Personality and Social Psychology, 35*, 767–82.

Sampson, E. E. (1981). Cognitive psychology as ideology. *American Psychologist, 36*, 730–43.

Sampson, E. E. (1983). Deconstructing psychology's subject. *Journal of Mind and Behavior, 4*, 135–64.

Shotter, J. (1975). *Images of man in psychological research*. London: Metheun.

Verhave, R. & van Hoorne, W. (1984). The temporalization of the self. In K. J. Gergen & M. M. Gergen (Eds). *Historical social psychology* (pp. 325–46). Hillsdale, NJ: Erlbaum.

Walkerdine, V. (1984). Developmental psychology and the child-centered pedagogy. In J. Henriques, W. Hollway, C. Urwin, V. Louze, & V. Walkerdine (Eds). *Changing the subject* (pp. 153–202). London: Metheun.

Wexler, P. (1983). *Critical social psychology*. Boston: Routledge & Kegan Paul.

4

knowledge as a language game

ludwig wittgenstein

Let us imagine a language ... meant to serve for communication between a builder A and an assistant B. A is building with building-stones: There are blocks, pillars, slabs, and beams. B has to pass the stones, of the type and in the order in which A needs them. For this purpose they use a language consisting of the words 'block', 'pillar', 'slab', 'beam'. A calls them out; – B brings the stone which he has learnt to bring at such-and-such a call. Conceive this as a complete primitive language.

An important part of the training will consist in the [builder's] pointing to the objects, directing the [assistant's] attention to them, and at the same time, uttering a word; for instance, the word 'slab' as he points to that shape.... This ostensive teaching of words can be said to establish an association between the word and the thing. But what does this mean? Well, it may mean various things; but one very likely thinks first of all that a picture of the object comes before the assistant's mind when it hears the word. But now, if this does happen – is it the purpose of the word? ... In the language [of the builder and the assistant] it is *not* the purpose of the words to evoke images.... Don't you understand the call 'Slab' if you act upon it in such-and-such a way?

In the practice of the use of language one party calls out the words, the other acts on them. In instruction in the language the following process will occur: the learner *names* the objects; that is, he utters the word when the teacher points to the stone. And there will be this still simpler exercise: the pupil repeats the words after the teacher – both of these being processes resembling language.

We can also think of the whole process of using words as one of those games by means of which children learn their native language. I will call these games 'language-games' and will sometimes speak of a primitive language as a language-game.

And the processes of naming the stones and of repeating words after someone might also be called language-games. Think of much of the use of words in games like ring-a-ring-a-roses.

I shall also call the whole, consisting of language and the actions into which it is woven, the 'language-game'.

[....] Think of the tools in a tool-box: there is a hammer, pliers, a saw, a screw-driver, a rule, a glue-pot, glue, nails and screws. The functions of words are as diverse as the functions of these objects.

It will be possible to say: In language we have different *kinds of words*. For the functions of the word 'slab' and the word 'block' are more alike than those of 'slab' and 'd'. But how we group words into kinds will depend on the aim of the classification, and on our own inclination.

Think of the different points of view from which one can classify tools or chess-men.

Do not be troubled by the fact this language consists only of orders. If you want to say that this shows them to be incomplete, ask yourself whether our language is complete; whether it was so before the symbolism of chemistry and the notation of the infinitesimal calculus were incorporated in it; for these are, so to speak, suburbs of our language. (And how many houses or streets does it take before a town begins to be a town?) Our language can be seen as an ancient city: a maze of little streets and squares, of old and new houses, and of houses with additions from various periods; and this surrounded by a multitude of new boroughs with straight regular streets and uniform houses.

It is easy to imagine a language consisting only of orders and reports in battle. Or a language consisting only of questions and expressions for answering yes and no. And innumerable others. And to imagine a language means to imagine a form of life.

economics as rhetoric

deirdre n. mccloskey

The idea that science is a way of talking, not a separate realm of Truth, has become common among students of science since Thomas Kuhn. The idea does not imply that science is inconclusive or that literature is cold-blooded. The point is that science uses art for urgent practical purposes daily. The aesthetic judgements necessary before one of the theories in particle physics is selected for the expensive experiment it requires for testing, does not make science arbitrary or flimsy. No one would have financed the British expedition to the South Seas in 1919 to test Einstein's theory had it been thought ugly.

The project here is to overturn the monopolistic authority of Science in economics by questioning the usefulness of the demarcation of science from art. To show that economics resembles literary criticism, philology, and social theory as much as particle physics and dam-building can either thrill economists with a wild surmise or leave them trembling from identity outraged.

PROOFS OF THE LAW OF DEMAND ARE MOSTLY LITERARY

Economics is scientific, I am claiming, but literary too. Saying that something is 'literary' is saying that you can talk of it in ways that sound like the things people say about drama, poetry, novels, and the study of them. Look for example at the performative character of the sentence 'Economics is scientific.' The sentence carries with it the implication that things can be said about economics and economies that use mathematics; the economists will emulate the rhetoric of controlled experiment; that the economists will have 'theorems' from the mathematics and 'findings' from the experiments; that it will be 'objective' (whatever the word might mean); and even that the world it constructs, to use Nelson Goodman's way of talking, will have a certain character, of maximizing and equilibrium, captured in the perspicacious phrase, 'the unreasonable effectiveness of mathematics.' All these implications about economics are persuasive.

But equally persuasive are other implications, usually and erroneously thought to be antithetical to science, implied by the sentence 'Economics is literary.' The literary character of economics shows at various levels, from most abstract to most concrete, from methodology down to the selling of diamonds.

The error is to think that you are engaged in mere making of propositions, about which formal logic speaks, when in fact you are engaged – all day, most days – in persuasive discourse, aimed at some effect about which rhetoric speaks. Scientists are trying to persuade other scientists when they affirm a law. Economics want to persuade themselves of the Law of Demand, that when the relative price of a good increases the quantity demanded of it declines. Consider the good reasons that economists believe the Law of Demand to be persuasive:

1. Sometimes, certain very sophisticated statistical tests of the law applied to entire economies, in which every allowance has been made for bias and incompleteness, have resulted, after a good deal of handwringing and computer-squeezing, in the diagonal elements of certain matrices being negative at the 5 percent level of significance.
2. Less comprehensive but more numerous demonstrations of the law have been attempted market by market. Agricultural economists, especially, have since 1924 been fitting demand curves to statistics on corn and hogs. Again, the curves sometimes give the right slope, and sometimes don't.
3. Some economists have tried to subject the law to a few experimental tests. After a good deal of throat-clearing they have found it to be true for clearheaded rats and false for confused humans, an interesting result which no one worries about too much.

These three arguments are properly 'scientific,' in the strange modern English usage of the word, although only the third quite matches the received view of scientific method. The Scientific arguments yield mixed results.

Does this leave economists uncertain about the Law of Demand? Certainly not. Belief in the Law of Demand is the distinguishing mark of an economist, demarcating her from other social scientists more even than her other peculiar beliefs, such as that assets equal liabilities plus net wealth. Economists believe it ardently. Only some part of their ardor, therefore, is properly Scientific. The rest is below the demarcation line:

4. Introspection is an important source of belief. The economic scientist asks herself, 'What would I do if the price of gasoline doubled?' If properly socialized in economics she will answer, 'I will consume less.' In similar fashion a poet might ask herself what she might do if she saw heather or a wave; a textural critic might ask himself how he would react to a line if *'quod, o patrona virgo'* were emended to *'quidem est, patroni et ergo.'*

5. Thought experiments (common in physics) are persuasive too. The economic scientist asks in view of her experience of life and her knowledge of economics what other people might do if the price of gasoline doubled? A novelist, likewise, might ask how Huck would respond to Jim's slavery, or a critic might ask how an audience would react to the sacrifice of Coriolanus?

6. Cases in point, though not controlled experiments or large samples, persuade to some degree. A big triumph for the Law of Demand in modern economic history was the oil embargo of 1973–1974: the doubling of gasoline prices caused gasoline consumption to decline, although non-economists predicted it would not.

7. The lore of the marketplace persuades. Business people, for instance, believe that the Law of Demand is true, for they cut prices when they wish to raise the quantity demanded. They have the incentive of their livelihood to know rightly. What mere professor would dispute such testimony?

8. The lore of the academy persuades as well. If many wise economists have long affirmed the Law of Demand, what mere latecomer would dispute their testimony? All sciences operate this way, building on the testimony of forerunners. The argument from authority is not decisive, of course, but gives weight. Science could not advance if all questions were reopened every five years.

9. Commonly the symmetry of the law will be a persuasive argument, because, to repeat Kenneth Burke, 'Yielding to the form prepares assent to the matter identified with it.' If there is a Law of Supply – and there is ample reason to think there is – it is hard to resist the symmetrical attractions of a Law of Demand.

10. Mere definition is a powerful argument, and is more powerful the more mathematical the talk. A higher price of gasoline, for instance, leaves less income to be spent on all things, including gasoline (at least by one definition of income, or of the law).

11. Above all, there is analogy. That the Law of Demand is true for purchases of ice cream and movies, which no one would want to deny, makes it more persuasive also for gasoline. Analogy gives the law its majesty.

These are all good reasons for believing the Law of Demand, but only the first three, I repeat, are scientific by the dichotomous definition of English modernism. The other eight are artistic and literary.

6

knowledge as a numbers game

gudmund r. iversen

WHO IS BETTER OFF?

The English weekly newsmagazine *The Economist* once showed this graph in an article as part of a series on statistics:

The purpose of the graph was to make a comparison between the wages of Bosses and Workers. The comparison was made with time-series data over a ten-year span, and the graphs plot three aspects of wages against time.

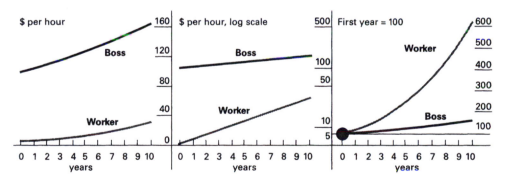

FIGURE 6.1   *A comparison of wages for bosses and workers.* (Source: *The Economist*, May 16, 1998, p. 79)

COMPARING GROUPS

Statisticians are very good at comparing groups. We typically translate the comparison of two groups into a comparison of two means or perhaps a comparison of two percentages. We can even compare two variances, if we have to. We are good at computing the proper test statistic and finding the proper p-value that will make us decide whether the difference between the groups is found to be statistically significant or not.

But are we doing the 'right' thing by making such comparisons? What does it mean to say that two groups are different on a statistical variable? A researcher brings me data on two interval/ratio variables for observations in two groups and asks me to help her find out whether the groups are different. She would typically have had a statistics course or two, particularly if she is doing biological research. If she is social scientist, we are on thinner ice. My immediate reaction is to do a t-test for the difference between two means, assuming no wild departure from normality and that the samples are large enough and that the underlying variances are not strikingly different. I will enter the data in a statistical software package of some kind and ask for the t-test. Based on the p-value returned by the software package, I will tell her whether there is a statistically significant difference between the two groups or not.

I am conditioned to do this from a long career in statistics, and hardly ever do I stop and consider whether I have done the right thing. Does it make any sense to compare the means? Forcing the comparison of two groups into a comparison of two means, implies that I have constructed a reality out there of the world for the researcher, whether she wanted it or not. Maybe our comparison of means forces researchers down paths they have not intended to take. After all, there are many ways in which things can be different.

Different can mean that all the observed values in one group are larger than the observed values in the other group. Different can mean that some of the values in one group are larger than some of the values for the second group. Different can mean that some type of an average is larger in one group than the other group, be it the mean, the median, or whatever our favorite average may turn out to be. So, what is the meaning of 'different' when it comes to a comparison between Workers and Bosses? What can we conclude about what that world out there really is like?

I must confess I enjoy taking this graph to class. First I probe the students to see what their thoughts are on the meaning of the statement that two groups are different. The end of the discussion usually consists of an agreement that two groups are different if their means are different. They sometimes go as far as saying that it could be that the two medians are different, since they remember something about skewed distributions. When I make the question more concrete and ask them to think of a comparison between wages for blue-collar worker and white-collar workers, they usually respond that the white-collar workers would be expected to have higher wages, and so the groups are different.

When I push the students, they propose that there is a list somewhere containing wages, and they base their answer on the existence of such data. The implication of their answer is that they base their thinking on the existence of a real fact out there, in the 'real world.' There are wages out there in the world, and different groups have different wages. That is a fact about the world.

The students think they know what they mean by the study of the difference between two groups, but do they really? Are there facts out there, waiting for statistics to be discovered? I venture to say that the same discussion among readers of this book would not have been very different; perhaps more sophisticated, but in the end not very different.

But when I present the graph about the wages for Workers and Bosses, they are no longer so certain about the factual world. There are three different graphs displaying the same factual world, but the conclusions from the three graphs are very different. According to the first graph, on the left, the wages in dollars per hour are plotted as a dependent variable against time as an independent variable. For ease of comparisons, the points for each group have been connected by curves, and we are left with two curves, one for the Bosses and one for the workers. The top hourly pay is $160, and I would not have minded that wage myself!

The first graph shows the curve for the Bosses to be considerably higher than the curve for the Workers across the ten years, and from that we draw the conclusion that the Bosses are better off than the Workers. Is that the way the world is? Is that a fact we have uncovered about the world? Or is this maybe simply a construction of the world we have created and are now, as statisticians, forcing on the researcher and thereby on those who read the research report? And does the researcher recognize that we, the statisticians, have added something to the research finding? The result is not just the data speaking, it is also a particular way of displaying the data that is speaking.

Turning to the middle graph, we see that the dependent variable has been changed. Instead of actual wages per hour, the wages have been transformed into logarithms. This bothers the students right away. They say they do not live on logarithms of money, they spend real dollars and cents. The student comments about logarithms may be a sign that as time has passed, not everything has become better. I used to think that such a statement was something old people made, but I actually grew up at a time when we used logarithms to perform multiplications and divisions. After some discussion, however, I usually get the students to accept that the use logarithms of wages makes it possible to see percentage increases over time, and that is what the middle chart shows.

The points for the years are again connected to give us two curves, one for the Workers and one for the Bosses. The curve for the Bosses still lies above the curve for the Workers, but now the curve for the Workers is rising faster than the curve for the Bosses. Somehow, the Workers are gaining on the Bosses. The Workers may not be as badly off, after all. This is a different reality. We are now using statistics to construct and paint for the researcher. What is the researcher to do? All of a sudden, maybe statistics are not as helpful as she thought they would be.

The third graph, on the right, again shows two curves. But this time the curve for the Workers lies above the curve for the Bosses. Here, we thought we had shown that the Bosses are better off than the Workers! The graph shows annual wages, and setting both wages equal to 100 at the beginning of the time period compares them over time from a common base. The curve for the Workers now goes up much more rapidly than the one for the Bosses, meaning that the Workers have gained more than the Bosses have.

CONSTRUCTION OF THE WORLD

Each statistical method paints a different picture of the world. Even for the same data, we get different regression lines from minimizing sums of squares and minimizing sums of absolute differences. Thus, we use the same data and different methods to construct two different realities of the world. So, which is the 'right picture'? The obvious answer is that neither of them is the right picture; it all depends upon how we look at it.... As statisticians we need ... to make researchers aware of the fact that the result of a research process is a particular construction of the world.

7

the egg and the sperm: knowledge as ideology

emily martin

The theory of the human body is always a part of a world-picture....The theory of the human body is always a part of a *fantasy*.[1]

As an anthropologist, I am intrigued by the possibility that culture shapes how biological scientists describe what they discover about the natural world. If this were so, we would be learning about more than the natural world in high school biology class; we would be learning about cultural beliefs and practices as if they were part of nature. In the course of my research I realized that the picture of egg and sperm drawn in popular, as well as scientific accounts of reproductive biology, relies on stereotypes central to our cultural definitions of male and female. The stereotypes imply not only that female biological processes are less worthy than their male counterparts but also that women are less worthy than men. Part of my goal in writing this article is to shine a bright light on the gender stereotypes hidden within the scientific language of biology. Exposed in such a light, I hope they will lose much of their power to harm us.

EGG AND SPERM: A SCIENTIFIC FAIRY TALE

At a fundamental level, all major scientific textbooks depict male and female reproductive organs as systems for the production of valuable substances, such as eggs and sperm.[2] In the case of women, the monthly cycle is described as being designed to produce eggs and prepare a suitable place for them to be fertilized and grown – all to the end of making babies. But the enthusiasm ends there. By extolling the female cycle as a productive enterprise, menstruation must necessarily be viewed as a failure. Medical texts describe menstruation as the 'debris' of the uterine lining, the result of necrosis or death of tissue. The descriptions imply that a system has gone awry, making products of no use, not to specification, unsaleable, wasted, scrap. An illustration in a widely used medical text shows menstruation as a chaotic disintegration of form, complementing the many texts that describe it as 'ceasing', 'dying', 'losing', 'denuding', 'expelling'.[3]

Male reproductive physiology is evaluated quite differently. One of the texts that sees menstruation as failed production employs sort of breathless prose when it describes the maturation of sperm. 'The mechanisms which guide the remarkable cellular transformation from spermatid to mature sperm remain uncertain....Perhaps the most amazing characteristic of spermatogenesis is its sheer magnitude: the normal human male may manufacture several hundred million sperm per day.'[4] In the classic text *Medical Physiology*, edited by Vernon Mountcastle, the male–female, productive–destructive comparison is more explicit: 'Whereas the female *sheds* only a single gamete each month, the seminiferous tubules *produce* hundreds of millions of sperm each day' (emphasis mine).[5] The female author of another text marvels at the length of the microscopic seminiferous tubules, which, if uncoiled and placed end to end, 'would span almost one-third of a mile!' She writes, 'In an adult male these structures produce millions of sperm cells each day.' Later she asks, 'How is this feat accomplished?'[6] None of these texts express such intense enthusiasm for any female processes. It is surely no accident that the 'remarkable' process of making sperm involves precisely what, in the medical view, menstruation does not: production of something deemed valuable.[7]

One could argue that menstruation and spermatogenesis are not analogous processes and, therefore, should not be expected to elicit the same kind of response. The proper female analogy to spermatogenesis, biologically, is ovulation. Yet ovulation does not merit enthusiasm in these texts either. Textbook descriptions stress that all of the ovarian follicles containing ova are already present at birth. Far from being *produced*, as sperm are, they merely sit on the shelf, slowly degenerating and aging like overstocked inventory: 'At birth, normal human ovaries contain an estimated one million follicles [each], and no new appear after birth. Thus, in marked contrast to the male, the newborn female already has all the germ cells she will ever have. Only a few, perhaps 400, are destined to reach full maturity during her active productive life. All the others degenerate at some point in their development so that few, if any, remain by the time she reaches menopause at approximately 50 years of age.'[8] Note the 'marked contrast' that this description sets up between male and female: the male, who continuously produces fresh germ cells, and the female, who has stockpiled germ cells by birth and is faced with their degeneration.

Nor are the female organs spared such vivid descriptions. One scientist writes in a newspaper article that a woman's ovaries become old and worn out from ripening eggs every month, even though the woman herself is still relatively young: 'When you look through a laparoscope ... at an ovary that has been through hundreds of cycles, even in a superbly healthy American female, you see a scarred, battered organ.'[9]

To avoid the negative connotations that some people associate with the female reproductive system, scientists could begin to describe male and female processes as homologous. They might credit females with 'producing' mature ova one at a time, as they're needed each month, and describes males as having to face problems of degenerating germ cells. This degeneration would occur throughout life among spermatogonia, the undifferentiated germ cells in the testes that are the long-lived, dormant precursors of sperm.

[...]

The real mystery is why the male's vast production of sperm is not seen as wasteful?[10] Assuming that a man 'produces' 100 million (10^8) sperm per day (a conservative estimate) during an average reproductive life of sixty years, he would produce well over two trillion sperm in his lifetime. Assuming that a woman 'ripens' one egg per lunar month, or thirteen per year, over the course of her forty-year reproductive life, she would total five hundred eggs in her lifetime. But the word 'waste' implies an excess, too much produced. Assuming two or three offspring, for every baby a woman produces, she wastes only around two hundred eggs. For every baby a man produces, he wastes more than one trillion (10^{12}) sperm.

How is it that positive images are denied to the bodies of women? A look at language – in this case, scientific language – provides the first clue. Take the egg and the sperm. It is remarkable how 'femininely' the egg behaves and how 'masculinely' the sperm.[11] The egg is seen as large and passive.[12] It does not *move* or *journey*, but passively 'is transported', 'is swept',[13] or even 'drifts'[14] along the fallopian tube. In utter contrast, sperm are small, 'streamlined',[15] and invariably active. They 'deliver' their genes to the egg, 'activate the developmental program of the egg',[16] and have a 'velocity' that is often remarked upon.[17] Their tails are 'strong' and efficiently powered.[18] Together with the forces of ejaculation, they can 'propel the semen into the deepest recesses of the vagina'.[19] For this they need 'energy',[20] 'fuel',[20] so that with a 'whiplash-like motion and strong lurches'[21] they can 'burrow through the egg coat'[22] and 'penetrate' it.[23]

At its extreme, the age-old relationship of the egg and the sperm takes on a royal or religious patina. The egg coat, its protective barrier, is sometimes called its 'vestments', a term usually reserved for sacred, religious dress. The egg is said to have a 'corona',[24] a crown, and to be accompanied by 'attendant cells'.[25] It is holy, set apart and above, the queen to the sperm's king. The egg is also passive, which means it must depend on sperm for rescue. Gerald Schatten and Helen Schatten liken the egg's role to that of Sleeping Beauty: 'a dormant bride awaiting her mate's magic kiss, which instills the spirit that brings her to life'.[26] Sperm, by contrast, have a 'mission',[27] which is to 'move through the female genital tract in quest of the ovum'.[28] One popular account has it that the sperm carry out a 'perilous journey' into the 'warm darkness', where some fall away 'exhausted'. Survivors' 'assault' the egg, the successful candidates 'surrounding the prize'.[29] Part of the urgency of this journey, in more scientific terms, is that 'once released from the supportive enviroment of the ovary, an egg will die within hours unless rescued by a sperm'.[30] The wording stresses the fragility and dependency of the egg, even though the same text acknowledges elsewhere that sperm also live for only a few hours.[31]

In 1948, in a book remarkable for its early insights into these matters, Ruth Herschberger argued that female reproductive organs are seen as biologically interdependent, while male organs are viewed as autonomous, operating independently and in isolation:

[...]

> The sperm is no more independent of its milieu than the egg, and yet from a wish that it
> were, biologists have lent their support to the notion that the human female, beginning with
> the egg, is congenitally more dependent than the male.[32]

An article in the journal *Cell* has the sperm making an 'existential decision' to penetrate the egg: 'Sperm are cells with a limited behavioral repertoire, one that is directed
toward fertilizing eggs. To execute the decision to abandon the haploid state, sperm
swim to an egg and there acquire the ability to effect membrane fusion.[33] Is this a
corporate manager's version of the sperm's activities—'executing decisions' while
fraught with dismay over difficult options that bring with them very high risk.

[...]

One depiction of sperm as weak and timid, instead of strong and powerful – the
only such representation in Western civilization, so far as I know – occurs in Woody
Allen's movie *Everything You Always Wanted To Know About Sex* *But Were Afraid
to Ask*. Allen, playing the part of an apprehensive sperm inside a man's testicles, is
scared of the man's approaching orgasm. He is reluctant to launch himself into the
darkness, afraid of contraceptive devices, afraid of winding up on the ceiling if the man
masturbates.

The more common picture – egg as damsel in distress, shielded only by her sacred
garments; sperm as heroic warrior to the rescue – cannot be proved to be dictated by
the biology of these events. While the 'facts' of biology may not *always* be constructed
in cultural terms, I would argue that in this case they are. The degree of metaphorical
content in these descriptions, the extent to which differences between egg and sperm
are emphasized, and the parallels between cultural stereotypes of male and female
behaviour and the character of egg and sperm all point to this conclusion.

One clear feminist challenge is to wake up sleeping metaphors in science, particularly those involved in descriptions of the egg and the sperm. Although the literary
convention is to call such metaphors 'dead', they are not so much dead as sleeping,
hidden within the scientific content of texts – and all the more powerful for it. Waking
up such metaphors, by becoming aware of when we are projecting cultural imagery
onto what we study, will improve our ability investigate and understand nature.
Waking up such metaphors, by becoming aware of their implications, will rob them of
their power to naturalize our social conventions about gender.

NOTES

1. James Hillman, *The Myth of Analysis* (Evanston, Ill.: Northwestern University
   Press, 1972), 220.
2. The textbooks I consulted are the main ones used in classes for undergraduate
   premedical students or medical students (or those held on reserve in the library

for these classes) during the past few years at Johns Hopkins University. These texts are widely used at other universities in the country as well.

3. Authur C. Guyton, *Physiology of the Human Body,* 6th edn. (Philadelphia: Saunders College Publishing, 1984), 624.

4. Arthur J. Vander, James H. Sherman, and Dorothy S. Luciano, *Human Physiology: The Mechanisms of Body Function,* 3rd edn. (New York: McGrawHill, 1980), 483–4.

5. Vernon B. Mountcastle, *Medical Physiology,* 14th edn. (London: Mosby, 1980), 2:1624.

6. Eldra Pearl Solomon, *Human Anatomy and Physiology* (New York: CBS College Publishing, 1983), 678.

7. For elaboration, see Emily Martin, *The Woman in the Body: A Cultural Analysis of Reproduction* (Boston: Beacon, 1987), 27–53.

8. Vander, Sherman, and Luciano, 568.

9. Melvin Konner, 'Childbearing and Age', *New York Times Magazine* (27 Dec. 1987), 22–3, esp. 22.

10. In her essay 'Have Only Men Evolved?' (in Sandra Harding and Merrill B. Hintikka (eds), *Discovering Reality: Feminist Perspectives on Epistemology, Metaphysics, Methodology, and Philosophy of Science* (Dordrecht: Reidel, 1983), 45–69, esp. 60–1, Ruth Hubbard points out that sociobiologists have said the female invests more energy than the male in the productions of her large gametes, claiming that this explains why the female provides parental care. Hubbard questions whether it 'really takes more "energy" to generate the one or relatively few eggs than the large excess of sperms required to achieve fertilization'.

11. See Carol Delaney, 'The Meaning of Paternity and the Virgin Birth Debate', *Man,* 21/3 (Sept. 1986), 494–513. She discusses the difference between this scientific view that women contribute genetic material to the fetus and the claim of long-standing Western folk theories that the origin and identity of the fetus comes from the male, as in the metaphor of planting a seed in soil.

12. For a suggested direct link between human behaviour and purportedly passive eggs and active sperm, see Erik H. Erikson, 'Inner and Outer Space: Reflections on Womanhood', *Daedalus,* 93/2 (Spring 1964), 582–606, esp. 591.

13. Guyton (n. 3 above), 619; and Mountcastle (n. 5 above), 1609.

14. Jonathan Miller and David Pelham, *The Facts of Life* (New York: Viking Penguin, 1984), 5.

15. Bruce Alberts *et al., Molecular Biology of the Cell* (New York: Garland, 1983), 796.

16. Ibid. 796.

17. See, e.g. William F. Ganong, *Review of Medical Physiology,* 7th edn. (Los Altos, Calif.: Lange Medical Publications, 1975), 322.

18. Alberts *et al.* (n. 15 above), 796.

19. Guyton, 615.

20. Solomon (n. 6 above), 683.

21. Vander, Sherman, and Luciano (n. 4 above), 4th edn. (1985), 580.

22. Alberts *et al.,* 796.

23. All biology texts quoted above use the word 'penetrate'.

24. Solomon, 700.

25. A. Beldecos *et al.,* 'The Importance of Feminist Critique for Contemporary Cell Biology', *Hypatia,* 3/1 (Spring 1988), 61–76.

26. Gerald Schatten and Helen Schatten, 'The Energetic Egg', *Medical World News*, 23 (23 Jan. 1984), 51–3, esp. 51.

27. Alberts *et al.*, 796.

28. Guyton (n. 3 above), 613.

29. Miller and Pelham (n. 14 above), 7.

30. Alberts *et al.* (n. 15 above), 804.

31. Ibid. 801.

32. Ruth Herschberger, *Adam's Rib* (New York: Pelligrini & Cudaby, 1948), esp. 84.

33. Bennett M. Shapiro, 'The Existential Decision of a Sperm', *Cell*, 49/3 (May 1987), 293–4, esp. 293.

part two

constructing the person: culture and critique

Our relationships give rise to our understandings of the real and the good. This is perhaps the major conclusion to be derived from the preceding readings. Although such a conclusion challenges longstanding beliefs in individual knowledge and truth-beyond-community, constructionist ideas go much further than unsettling these beliefs. As many see it, they also possess an enormous liberating potential. Our commonly shared assumptions of the real and the good serve as anchors for our daily activities. The world of medicine, for example, is vitally dependent upon shared assumptions about 'illness' and 'cure,' and why the latter is preferred over the former. Our educational systems are premised in beliefs about 'ignorance' and 'individual knowledge,' and why the latter is preferred. So powerful are these realities and values that one can scarcely imagine an alternative. It is precisely at this juncture that constructionist ideas become potent. This is so because a constructionist regards all our assumptions and related practices open to reflexive recon-sideration. Illness and cure, ignorance and knowledge, for example, are not 'out there' in the world as unquestionable realities, and the benefits of 'cure' and 'knowledge' are not handed from the heavens. We are free to consider alternatives. And, as Emily Martin's work on the sperm and the egg makes clear (Reading 7), our hand-me-down assumptions often contain implications that can be oppressive to many people. It is not only that we can question our traditions, but that in many cases we should.

These liberating potentials have unleashed an enormous scholarship of critique and reconsideration across the sciences and humanities. Feminist scholars, for example, have brought into question the masculine biases inherent in prevailing concepts of moral princi-ple (Gilligan, 1982), human experimentation (Gergen, 1988), and laws of physical science (Keller, 1985). These efforts have been have joined by scholars questioning the racist and nationalist biases inherent in everyday language (Wetherell and Potter, 1992; Billig, 1995), and the Eurocentric biases that inhabit our research into other cultures (Marcus and Fischer, 1986; Said, 1973). These critiques have also been directed to various social practices that otherwise seem 'just normal.' For example, critics have explored the class and racial biases inherent in our codes of law (Douzinas and Warrington, 1991), common television fare (Miller, 1988), and popular styles (Ewen, 1999). Other scholars have illuminated the constructed character of daily news stories (Dayan and Katz, 1992; Fiske, 1996), motherhood (Badinter, 1980), the mind (Coulter, 1979), sex differences (Laqueuer, 1990), old age (Hazan, 1994), and world geography (Gregory, 1994). In all cases the hope is that by disclosing otherwise hidden biases we are sensitized to the possibilities of human transfor-mation. From the enormous body of emancipatory literature we offer here illustrations from two specific domains.

THE NATURAL AS CULTURAL

One of the greatest impediments to social change is the assumption that many of our actions are 'just natural,' built in to the nervous system, biologically required. Particularly in the case of human behavior, we view 'natural' behavior as something fixed and permanent. We can do little about it, except channel or control it. If we hold that male aggression is natural – an evo-lutionary necessity – we are discouraged from 'changing human nature.' Rather, we look for means of controlling the aggression, for example, through laws, police and prisons. Power and control become favored ways of achieving the good society as opposed, for example, to more collaborative and dialogic possibilities.

The four contributions in this section all form significant challenges to the presumption of the natural in human behavior. Each considers a form of activity or experience that we generally consider intrinsic to human nature and attempts to demonstrate its culturally constructed character. In each case we are encouraged to deliberate on more promising alternatives.

Anthropologist Catherine Lutz has written extensively on the cultural construction of emotions. *Unnatural Emotions* is a landmark volume demonstrating how the people of a micronesian island understand and express emotions. As she demonstrates, the emotional vocabulary of the Ifaluk cannot be translated into Western terms, and the forms of expression are very particular to the kinds of cultural and physical conditions specific to their existence. For Lutz, as for many other anthropologists, emotions are not universal, biologically determined tendencies, but socially constituted for use within specific cultural contexts. In the present excerpt from Lutz's work (Reading 8), she explores the ideology carried by our Western views of emotion. As she explores, the very concept of the emotions in the West is loaded with political and social value. To challenge these understandings of emotion is to open new paths of action – particularly in gender relations.

While many readers can appreciate how the emotions are culturally constituted, they are likely to draw the line at pain. It's one thing to say, for example, that 'romantic love is a cultural construction,' but surely pain is universal. Do we not know directly our pain even before we have any significant relationships? Yet, it is precisely this possibility that David Morris explores in Reading 9. By moving across cultures and history, Morris draws our attention to the many different ways in which pain has been interpreted. In many cases, for example, men wounded in battle have failed to experience pain at all. The chapter raises profound questions about pain management in society: is it possible that what is commonly experienced as pain could, through social intervention, actually be experienced as pleasure? The pleasure that many men derive from physical contact sports seems to support such a possibility. Perhaps the reader can press this possibility forward in new ways.

POWER AND RESISTANCE

Michel Foucault's writings are among the most catalytic and hotly contested within the constructionist dialogues. Perhaps Foucault's most important contribution is to link the construction of truth with the emergence of power and control (see especially Foucault, 1979; 1980). As a group comes to develop its local truths or knowledge, it will first attempt to bind its members to these views. One is not free within an autocratic society or religion, for example, to challenge what Foucault calls 'the dominant discourse.' Indeed, history is replete with eradications of heretics. And, once committed to its particular vision of knowledge, groups will typically attempt to convert others in various ways – proselytizing, educating, enforcing. In effect, social convergence around 'the truth' gives rise to structures of power and domination. Although this proposal seems compelling enough, Foucault sees many more subtle and profound implications. While many readers are perhaps already suspicious of claims to Truth, the concept of 'knowledge' seems far more acceptable. As a culture we tend to celebrate the accumulation and dissemination of knowledge. Yet, if what we call knowledge essentially represents the constructions of particular, value invested groups, then education, research, and science all represent the subtle expansion of power. For Foucault, the disciplines of knowledge (e.g. biology, psychology, physics, economics), not only keep their participants under control, but also order the minds and actions of those who come to learn.

We include here (Reading 10) but a single argument from Foucault's sprawling and often disordered work, but one with important implications. Here Foucault centers on the practice of confession, first as it functioned in traditions of religion and then in its later forms, including the research interview. As Foucault proposes, the confession functions in all these cases as a means of generating truth. But so long as one opens oneself to responding to the questions, the truths that result from confessional practices are under the control of the agent who questions. From the priest to the contemporary researcher, it is the one who puts the question who will determine the reality emerging from the answer. Simply responding to a questionnaire as to whether one is male or female will, for example, contribute to the reality of two genders. In this reading Foucault goes on to show how assumptions of causality and the unconscious mind worked in concert with confessional practices to create a scientific vocabulary of sexual deviance. As this knowledge is disseminated to the public, so is the public brought under the control of the scientific profession.

One of the most troubling aspects of Foucault's work on power concerns the possibility of resistance. While his writings stimulate the reader to resist, recalling the revolutionary spirit that brought down the French throne in the 1700s, he offers very little on the means by which resistance to the dominant discourse can be mounted. In his late works he suggests that the individual should resist societal constructions through self-creativity (Foucault, 1986). However, it remains difficult to envision a self-constructing individual whose visions of a personal self are not saturated with cultural meanings. At least one significant answer to the question of resistance emerges from the constructionist dialogues themselves. If people come together to create meanings, and these constructions are ultimately used to dominate others, then the chief means of resistance lies in counter culture creation. That is, people may best resist by generating an alternative and more compelling reality. This process is nicely illustrated in Reading 11, where Paul Willis reports on the way in which laboring class youth in England create together a reality enabling them to resist mainstream education. These adolescents develop their own language of understanding, a language that enables them to ridicule both teachers and their more proper 'earhole' classmates. This reading should also create useful deliberation on the values of revolutionary resistance. Is resistance always desirable; when and where should it be supported? The dialogue remains open.

REFERENCES

Badinter, E. (1980). *Mother love, myth and reality.* New York: Macmillan.

Billig, M. (1995). *Banal nationalism.* London: Sage.

Coulter, J. (1979). *The social construction of the mind.* New York: Macmillan.

Dayan, D., and Katz, E. (1992). *Media events: The live broadcasting of history.* Cambridge, MA: Harvard University Press.

Douzinas, C., & Warrington, R. (1991). *Postmodern jurisprudence: The law of text in the texts of law.* London: Routledge.

Ewen, S. (1999). *All consuming images: The politics of style in contemporary culture.* New York: Basic Books.

Fiske, J. (1996). *Media matters: Race and gender in U. S. Politics.* Minneapolis: University of Minnesota Press.

Foucault, M. (1979). *Discipline and punish: The birth of the prison.* New York: Vintage.

Foucault, M. (1980). *The history of sexuality, Vol. 1.* (Tr. Robert Hurley). New York: Vintage.

Foucault, M. (1986). *The care of the self.* (Translated by Robert Hurley). New York: Pantheon.

Gergen, M. M. (1988). Towards a feminist methodology. In M. Gergen (Ed.) *Feminist Thought and the Structure of Knowledge.* (pp. 87–104). New York: New York University Press, 1988.

Gilligan, C. (1982). *In a different voice.* Cambridge, MA: Harvard University Press.

Gregory, D. (1994). *Geographical imaginations.* Cambridge: Blackwell.

Hazan, H. (1994). *Old age, constructions and deconstructions.* Cambridge: Cambridge University Press.

Keller, E. F. (1985). *Reflections on gender and science.* New Haven, CT: Yale University Press.

Laqueuer, T. (1990). *Making sex: Body and gender from the Greeks to Freud.* Cambridge, MA: Harvard University Press.

Lutz, C. A. (1988). *Unnatural emotions: Everyday sentiments on a Micronesian Atoll & their challenge to Western theory.* Chicago: University of Chicago Press.

Marcus, G. E., & Fischer, M. M. J. (1986). *Anthropology as cultural critique.* Chicago: University of Chicago Press.

Miller, M. C. (1988). *Boxed in: The culture of TV.* Evanston, IL: Northwestern University Press.

Said, E. (1973). *Culture and imperialism.* London: Chatto & Windus.

Wetherell, M. & Potter, J. (1992). *Mapping the language of racism: Discourse and the legitimation of exploitation.* Hemel Hempstead, England: Harvester Wheatsheaf.

8

emotion: the universal as local

catherine a. lutz

> The emotion here is nothing but the feeling of a bodily state, and it has a purely bodily cause.
>
> *W. James* (1967:110)

> Emotions are the life force of the soul, the source of most of our values ... the basis of most other passions.
>
> *R. Solomon* (1977:14)

> 'Joy' designates nothing at all. Neither any inward nor any outward thing.
>
> *L. Wittgenstein* (1966:487)

The extensive discussions of the concept of the emotions that have occurred in the West for at least the past 2,000 years have generally proceeded with either philosophical, religious, moral, or, more recently, scientific–psychological purposes in mind. This discourse includes Plato's concern with the relation between pleasure and the good; the Stoic doctrine that the passions are naturally evil; early Christian attempts to distinguish the emotions of human frailty from the emotions of God; Hobbes's view that the passions are the primary source of action, naturally prompting both war and peace; the argument of Rousseau that natural feelings are of great value and ought to be separated from the 'factitious' or sham feelings produced by civilization; the nineteenth-century psychologists' move to view emotions as psychophysiological in nature, with consciousness seen less and less as an important component of the emotions. One of the notable aspects of this discourse is its concern with emotion as essence; whether the passions are portrayed as aspects of a divinely inspired human nature or as genetically encoded biological fact, they remain, to varying degrees, things that have an inherent and unchanging nature. With the exceptions of Rousseau, to some extent, and of Wittgenstein more recently, emotions have been sought in the supposedly more permanent structures of human existence – in spleens, souls, genes, human nature, and individual psychology rather than in history, culture, ideology, and temporary human purposes.

I begin here, then, not with a definition of what emotion is but with an exploration of the concept of emotion as a master cultural category in the West. An examination of the unspoken assumptions embedded in the concept of emotion is my first interpretive task for several reasons. It is necessary, first, because the concept of emotion is cultural, which is to say, constructed primarily by people rather than by nature. I explicitly went to conduct fieldwork among the Ifaluk to explore how the people of that atoll experienced emotions in their everyday lives. That concept, therefore, represented one of the primary cultural frameworks through which, or occasionally against which, my understandings of the Ifaluk proceeded. Exploration of the culture 'schema' with which any anthropological observer begins fieldwork provides a methodological key because translating between two cultural systems requires explication of the relevant meaning systems on *both* sides of the cultural divide. The cultural meaning system that constitutes the concept of emotion has been invisible because we have assumed that it is possible to identify the 'essence' of emotion, that the emotions are universal, and that they are separable from both their personal and social contexts.

Second, to look at the Euramerican construction of emotion is to unmask how that schema unconsciously serves as a normative device for judging the mental health of culturally different peoples. Despite an assiduous rejection within anthropology of explicit value judgments in the description of other cultural systems, we necessarily import a variety of Western value orientations toward emotions (as good or bad things to have, in particular quantities, shapes, and sizes) whenever we use that concept without alerting the reader to the attitudes toward it that have developed in the West.

The concept of emotion has this and other sorts of ideological functions; that is, it exists in a system of power relations and plays a role in maintaining it. As we will see, emotion occupies an important place in Western gender ideologies. In identifying emotion primarily with irrationality, subjectivity, the chaotic, and other negative characteristics, and in subsequently labeling women the emotional gender, cultural belief reinforces the ideological subordination of women. The more general ideological role that the concept has played consists in reinforcing the split between 'facts' and 'values,' as cognition, which can theoretically achieve knowledge of facts, is dichotomized in relation to emotion, which is 'only' an index of value and personal interest.

EMOTION AGAINST THOUGHT, EMOTION AGAINST ESTRANGEMENT

Emotion stands in important and primary contrast relationship to two seemingly contradictory notions. It is opposed, on the one hand, to the positively evaluated process of thought and, on the other, to a negatively evaluated estrangement from the world. To say that someone is 'unemotional' is either to praise that person as calm, rational, and deliberate or to accuse them of being withdrawn or uninvolved, alienated, or even catatonic. Emotion is, at one time, a residual category of almost-defective personal process; at others, it is the seat of the true and glorified self. As we will see, these two views represent both a cultural contradiction and a necessary feature of any dualism whose simplicities cannot hold in the face of the demands social processes will put on it. Although each of these two senses of the emotional has played an important role in discourse, the contrast with rationality and thought is currently the more dominant in evaluative force, salience, and frequency of use. It is more often used to damn than to praise, and so I begin with an analysis of that contrast.

The split between emotion and thought goes under several other rubrics, including the more academic and psychological 'affect' and 'cognition,' the more romantic and philosophical 'passion' and 'reason,' and the more prosaic 'feeling' and 'thinking.' The distinction between them takes as central a place in Western psychosocial theory as do those between mind and body, behavior and intention, the individual and the social, or the conscious and the unconscious, structuring (as do those other contrasts) innumerable aspects of experience and discourse. Encoded in or related to that contrast is an immense portion of the Western worldwide of the person, of social life, and of morality.

It is first important to note, however, that emotion shares a fundamental character-istic with thought in this ethnopsychological view, which is that both are internal char-acteristics of persons. The essence of both emotion and thought are to be found within the boundaries of the person; they are features of individuals rather than of situations, relationships, or moral positions. In other words, they are construed as psycho-logical rather than social phenomena. Although social, historical, and interpersonal processes are seen as correlated with these psychic events, thought and emotion are taken to be the property of individuals. Thought and emotion also share the quality of being viewed as more authentic realities and more truly the repository of the self in comparison with the relative inauthenticity of speaking and other forms of interaction.

The contrast drawn culturally between emotion and thought can be outlined initially by looking at the large set of paired concepts associated with the two terms and like-wise set in contrast to each other. Thus, emotion is to thought as energy is to informa-tion, heart is to head, the irrational is to the rational, preference is to inference, impulse is to intention, vulnerability is to control, and chaos is to order. Emotion is to thought as knowing something is good is to knowing something is true, that is, as value is to fact or knowledge, the relatively unconscious is to the relatively conscious, the subjective is to the objective, the physical is to the mental, the natural is to the cultural, the expres-sive is to the instrumental or practical, the morally suspect is to the ethically mature, the lower classes are to the upper, the child is to the adult, and the female is to the male. Although people in the West of course vary in the extent to which they would empha-size the connection between emotion and thought and any of these other paired associ-ations, each pair appears as a cultural theme underlying much academic and everyday discussion of the nature of emotion. What is clear is that the evaluative bias in each of the associated pairs follows the bias evident in the distinction of emotion from thought itself, that is, as the inferior is to the superior, the relatively bad to the relatively good.

In the second major contrast set, emotion stands against estrangement or disengagement. The concept pairs that participate in the meaning of this contrast include life against death; community and connection against alienation; relationship against individualism; the subjective against the objective; the natural against the cultural; the authentic against the contrived; commitment and value against nihilism or morality against amorality; and the female against the male. While the emotional is generally treated as the inferior member of the set in the emotion/thought contrast, here the evaluation is reversed. It is better, most would agree, to be emotional than to be dead or alienated.

This sense of emotional is a Romantic one. The nineteenth-century tubercular patient is one cultural exemplar of the value placed then as now on feeling. Tuberculosis was the result of its bearer's 'sensitive' soul: 'TB was thought to come from too much passion, afflicting the reckless and sensual ... [It] was celebrated as a disease of passion' (Sontag, 1977:21). Emotionality in this sense may be tragic, but it is correspondingly heroic to feel. To be emotional is to understand deeply (even if too deeply) rather than to fail to see and know. If emotion in this sense is not necessarily affiliated with the notion of 'rationality,' it is at least a cousin to 'wisdom.'

While these two views of emotion – as the unthoughtful and as the unalienated – might at first appear to represent a logical contradiction, there are other more fruitful ways of conceptualizing the 'problem' that the existence of these two contrasts presents. The two can be seen, in psychological context, as being formed by and creating the potential for ambivalence; the emotional is, for individual Americans, simultaneously good and bad, antithought and against estrangement, core of the self and residual effect. The two sets can also be seen as separately activated or drawn on for particular purposes in different contexts, as will be illustrated in a moment. Like their Ifaluk counterparts, these American notions are ideological practices whose meanings are found in the diverse uses to which they are put. The meaning of emotion is sensitive to the context, and particularly the social relations, within which its use occurs.

REFERENCES

James, W. (1967). The emotions. In C. Lange & W. James (Eds). *The emotions.* New York: Hafner.

Solomon, R. C. (1977). *The passions.* New York: Anchor.

Sontag, S. (1977). *Illness as metaphor.* New York: Farrar, Straus & Giroux.

Wittgenstein, L. (1966). *Zettel.* (Trans. By G. Anscombe). London: Blackwell.

9

the meanings of pain

david morris

The human body is the best picture of the human soul.

Ludwig Wittgenstein

Anyone who has endured a period of intense pain has probably asked, silently or openly, the following incessant questions: Why me? Why is this happening? Why won't it stop? Suddenly we simply do not possess the knowledge we need. The combination of doubt and fear can loosen an avalanche of related questions. How will I earn a living if I can't go back to work? Will my sex drive ever return? Am I doomed to spend the rest of my life in pain? To be in pain is often to be in a state of crisis. It is a state in which we experience far more than physical discomfort. Pain has not simply interrupted our normal feeling of health. It has opened a huge fault or fissure in our world. We need answers. We want to know what all this torment in our bones – the disarrangement of our personal cosmos – adds up to. What does it mean?

Today, of course, we seek the meaning of pain at the doctor's office. Sometimes, mercifully, the answer is straightforward. The pain you feel is caused by a ruptured disk or an infected ear. An operation or a course of antibiotics will set you right and eliminate your questions. But suppose that a successful operation still leaves you with constant pain. Suppose x-rays and lab tests reveal no hidden organic cause. Suddenly the questions multiply and seem more urgent. Your doctor refers you to a specialist, who finds nothing and refers you to another specialist, who also finds nothing wrong, but still the pain continues. The meaning of pain seems a nonissue as long as medicine can provide its reassuring explanations and magical cures. When cures repeatedly fail, however, or when the explanations patently fall flat, we must confront once again – with renewed seriousness, even desperation – the ever-implicit question of meaning.

Ivan Ilych was an ordinary man: intelligent, cheerful, capable, sociable, good-natured. After his graduation from law school, he became a successful magistrate, performing his duties with honesty and exactness. He made a good salary, married an attractive young woman, and settled down to a life of domestic comfort. In due course, several children arrived. Soon he was promoted to Assistant Public Prosecutor and – after experiencing a slight but unpleasant friction in his marriage – thereafter redoubled his application to the law. His greatest pleasure was playing bridge. A life so pleasant and so industrious brought further rewards. Before long he and his wife, who now got along better, moved into the house of their dreams.

It was in climbing a ladder (the metaphor is almost too common) while decorating the new house that Ivan Ilych slipped and fell, bruising his side. The bruise was painful but the pain quickly passed. Soon, however, he noticed a queer taste that lingered in his mouth and an uncomfortable pressure where the bruise had subsided. He grew worried, uncharacteristically irritable, and at times quarreled openly with his wife. Eventually he developed in his side a dull, gnawing ache that never left him. He saw a doctor, got a prescription, consulted new doctors, got new prescriptions. There was no improvement. The pain in his side was like a slow poison relentlessly destroying his sense of satisfaction with life. He felt changed, alone, as if on the edge of a precipice.

The physical change in his appearance shocked him. At length even his family recognized that something was terribly wrong. It occurred to Ivan Ilych that he was dying, but the thought was impossible to grasp or understand. All the ordinary events at home and at work now seemed a sham or falsehood. He could not concentrate on them. His pain alone occupied his mind. His pain alone seemed real. It grew worse – and worse still because his family (wishing to encourage him) steadfastly maintained the pretense that he was not dying. As his pain increased, Ivan Ilych began to wonder whether his entire life had been a lie: a carefully maintained structure of fraud and self-deception. When the crisis finally came, he began to scream, and he screamed continuously for three days. It is said that one could not hear the screaming through two closed doors without feeling horror.

Tolstoy's spare, parablelike story *The Death of Ivan Ilych* (1886) provides a useful beginning, because it introduces us so clearly to what specialists might want to call the hermeneutics of pain. Borrowing its name from Hermes, the Greek messenger-god who presided over dreams and rites of divination, hermeneutics concerns the art or science of interpretation. The Greeks and Romans seldom took important actions – an invasion, say, or a long journey – without the support of a favorable omen, but dreams and sacrificial rites were often full of ambiguous images (snakes killing eagles, discolored intestines, strange patterns in the rising smoke). Someone in a position of authority, usually a priest, was needed to interpret the omen. Pain, while perhaps less eloquent than a discolored intestine, is something that almost intrinsically calls for interpretation.

[...]

Pain, whatever else philosophy or biomedical science can tell us about it, is almost always the occasion for an encounter with meaning. It not only invites interpretation: like an insult or an outrageous act, it seems to *require* an explanation. As David Bakan writes:

To attempt to understand the nature of pain, to seek to find its meaning, is already to respond to an imperative of pain itself. No experience demands and insists upon interpretation in the same way. Pain forces the question of its meaning, and especially of its cause, insofar as cause is an important part of its meaning. In those instances in which pain is intense and intractable and in which its causes are obscure, its demand for interpretation is most naked, manifested in the sufferer asking, 'Why?'

Generally, of course, the explanations we expect today center on questions of medicine, and Bakan is especially useful in reminding us that such medical diagnoses constitute an interpretation. They implicitly help us to make sense of pain: to give it a meaning.

The interpretation of pain, however, has not always centered so exclusively on questions of medicine. The impulse to phone our local physician, which seems now almost instinctive and certainly belongs to the domain of absolute common sense, has required over the centuries significant learning and unlearning. Consider the biblical patriarch Job as he sits on his dunghill, covered with boils, struggling to figure out why God has punished him. What from a medical perspective appears to be simply a problem in dermatology lies at the distant horizon, not the center, of his experience with pain.

[...]

The Death of Ivan Ilych offers a vivid illustration of the mobility of pain. The accident that Ivan Ilych first dismissed as insignificant, a trivial event in the course of an ordinary life, becomes over time subject to reinterpretation. Understood with hindsight, his pain sheds its original air of meaninglessness and at last exposes the origin of an unseen chain of events. An insignificant pain finally turns scandalous and terrifying. Like the devil impersonating a country salesman, its insignificance turns out to be merely a clever disguise that death has employed in forcing an entry into Ivan Ilych's otherwise well-insulated life...

The meaning of pain, as Tolstoy develops the story of Ivan Ilych, expands beyond a symbolic union with death. Tolstoy shows us with remarkable clarity how pain continues to change over time. In fact, the specific changes he describes also reveal the larger sense in which pain – far from constituting a single, simple, unified entity – is inherently changeable. *The Death of Ivan Ilych* suggests that pain does not possess an unchanging essence but rather continues to move between the poles of meaninglessness and meaning, even as its meanings continue to change. It is as if pain were never fixed but perpetually in motion across the plane of a human life.

The variable meanings of pain in *The Death of Ivan Ilych* do not stop with the terrifying revelation of its link with death. All at once, after three days spent in screaming and struggle, Ivan Ilych suddenly experiences a deep calm, and his relation to pain changes once again. In effect, he passes through pain to a state of spiritual awakening. After this awakening, he is still aware of his pain – the pain has not diminished or disappeared – but now it somehow no longer matters, no longer torments him. He can address it as one might address an old enemy, long forgiven:

'And the pain?' he asked himself, 'What has become of it. Where are you, pain.'
He turned his attention to it.
'Yes, here it is. Well, what of it? Let the pain be.'

The pain of Ivan Ilych now stands stripped of its terrors. His pain is, once again, simply pain.

Tolstoy's narrative describes a kind of circular motion. For Ivan Ilych, the pain which began in meaninglessness and later revealed its symbolic link with death finally came to rest once more in meaninglessness. Yet the two types of significance are profoundly different. Ivan Ilych's final disregard of pain marks the attainment of a spiritual, almost otherworldly vision in which human life looks vastly different than it did in his period of career-building and social-climbing. At the very end of his life, Ivan Ilych unexpectedly scales a religious height from which he views his pain – even agonizing, excruciating, terminal pain – as truly insignificant. His final *understanding* of his pain (his acceptance of its place and meaning in his life) is Ivan Ilych's profoundest act. It is, needless to say, an act of interpretation.

The peculiarly changeable nature of pain – its power to take on new meaning or abruptly to lose, to regain, or to transform the meaning it temporarily possesses – requires that we understand this most ancient and personal of human experiences as indelibly stamped by a specific place and time. Pain seems the quintessential solitary experience. We are probably never more alone than when severe pain invades us. Others appear to go about their business mostly unchanged, thinking that the world is just the same, but we know differently. The isolation of pain is undeniable. Yet it is thus especially important to recognize that pain is also always deeply social. The pain we feel has in large part been constructed or shaped by the culture from which we now feel excluded or cut off.

REFERENCES

Tolstoy, L. (1967). *Great short stories of Leo Tolstoy* (Trans. L. & A. Maude) New York: Harper & Row.

10

power and confession

michel foucault

S ince the Middle Ages at least, Western societies have established the confession as one of the main rituals we rely on for the production of truth: the codification of the sacrament of penance by the Lateran Council in 1215, with the resulting development of confessional techniques, the declining importance of accusatory procedures in criminal justice, the abandonment of tests of guilt (sworn statements, duels, judgments of God) and the development of methods of interrogation and inquest, the increased participation of the royal administration in the prosecution of infractions, at the expense of proceedings leading to private settlements, the setting up of tribunals of Inquisition: all this helped to give the confession a central role in the order of civil and religious powers. The evolution of the word *avowal* and of the legal function it designated is itself emblematic of this development: from being a guarantee of the status, identity, and value granted to one person by another, it came to signify someone's acknowledgement of his own actions and thoughts. For a long time, the individual was vouched for by the reference of others and the demonstration of his ties to the commonweal (family, allegiance. protection); then he was authenticated by the discourse of truth he was able or obliged to pronounce concerning himself. The truthful confession was inscribed at the heart of the procedures of individualization by power.

In any case, next to the testing rituals, next to the testimony of witnesses, and the learned methods of observation and demonstration, the confession became one of the West's most highly valued techniques for producing truth. We have since become a singularly confessing society. The confession has spread its effects far and wide. It plays a part in justice, medicine, education, family relationships, and love relations, in the most ordinary affairs of everyday life, and in the most solemn rites; one confesses one's crimes, one's sins, one's thoughts and desires, one's illnesses and troubles; one goes about telling, with the greatest precision, whatever is most difficult to tell. One confesses in public and in private, to one's parents, one's educators, one's doctor, to those one loves; one admits to oneself, in pleasure and in pain, things it would be impossible to tell to anyone else, the things people write books about.

[...]

From the Christian penance to the present day, sex was a privileged theme of confession. A thing that was hidden, we are told. But what if, on the contrary, it was what, in a quite particular way, one confessed? Suppose the obligation to conceal it was but another aspect of the duty to admit to it (concealing it all the more and with greater care as the confession of it was more important, requiring a stricter ritual and promising more decisive effects)? What if sex in our society, on a scale of several centuries, was something that was placed within an unrelenting system of confession? The transformation of sex into discourse, which I spoke of earlier, the dissemination and reinforcement of heterogeneous sexualities, are perhaps two elements of the same deployment: they are linked together with the help of the central element of a confession that compels individuals to articulate their sexual peculiarity – no matter how extreme. In Greece, truth and sex were linked, in the form of pedagogy, by the transmission of a precious knowledge from one body to another; sex served as a medium for initiations into learning. For us, it is in the confession that truth and sex are joined, through the obligatory and exhaustive expression of an individual secret. But this time it is truth that serves as a medium for sex and its manifestations.

The confession is a ritual of discourse in which the speaking subject is also the subject of the statement; it is also a ritual that unfolds within a power relationship, for one does not confess without the presence (or virtual presence) of a partner who is not simply the interlocutor but the authority who requires the confession, prescribes and appreciates it, and intervenes in order to judge, punish, forgive, console, and reconcile; a ritual in which the truth is corroborated by the obstacles and resistances it has had to surmount in order to be formulated; and finally, a ritual in which the expression alone, independently of its external consequences, produces intrinsic modifications in the person who articulates it: it exonerates, redeems, and purifies him; it unburdens him of his wrongs, liberates him, and promises him salvation.

For centuries, the truth of sex was, at least for the most part, caught up in this discursive form. Moreover, this form was not the same as that of education (sexual education confined itself to general principles and rules of prudence); nor was it that of initiation (which remained essentially a silent practice, which the act of sexual enlightenment or deflowering merely rendered laughable or violent). As we have seen, it is a form that is far removed from the one governing the 'erotic art.' By virtue of the power structure immanent in it, the confessional discourse cannot come from above, as in the *ars erotica,* through the sovereign will of a master, but rather from below, as an obligatory act of speech which, under some imperious compulsion, breaks the bonds of discretion or forgetfulness. What secrecy it presupposes is not owing to the high price of what it has to say and the small number of those who are worthy of its benefits, but to its obscure familiarity and its general baseness. Its veracity is not guaranteed by the lofty authority of the magistery, nor by the tradition it transmits, but by the bond, the basic intimacy in discourse, between the one who speaks and what he is speaking about. On the other hand, the agency of domination does not reside in the one who speaks (for it is he who is constrained), but in the one who listens and says nothing;

not in the one who knows and answers, but in the one who questions and is not supposed to know. And this discourse of truth finally takes effect, not in the one who receives it, but in the one from whom it is wrested. With these confessed truths, we are a long way from the learned initiations into pleasure, with their technique and their mystery. On the other hand, we belong to a society which has ordered sex's difficult knowledge, not according to the transmission of secrets, but around the slow surfacing of confidential statements.

The confession was, and still remains, the general standard governing the production of the true discourse on sex. It has undergone a considerable transformation, however. For a long time, it remained firmly entrenched in the practice of penance. But with the rise of Protestantism, the Counter Reformation, eighteenth-century pedagogy, and nineteenth-century medicine, it gradually lost its ritualistic and exclusive localization; it spread; it has been employed in a whole series of relationships: children and parents, students and educators, patients and psychiatrists, delinquents and experts. The motivations and effects it is expected to produce have varied, as have the forms it has taken: interrogations, consultations, autobiographical narratives, letters; they have been recorded, transcribed, assembled into dossiers, published, and commented on. But more important, the confession lends itself, if not to other domains, at least to new ways of exploring the existing ones. It is no longer a question simply of saying what was done – the sexual act – and how it was done; but of reconstructing, in and around the act, the thoughts that recapitulated it, the obsessions that accompanied it, the images, desires, modulations, and quality of the pleasure that animated it. For the first time no doubt, a society has taken upon itself to solicit and hear the imparting of individual pleasures.

A dissemination, then, of procedures of confession, a multiple localization of their constraint, a widening of their domain: a great archive of the pleasure of sex was gradually constituted. For a long time this archive dematerialized as it was formed. It regularly disappeared without a trace (thus suiting the purposes of the Christian pastoral) until medicine, psychiatry. and pedagogy began to solidify it: Campe, Salzmann, and especially Kaan, Krafft-Ebing, Tardieu, Molle, and Havelock Ellis carefully assembled this whole powerful typical outpouring from the sexual mosaic. Western societies thus began to keep an indefinite record of these people's pleasures. They made up a herbal of them and established a system of classification. They described their everyday deficiencies as well as their oddities or exasperations. This was an important time. It is easy to make light of these nineteenth-century psychiatrists, who made a point of apologizing for the horrors they were about to let speak, evoking 'immoral behavior' or 'aberrations of the genetic senses,' but I am more inclined to applaud their seriousness: they had a feeling for momentous events. It was a time when the most singular pleasures were called upon to pronounce a discourse of truth concerning themselves, a discourse which had to model itself after that which spoke, not of sin and salvation, but of bodies and life processes – the discourse of science. It was enough to make one's voice tremble, for an improbable thing was then taking shape: a confessional science, a science which relied on a many-sided extortion, and took for its object what was unmentionable but admitted to nonetheless.

learning to labour

T he difficult thing to explain about how middle-class kids get middle-class jobs is why others let them? The difficult thing to explain about how working-class kids get working-class jobs is why they let themselves?

It is much too facile simply to say that they have no choice. The way in which manual labour is applied to production can range in different societies from the coercion of machine guns, bullets and trucks to the mass ideological conviction of the voluntary industrial army. Our own liberal democratic society is somewhere in between. There is no obvious physical coercion and a degree of self direction. This is despite the inferior rewards for, undesirable social definition, and increasing intrinsic meaninglessness, of manual work: in a word its location at the bottom of a class society.

Too often occupational and educational talents are thought of as on a shallowing line or shrinking capacity with working class people at its lower reaches unquestion-ningly taking on the worst jobs thinking somehow, 'I accept that I'm so stupid that it's fair and proper that I should spend the rest of my life screwing nuts onto wheels in a car factory'. This gradient model must, of course, assume a zero or near zero reading at its base. The real individuals at the bottom end would scarcely rate a score for being alive, never mind for being human. Since these individuals are currently far from walk-ing corpses but are actually bringing the whole system into crisis, this model is clearly in need of revision. The market economy of jobs in a capitalist society emphatically does not extend to a market economy of satisfactions.

I want to suggest that 'failed' working-class kids do not simply take up the falling curve of work where the least successful middle-class, or the most successful working-class kids, leave off. Instead of assuming a continuous shallowing line of ability in the occupational/class structure we must conceive of radical breaks represented by the interface of cultural forms. We shall be looking at the way in which the working class cultural pattern of 'failure' is quite different and discontinuous from the other patterns. Though in a determined context it has its own processes, its own definitions, its own account of those other groups conventionally registered as more successful. And this class culture is not a neutral pattern, a *mental* category, a set of variables impinging on the school from the outside. It comprises experiences, relationships, and ensembles of systematic types of relationship which not only set particular 'choices' and 'decisions' at particular times, but also structure, really and experientially, how these 'choices' come about and are defined in the first place …

Labour power is the human capacity to work on nature with the use of tools to produce things for the satisfaction of needs and the reproduction of life. Labouring is not a universal transhistorical changeless human activity. It takes on specific forms and meanings in different kinds of societies. The processes through which labour power comes to be subjectively understood and objectively applied and their interrelationships is of profound significance for the type of society which is produced and the particular nature and formation of its classes. These processes help to construct both the identities of particular subjects and also distinctive class forms at the cultural and symbolic level as well as at the economic and structural level …

The specific milieu, I argue, in which a certain subjective sense of manual labour power, and an objective decision to apply it to manual work is produced, is the working class counter-school culture. It is here where working-class themes are mediated to individuals and groups in their own determinate context and where working-class kids creatively develop, transform and finally reproduce aspects of the larger culture in their own praxis in such a way as to finally direct them to certain kinds of work […] I argue that it is their own culture which most effectively prepares some working-class lads for the manual giving of their labour power. We may say that there is an element of self-damnation in the taking on of subordinate roles in Western capitalism. However, this damnation is experienced, paradoxically, as true learning, affirmation, appropriation, and as a form of resistance.

The qualitative methods, and Participant Observation used in the research, and the ethnographic format of the presentation were dictated by the nature of my interest in 'the cultural'. These techniques are suited to record this level and have a sensitivity to meanings and values as well as an ability to represent and interpret symbolic articulations, practices and forms of cultural production. In particular the ethnographic account, without always knowing how, can allow a degree of the activity, creativity and human agency within the object of study to come through into the analysis and the reader's experience. This is vital to my purposes where I view the cultural, not simply as a set of transferred internal structures (as in the usual notions of socialisation) nor as the passive result of the action of dominant ideology downwards (as in certain kinds of Marxism), but a least in part as the product of collective human praxis …

The main study was of a group of twelve non-academic working-class lads from a town we shall call Hammertown and attending a school we shall call Hammertown Boys. They were selected on the basis of friendship links and membership of some kind of an oppositional culture in a working-class school. The school was built in the inter-war years and was composed of standard, often terraced, reasonably well maintained houses interlinked with a maze of roads, crescents and alleys and served by numerous large pubs and clusters of shops and small supermarkets.

During the period of the research this school was a boys only, non-selective secondary modern school twinned with a girls' school of the same status.

OPPOSITION TO AUTHORITY AND REJECTION OF THE CONFORMIST

The most basic, obvious and explicit dimension of counter-school culture is entrenched general and personalised opposition to 'authority'. This feeling is easily verbalised by 'the lads' (the self-elected title of those in the counter-school culture).

[In a group discussion on teachers]

Joey   (...) they're able to punish us. They're bigger than us, they stand for a bigger establishment than we do, like, we're just little and they stand for bigger things, and you try to get your own back. It's, uh, resenting authority I suppose.

Eddie   The teachers think they're high and mighty 'cos they're teachers, but they're nobody really, they're just ordinary people ain't they?

Bill   Teachers think they're everybody. They are more, they're higher than us, but they think they're a lot higher and they're not.

Spanksy Wish we could call them first names and that ... think they're God.

Pete   That would be a lot better.

PW   I mean you say they're higher. Do you accept at all that they know better about things?

-

Joey   Yes, but that doesn't rank them above us, just because they are slightly more intelligent.

Bill   They ought to treat us how they'd like us to treat them.

(...)

Joey   (...) the way we're subject to their every whim like. They want something doing and we have to sort of do it, 'cos, er, er, we're just, we're under them like. We were with a woman teacher in here, and 'cos we all wear rings and one or two of them bangles, like he's got one on, and bout of the blue, like for no special reason, she says, 'take all that off'.

PW   Really?

Joey   Yeah, we says, 'One won't come off', she says, 'Take yours off as well'. I said, 'You'll have to chop my finger off first'.

PW   Why did she want you to take your rings off?

Joey   Just a sort of show like. Teachers do this, like all of a sudden they'll make you do your ties up and things like this. You're subject to their every whim like. If they want something done, if you don't think it's right, and you object against it, you're down to Simmondsy [the head], or you get the cane, you get some extra work tonight.

PW   You think of most staff as kind of enemies (...)?

-       Yeah.

-       Yeah.

-       Most of them.

Joey   It adds a bit of spice to yer life, if you're trying to get him for something he's done to you.

This opposition involves as apparent inversion of the usual values held up by authority. Diligence, deference, respect – these become things which can be read in quite another way.

[In a group discussion]
PW   Evans [the Careers Master] said you were all being very rude (...) you didn't have the politeness to listen to the speaker [during a careers session]. He said why didn't you realise that you were just making the world very rude for when you grow up and God help you when you have kids 'cos they're going to be worse. What did you think of that?
Joey   They wouldn't. They'll be outspoken. They wouldn't be submissive fucking twits. They'll be outspoken, upstanding sort of people.
Spanksy   If any of my kids are like this, here, I'll be pleased.

This opposition is expressed mainly as a style. It is lived out in countless small ways which are special to the school institution, instantly recognised by the teachers, and an almost ritualistic part of the daily fabric of life for the kids. Teachers are adept conspiracy theorists. They have to be. It partly explains their devotion to finding out 'the truth' from suspected culprits. They live surrounded by conspiracy in its most obvious – though often verbally unexpressed – forms. It can easily become a paranoiac conviction of enormous proportions.

As 'the lads' enter the classroom or assembly, there are conspiratorial nods to each other saying, 'Come and sit here with us for a laff', sidelong glances to check where the teacher is and smirking smiles. Frozen for a moment by a direct command or look, seething movement easily resumes with the kids moving about with that 'I'm just passing through, sir' sort of look to get closer to their mates. Stopped again, there is always a ready excuse. 'I've got to take my coat off sir', 'So and So told me to see him sir'. After assembly has started, the kid still marooned from his mates crawls along the backs of the chairs or behind a curtain down the side of the hall, kicking other kids, or trying to dismantle a chair with somebody on it as he passes.

'The lads' specialise in a caged resentment which always stops just short of outright confrontation. Settled in class, as near a group as they can manage, there is a continuous scraping of chairs, a bad tempered 'tut-tutting' at the simplest request, and a continuous fidgeting about which explores every permutation of sitting or lying on a chair. During private study, some openly show disdain by apparently trying to go to sleep with their head sideways down on the desk, some have their backs to the desk gazing out of the window, or even vacantly at the wall. There is an aimless air of insubordination ready with spurious justification and impossible to nail down. If someone is sitting on the radiator it is because his trousers are wet from the rain, if someone is drifting across the classroom he is going to get some paper for written work, or if someone is leaving class he is going to empty the rubbish 'like he usually does'. Comics, newspapers and nudes under half-lifted desks melt into elusive textbooks. A continuous hum of talk flows around injunctions not to, like the inevitable tide over barely dried sand and everywhere there are rolled-back eyeballs and exaggerated mouthings of conspiratorial secrets.

During class teaching a mouthed imaginary dialogue counterpoints the formal instruction: 'No, I don't understand, you cunt'; 'What you on about, twit?'; 'Not fucking likely'; 'Can I go home now please?' At the vaguest sexual double meaning giggles and 'whoas' come from the back accompanied perhaps by someone masturbating a gigantic penis with rounded hands above his head in compressed lipped lechery. If the secret of the conspiracy is challenged, there are V signs behind the teacher's back, the gunfire of cracked knuckles from the side, and evasive innocence at the front. Attention is focused on ties, rings, shoes, fingers, blots on the desk – anything rather than the teacher's eyes...

It is essentially what appears to be their enthusiasm for, and complicity with, immediate authority which makes the school conformists – or 'ear'oles' or 'lobes' – the second great target for 'the lads'. The term 'ear'ole' itself connotes the passivity and absurdity of the school conformists for 'the lads'. It seems that they are always listening, never *doing*: never animated with their own internal life, but formless in rigid reception. The ear is one of the least expressive organs of the human body: it responds to the expressivity of others, It is pasty and easy to render obscene. That is how 'the lads' liked to picture those who conformed to the official idea of schooling.

Crucially, 'the lads' not only reject but feel *superior* to the 'ear'oles'. The obvious medium for the enactment of this superiority is that which the 'ear'oles' apparently yield – fun, independence and excitement: having a 'laff'.

[In a group discussion]

PW	(...) why not be like the ear'oles, why not try and get CSEs?
-	They don't get any fun, do they?
Derek	Cos they'm prats like, one kid he's got on his report now, he's got five As and one B.
-	-Who's that?
Derek	Birchall.
Spanksy	I mean, what will they remember of their school life? What will they have to look back on? Sitting in a classroom, sweating their bollocks off, you know, while we've been ... I mean look at the things we can look back on, fighting on the Pakis, fighting on the JAs [i.e. Jamaicans]. Some of the things we've done on teachers, it'll be a laff when we look back on it.
(...)	
Perce	Like you know, he don't get much fun, well say Spanksy plays about all day, he gets fun. Bannister's there sweating, sweating his bollocks off all day while Spanksy's doing fuck all, and he's enjoying it.
Spanksy	In the first and second years I used to be brilliant realy. I was in 2A, 3A you know and when I used to get home, I used to lie in bed thinking, 'Ah, school tomorrow', you know, I hadn't done that homework, you know ... 'Got to do it'.
-	Yeah, that's right, that is.
Spanksy	But now when I go home, it's quiet, I ain't got nothing to think about, I say, 'Oh great, school tomorrow, it'll be a laff', you know.
Will	You still never fucking come!

Spanksy	Who?
Will	You.
[Laughter]	
(...)	
-	You can't imagine ...
-	You can't imagine [inaudible] going into the Plough and saying, 'A pint of lager please'.
Fred	You can't imagine Bookley goin' home like with the missus, either, and having a good maul on her.
-	I can, I've seen him!
-	He's got a bird, Bookley!
-	He has.
Fred	I can't see him getting to grips with her, though, like we do you know.

It was in the sexual realm especially that 'the lads' felt their superiority over the 'ear'oles'. 'Coming out of your shell', 'losing your timidness' was part of becoming 'one of the lads', but it was also the way to 'chat up birds' successfully. In an odd way there was a distorted reflection here of the teachers' relationships to the 'ear'oles'. 'The lads' felt that they occupied a similar structural role of superiority and experience, but in a different and more antisocial mode.

[In an individual interview]

Joey	We've [the lads] all bin with women and all that (...) we counted it up the other day, how many kids had actually been with women like, how many kids we know been and actually had a shag, and I think it only come to, I think we got up to twenty-four (...) in the fifth year out of a hundred kids, that's a quarter.
PW	Would you always know though?
Joey	Yes I would (...) It gets around you know, the group within ourself, the kids who we know who are sort of semi-ear'oles like ... they're a separate group from us and the ear'oles. Kids like Dover, Simms and Willis, and one or two others like. They all mess about with their own realm, but they're still fucking childish, the way they talk, the way they act like. They can't mek us laff, we can mek them laff, they can fucking get in tears when they watch us sometimes, but it's beyond their powers to mek one of us laff, and then there's us (...) some of them [the semi-ear'oles] have been with women and we know about it like. The ear'oles (...) they've got it all to come. I mean look at Tom Bradley, have you ever noticed him? I've always looked at him and I've thought, Well ... we've been through all life's pleasures and all its fucking displeasures, we've been drinking, we've been fighting, we've known frustration, sex, fucking hatred, love and all this lark, yet he's known none of it. He's never been with a woman, he's never been in a pub. We don't know it, we assume it – I dare say he'd come and tell us if he had – but he's never been with a woman, he's never been drinking, I've never known him in a fight. He's not known so many of the emotions as we've had to experience, and he's got it all to come yet...

THE INFORMAL GROUP

On a night we go out on
the street
Troubling other people,
I suppose we're anti-social,
But we enjoy it.

The older generation
They don't like our hair,
Or the clothes we wear
They seem to love running
us down,
I don't know what I would
do if I didn't have the gang.

(Extract from a poem by Derek written in an English class)

In many respects the opposition we have been looking at can be understood as a classic example of the opposition between the formal and the informal. The school is the zone of the formal. It has a clear structure: the school building, school rules, peda-gogic practice, a staff hierarchy with powers ultimately sanctioned – as we have seen in small way – by the state, the pomp and majesty of the law, and the repressive arm of state apparatus, the police. The 'ear'oles' invest in this formal structure, and in exchange for some loss in autonomy expect the official guardians to keep the holy rules – often above and beyond their actual call to duty. What is freely sacrificed by the faithful must be taken from the unfaithful.

Counter-school culture is the zone of the informal. It is where the incursive demands of the formal are denied – even if the price is the expression of opposition in style, micro-interactions and non-public discourses. In working class culture generally oppo-sition is frequently marked by a withdrawal into the informal and expressed in its characteristic modes just beyond the reach of 'the rule'.

Even though there are no public rules, physical structures, recognised hierarchies or institutionalised sanctions in the counter-school culture, it cannot run on air. It must have its own material base, its own infrastructure. This is, of course, the social group. The informal group is the basic unit of this culture, the fundamental and elemental source of its resistance. It locates and make possible all other elements of the culture, and its presence decisively distinguishes 'the lads' from the 'ear'oles'.

The importance of the group is very clear to members of the counter-school culture.

[In a group discussion]
Will   (...) we see each other every day, don't we, at school (...)
Joey   That's it, we've developed certain ways of talking, certain ways of acting, and we developed disregards for Pakis, Jamaicans and all different ... for all the scrubs and the fucking ear'oles and all that (...) We're getting to know it now, like we're getting to know all the cracks, like, how to get out of lessons and things, and we know where to have a crafty smoke. You can

come over here to the youth wing and do summat, and er'm … all your friends are here, you know, it's sort of what's there, what's always going to be there for the next year, like, and you know you have to come to school today, if you're feeling bad, your mate'll soon cheer yer up like, 'cos you couldn't go without ten minutes in this school, without having a laff at something or other.

PW	Are your mates a really big important thing at school now?
-	Yeah.
-	Yeah.
-	Yeah.
Joey	They're about the best thing actually.

The essence of being 'one of the lads' lies within the group. It is impossible to form a distinctive culture by yourself. You cannot generate fun, atmosphere and a social identity by yourself. Joining the counter-school culture means joining a group, and enjoying it means being with the group:

[In a group discussion on being 'one of the lads']

Joey	(…) when you'm dossing on your own, it's no good, but when you'm dossing with your mates, then you're all together, you're having a laff and it's a doss.
Bill	If you don't do what the others do, you feel out.
Fred	You feel out, yeah, yeah. They sort of, you feel, like, thinking the others are …
Will	In the second years …
Spanksy	I can imagine … you know, when I have a day off school, when you come back the next day, and something happened like in the day you've been off, you feel, 'Why did I have that day off', you know, 'I could have been enjoying myself. You know what I mean? You come back and they're saying, 'Oorh, you should have been here yesterday', you know.
Will	(…) like in the first and second years, you can say er'm … you're a bit of an ear'ole right. Then you want to try what it's like to be er'm … say, one of the boys like, you want to have a taste of that, not an ear'ole, and so you like the taste of that.

Though informal, such groups nevertheless have rules of a kind which can be described – though they are characteristically framed in contrast to what 'rules' are normally taken to mean.

PW	(…) Are there any rules between you lot?
Pete	We just break the other rules.
Fuzz	We ain't got no rules between us though, have we?
(…)	
Pete	Changed 'em round.
Will	We ain't got rules but we do things between us, but we do things that y'know, like er … say, I wouldn't knock off anybody's missus or Joey's missus, and they wouldn't do it to me, y'know what I mean? Things like

	that or, er … yer give 'im a fag, you expect one back, like, or summat like that.
Fred	T'ain't rules, it's just an understanding really.
Will	That's it, yes.
PW	(…) What would these understandings be?
Will	Er … I think, not to … meself, I think there ain't many of us that play up the first or second years, it really is that, but y'know, say if Fred had cum to me and sez, 'er … I just got two bob off that second year over there'. I'd think, 'What a cunt', you know.
(…)	
Fred	We're as thick as thieves, that's what they say, stick together.

horizons of inquiry

Part three

The concept of 'knowledge' walks hand in hand with the idea of 'research methods.' By usual scientific standards, knowledge is an accurate and unbiased representation of the world as it is. The scientist's task is to report with fidelity on 'what is the case?' If this is our view of knowledge, then we will seek out methods that accurately reflect the world. An accurate representation should function something like a mirror, catching every nuance of that which it reflects. If the mirror is clouded or cracked, it will interfere with the representational process. And so it is with methods of research. If the researcher is biased by ideology we cannot trust his or her results. Distance is also required between the researcher and the researched, lest the relationship between them 'contaminate' the results. Quantitative methods are preferred over qualitative interpretations, as the former are viewed as more unbiased and precise and can also be subjected to the formal requirements of statistical analysis. At least, these are our traditional beliefs.

Social constructionist ideas pose a major challenge to the traditional account of knowledge and research methods. For the constructionist what passes as knowledge is generated within communities for purposes shared by the participants. A method is only accurate or objective in terms of the particular conventions shared within the community. For example, communities of artists have a highly differentiating vocabulary of color, while communities of psychophysiologists propose that there are no color differences in the world, only differences in light reflected on the retina. Further, every community shares certain values, and these will inevitably be reflected in the results of inquiry. Research that studies the differences between 'men' and 'women,' for example, sustains a way of life in which it is important to notice differences of this kind. Thus, for the constructionist, any demands for universal methods of research function oppressively. They sustain the realities and morality of a particular group. The constructionist invitation, then, is first, to open the door to multiple traditions, each with their own particular view of knowledge and methodology. Second, we are challenged to be creative, to initiate new ways of producing knowledge that are tied to our particular values or ideals.

The constructionist invitation to expand the domain of research practices has an additional advantage. Every method of research also carries with it certain assumptions about the nature of the world. To select a method, then, is to constrain our way of understanding. For example, if we are trained to carry out laboratory experiments, we will presume that the world functions according to laws of cause and effect. Once we have put on the glasses of the experimentalist, the entire world will appear to us as a set of cause and effect relationships. Contrast the experimental method with that of the phenomenologist. The phenomenologist assumes that the most important thing you can know about the individual is how he or she privately sees, interprets, feels, or understands the world. Each individual may be unique in this regard. The preferred methods of the phenomenologist are sensitive interviews that delve into the individual's subjective state. The interview will thus translate the world into subjective states; cause and effect relations will seldom be mentioned. In effect, a choice of research method is also a choice about the way we shall understand the world. To expand the vocabulary of research methods is thus to enrich the ways we have of constructing the world and our actions within it.

This invitation to enrichment has unleashed an enormous range of innovative research activity – especially within the social sciences. We recommend, for example, Denzin and Lincoln's voluminous *Handbook of Qualitative Research* (2000), and Reason and Bradbury's *Handbook of action research: Participatory inquiry and practice* (2000). The interested reader will also find a wealth of innovative work described in Kvale's *InterViews* (1996), Wetherell, Taylor and Yates' *Discourse as Data* (2001), and Reinharz *Feminist Methods in Social Research* (1992), along with the journal, *Qualitative Inquiry*. In the present volume we offer close-up views of several newly developing domains, the first emphasizing discourse, the second the expansion of voices expressed in the research itself, and the third the action potentials of research.

EXPLORING DISCOURSE

If we favor a constructionist view of social life, we are immediately drawn to the importance of language. It is through language that we create the sense of the real and the good, that we create our histories and our destinies. This should be clear from the preceding readings. With this realization has grown an immense body of research on discourse. This is scarcely to say that the study of language is itself novel within the social sciences. However, for the constructionist the study of language takes on a very special character. It differs from the psychologist's approach to language, for example, because for psychologists, language is considered an outward expression of mental life. Thus, for the psychologist it is not the words that are important in themselves, so much as what they might say about cognitive process or 'underlying' meaning. In contrast, for the constructionist making meaning is a public process; discourse is important in terms of the relationships in which it is embedded. The major questions, then, concern the public process and not an underlying mental life. In fact, as you may surmise from Lutz's work on emotions (Reading 8), constructionists often hold that the very idea of 'mental life' is a cultural construction. Constructionist inquiry also differs from most linguistic study. Many linguists are indeed concerned with the public patterns of language, for example, the structure of grammar or the diffusion of language usage across culture or history. However, such research is typically wedded to a traditional scientific investment in the value neutral accumulation of knowledge – 'getting it right' about language. In contrast, most constructionist inquiry into language carries with it a liberatory goal. The point is not simply to record language usage, but to focus on linguistic forms that affect our well-being, that are potentially injurious and oppressive, or that are releasing and joyful. Here the interest is not so much in accumulating knowledge about a stable phenomenon, but in changing our patterns of language – and thus of cultural life.

A central topic in the study of discourse is that of narrative. As investigators reason, one of our major ways of making sense of the world is through stories. We understand our lives as a story, history as a story, the cosmos as a story, and so on. In effect, the story form structures our understandings and thus our actions. Such reasoning has given rise to a substantial body of study, and the interested reader might wish to see Sarbin's *Narrative Psychology* (1986), Carr's *Time, Narrative, and History* (1986), Spence's *Narrative Truth and Historical Truth* (1982), Church's *Forbidden Narratives: Critical Autobiography as Social Science* (1995), Coles', *The Call of Stories: Teaching and the Moral Imagination* (1989), the Josselson, Lieblich, and McAdams edited series, *The Narrative Study of Lives*, as well as issues of the journal, *Narrative Inquiry*. We offer here but one exemplar of narrative study. Mary Gergen's particular concern (Reading 12) is with the ways in which life stories shape people's visions of what they can and should do. As we share and disseminate stories of heroes and villains, success and failure, for example, so are our own life decisions shaped. In this respect, Gergen is particularly concerned about the lack of heroic success stories for women in the culture, and the possibility that this scarcity may contribute to the low percentage of women at the higher echelons of government and business. Gergen's study of the life story accounts of famous men and women does indeed demonstrate a strong hero myth within the male stories, and little in the way of well-structured narrative among the women. However, rather than rueing the lack of heroine stories among the women, Gergen reveals characteristics of the male story that make them far from ideal. From her standpoint society might be far better off with a greater prevalence of the woman's narrative.

EXPANDING VOICE

In traditional research 'the investigator' reports on the results of his or her observations. It is thus the observer's responsibility to report on 'what I observed,' or 'my findings.' Essentially this means that the researcher controls the language of the research report. Or in constructionist terms, the reality constructed in the research report is that of the researcher him or herself. Even in cases where the researcher is reporting on what the research subjects said (as in the research interview), the subjects' voices are translated in such a way that the researcher's interpretations and interests are sustained. In this sense traditional research is *monologic*; a single voice dominates.

The constructionist dialogues generate reflective pause. Why should the researcher be the sole arbiter of the real; why should he or she be granted ultimate authority; why are the voices of those we 'study' not granted the right to speak for themselves; are there means of shifting research in a more dialogic direction? Questions such as these have stimulated a wave of new and innovative research methodologies – all expanding the range of voices contributing to the creation of meaning. We select three of these creative ventures to illuminate the possibilities.

Lisa Tillmann-Healy's treatment of bulimia (Reading 13) is an illustration of *autoethnography* in action. Autoethnography has emerged in recent years as a means of enabling 'researchers' to become 'witnesses.' That is, rather than reporting on 'subjects under observation,' the autoethnographer serves as the subject. He or she gives first-hand insight into a form of life, making it available to the broader community. Tillmann-Healy's offering is especially significant because she is able to combine the skills of dramatic story-telling with her clinician's sense of the dynamics of bulimia. We come away not only with a sense of enhanced understanding, but an experience of 'feeling with.'

In the educational sphere Patti Lather, has been a major figure in the development of constructionist theory, research methodology, and educational practices. Her work, *Getting Smart: Feminist Research and Pedagogy With/in the Postmodern*, has found a global audience. The present offering (Reading 14) provides a glimpse into her creative work with Chris Smithies and a group of women diagnosed as HIV positive. The book from which this is excerpted, *Troubling the Angels*, provides intimate portraits of the lives of these women – touching, illuminating, and inspirational. The reader is also introduced to a welter of information, along with significant glimpses into the emotional and intellectual complexities of carrying out such work. And herein lies the particular importance of the work in the present context: Lather and Smithies provide an outstanding example of a text open to multiple voices. The women are allowed ample space to tell their stories, to share their dialogues, and even to comment on the research itself. At the same time, Lather and Smithies include their own views, not only on the broader issues at stake in the research, but on their own complex positions in the support group, and in relationship to their own intellectual work.

In this thrust toward the expansion of voice, an offering that has fascinated us is included (in edited form) as Reading 15. Here Karen Fox, a therapist, explores a case of child sexual abuse. Traditionally such work would focus on the experiences of the victim/survivor, helping us to understand his or her complex emotional world. However, Fox is not content with a one-dimensional understanding. Rather, in addition to the victim, she also includes excerpts from interviews with the step-grandfather, a sex offender. Finally, so that the reader can also understand that Fox herself is not simply a neutral bystander in the work, she secretes her own voice within the assortment. This is especially important, because Fox was also a victim of child sexual abuse. Yet, it is not simply the inclusion of the three voices that makes this such a rich offering. Fox situates the voices so that a vital inter-animation results. The interview excerpts are arrayed so that they form a complex trialogue, with each entry playing off against the others – resonating, elaborating, questioning. We come away as readers with a sense of the multi-textured character of sex abuse and an appreciation for the possible unfolding of meaning as conversation continues.

MOVING TOWARD ACTION

Discourse is a form of social action – a 'doing with' in the world. This is certainly a prevailing theme within the constructionist dialogues. Yet, the implications of this view are only slowly being unpacked; one cannot see the entire terrain of possibility at once. At present there are two directions that are being creatively and energetically explored, and both are represented in the two final readings in this section. In the first case, many researchers have long been discontent with a science that watches the world from the sidelines, and hopes that somehow its recordings will improve world conditions. Rather, the constructionist researcher is given license to be engaged in social change itself. One significant expression of this impulse is called 'participatory action research.' And, while long extant as a form of inquiry, the constructionist dialogues have added new and important dimension to such work (see, for example, Reason and Bradbury, 2000). In participatory action research the scientist makes him/herself available to a community in need, and using all his or her skills, participates with this community in bringing about change. Participatory action research may take many different forms, depending on the researcher and the context. We present only one, exemplary case, Gustav de Roux's work with a rural Colombian community (Reading 16). Here de Roux describes his efforts to help a community combat the oppressive force of an electric company that was economically exploiting the people. The chapter provides an inspiring example of how the participatory action paradigm can be used to improve the human condition.

If discourse is a form of action, then we can also begin to ask about the discursive actions of scholars and scientists themselves. Why do we typically write in such formal, abstract, impersonal, and dispassionate prose? Is such writing not intended for an audience that considers itself elite or superior in some way to the public at large? Does the very complexity of such writing not function in such a way as to exclude others from 'the club?' These are only some of the questions now being asked of academic writing. And, simultaneous with such questioning, there has been an explosion in experimental writing. We include here an attempt by Marcelo Diversi (Reading 17) to use the short story form to help us understand street life among urban homeless children in Brazil. As Diversi proposes, 'short stories as a writing genre have a unique potential to ... touch the feelings and emotions of people whose only channel of access to street kids' lives is the slanderous representations of the printed and televised media ... Short stories have the power to move readers from abstract, sterile notions to the lively imagery of otherwise distant social realities'. To be sure, these stories are based on intense immersion in the lives of the children. And the form in which their lives are represented beckons us as well to think imaginatively about possible modes of academic expression.

REFERENCES

Carr, D. (1986). *Time, Narrative, and History*. Bloomington: Indiana University Press.

Church, K. (1995). *Forbidden Narratives: Critical Autobiography as Social Science*. Newark, NJ: Gordon & Breach.

Coles, R. (1989). *The Call of Stories: Teaching and the Moral Imagination*. Boston, MA: Houghton-Mifflin.

Denzin, N. K. and Lincoln, Y. S. (Eds) (2000). *Handbook of Qualitative Research* (2nd. ed.) Thousand Oaks, CA: Sage.

Josselson, R., Lieblich, A. & McAdams, D. (Eds) (1993–2003). *The Narrative Study of Lives* series. Washington, D.C.: American Psychological Association Press.

Kvale, S. (1996). *InterViews: An Introduction to Qualitative Research Interviewing*. London, Thousand Oaks, CA: Sage.

Lather, P. (1991). *Getting smart: Feminist Research and Pedagogy With/in the Postmodern*, London, New York: Routledge, Kegan Paul.

Lather, P. and Smithies, C. (1997). *Troubling the Angels: Women Living with HIV/AIDS*. Boulder, CO: Westview Press.

Reason, P. and Bradbury, H. (Eds) (2000). *Handbook of Action Research: Participatory Inquiry and Practice*. London: Sage.

Reinharz, S. (1992). *Feminist Methods in Social Research*. New York: Oxford University Press.

Sarbin, T. R. (Ed.) (1986). *Narrative Psychology: The storied nature of human conduct*. New York: Praeger.

Spence, D. P. (1982). *Narrative Truth and Historical Truth*. New York: Norton.

Wetherell, M., Taylor, S. and Yates, S. J. (2001). *Discourse as Data: A guide for analysis*. London, Thousand Oaks, CA: Sage.

12

life stories: pieces of a dream

mary gergen

Mermaids' Songs
'I have heard the mermaids singing, each to each'.

T.S. Eliot

The songs of mermaids are not like other songs. Mermaids' voices sing beyond the human range – notes not heard, forms not tolerated, and each to each, not one to many, one above all. If we imagine the mermaids, we might almost hear them singing. Their voices blending, so that each, in its own special timbre, lends to the harmony of the whole. So it might be as one writes – a voice in a choir at the threshold of sensibility. My voice shall be only one of many to be heard.

When you hear one voice it is the voice of authority, the father's voice. One voice belongs to an androcentric order. Will our singing mute the single voice before we drown?

'We need to learn how to see our theorizing projects as ... 'riffing' between and over the beats of patriarchal theories' (Sandra Harding, 1986, 649).

This is an interwoven etude about life stories; it seeks to disrupt the usual narrative line, the rules of patriarchal form. I wish to escape the culturally contoured modes of discourse. Yet I, too, am mired in convention. If I write in all the acceptable ways, I shall only recapitulate the patriarchal forms. Yet, if I violate expectations too grievously, my words will become nonsense. Still, the mermaids sing.

'Finding voices authentic to women's experience is appallingly difficult. Not only are the languages and concepts we have ... male oriented, but historically women's experiences have been interpreted for us by men and male norms' (Kathryn Rabuzzi, 1988, 12).

We play at the shores of understanding. If you assent to the bending of traditional forms, then perhaps our collective act may jostle the sand castles of the ordered kingdom. We need one another, even if we do not always agree.

'If we do our work well, "reality" will appear even more unstable, complex, and disorderly than it does now' (Jane Flax, 1987, 643).

THE PARADOX OF THE PRIVATE: OUR PUBLIC SECRETS

When we tell one another our deepest secrets we use a public language. The nuances of consciousness, emotions both subtle and profound, inner yearnings, the whispering of conscience – all of these are created in the matrix of this language. The words form and deform around us as we speak and listen. We swim in a sea of words. Only that which is public can be private. We dwell in a paradox.

'Individual consciousness is a socio-ideological fact. If you cannot talk about an experience, at least to yourself, you did not have it' (Caryl Emerson, 1983, 10).

Our cultures provide models not only for the contents of what we say but also for the forms. We use these forms unwittingly; they create the means by which we interpret our lives. We know ourselves via the mediating forms of our cultures, through telling, and through listening.

'What created humanity is narration' (Pierre Janet, 1928, 42).

'Know thyself,' a seemingly timeless motto, loses clarity when we hold that our forms of self-understanding are the creation of the unknown multitudes who have gone before us. We have become, we are becoming because 'they' have set out the linguistic forestructures of intelligibility. What then does a personal identity amount to?

'Every text is an articulation of the relations between texts, a product of intertextuality, a weaving together of what has already been produced elsewhere in discontinuous form; every subject, every author, every self is the articulation of an intersubjectivity structured within and around the discourses available to it at any moment in time' (Michael Sprinker, 1980, 325).

If self-understanding is derived from our cultures, and the stories we can tell about ourselves are prototypically performed, what implications does this have for our life affairs? The reverberations of this question will ring in our ears.

'Every version of an "other" ... is also the construction of a "self"' (James Clifford, 1986, 23).

And, I add, every version of a self must be a construction of the other.

Our first mark of identity is by gender. We are called 'boy' or 'girl' in our first moment of life. Our personal identities are always genderized, then so must life stories be. I am concerned with the gendered nature of our life stories. What are manstories and womanstories? How do they differ? And what difference do these differences make?

'The literary construction of gender is always artificial ... one can never unveil the essence of masculinity or femininity. Instead, all one exposes are other representations' (Linda Kauffman, 1986, 314).

This overture suggests the major themes. Countertones may resist articulation. You may not find what you want. The voices mingle and collide. Only in the confluence will the totality be fixed ... temporarily.

DEFINING POWERS: DOUBTS ABOUT THE STRUCTURE

What do I mean by the narratives or stories of our lives? When we began our work on the traditional narrative, Kenneth Gergen and I described it as being composed of a valued end point; events relevant to this end point; the temporal ordering of these events toward the endpoint; the casual linkages between events (see also Gergen and Gergen, 1983; 1984; 1988).

Now I become uneasy. I wonder why this definition must be as it is? Doesn't a definition defend an order of discourse, an order of life? Whose lives are advantaged by this form and whose disadvantaged? Should we ask?

What are the forms of our life stories? We recognize them – a comedy, a tragedy, a romance, a satire. We know them as they are told. Their plots are implicated in their structures. A climax is a matter of form as well as content. Though separating form and content may be desirable from an analytic point of view, it is also arbitrary. (What are the forms of a womanstory and a manstory? How do they differ?)

'The dramatic structure of conversion ... where the self is presented as the stage for a battle of opposing forces and where a climactic victory for one force – spirit defeating flesh – completes the drama of the self, simply does not accord with the deepest realities of women's experience and so is inappropriate as a model for women's life-writing' (Mary G. Mason, 1980, 210).

Should we question the ways in which patriarchal authority has controlled the narrative forms? We would be in good company. Many feminist literary critics have expanded this perspective (see also Shari Benstock, 1988; Rachel Duplessis, 1985; Sidonie Smith, 1987). Such writers as Virginia Woolf (1957, 1958) have also struggled with how male domination in literary forms has made some works great and others trivial, some worthy and some not. What has been judged by the figures of authority as correct, has been granted publication, critical acclaim, and respect; the rest has often been ignored or abused.

'... both in life and in art, the values of a woman are not the values of a man. Thus, when a woman comes to write a novel, she will find that she is perpetually wishing to alter the established values – to make serious what appears insignificant to a man and trivial what is to him important' (Virginia Woolf, 1958, 81).

Although androcentric control over literary forms is a serious matter, how much graver is the accusation that the forms of our personal narratives are also under such control? The relation between one and the other is strong, but the more pervasive nature and consequence of male-dominated life stories is certainly more threatening to me.

'Narrative in the most general terms is a version of, or a special expression of, ideology; representations by which we construct and accept values and institutions' (Rachel DuPlessis, 1985, x).

I would add, construct and accept ourselves!

Thus, I become increasingly skeptical of our classical definitions of the narrative. Judgments of what constitutes a proper telling are suspect on the grounds that what seem to be simple canons of good judgment, aesthetic taste, or even familiar custom may also be unquestioned expressions of patriarchal power. Under the seemingly innocent guise of telling a true story, one's life story validates the status quo.

GENDERIZING: TENDERIZING THE MONOMYTH

Myths have carried the form and content of narratives throughout the centuries. They tell us how great events occur as well as how stories are made. Joseph Campbell (1956) has analyzed these ancient myths. He proposes that there is one fundamental myth – the 'monomyth.' This myth begins as the hero, having been dedicated to a quest, ventures forth from the everyday world. He goes into the region of the super-natural, where he encounters strange, dangerous, and powerful forces, which he must vanquish. Then the victorious hero returns and is rewarded for his great deeds. The monomyth is the hero's myth and the major manstory. (Where is the woman in this story? She is only to be found as a snare, an obstacle, a magic power, or a prize.)

'The whole ideology of representational significance is an ideology of power' (Stephen Tyler, 1986, 131).

This monomyth is not just a historical curiosity. It is the basic model for the stories of achievement in everyday lives. Life stories are often about quests; they, like the monomyth, are stories of achievement. The story hangs on the end point – will the goal be achieved or not? In such stories all is subsumed by the goal. The heroic character must not allow anything to interfere with the quest.

Do you assume that a heroine is the same as a hero, except for gender? Some might say that narratives of heroes are equally available to women. I doubt this is so. Cultural expectations about how the two genders should express their heroism are clearly divergent.

Consider the central characters and the major plots of life stories codified in literature, history, or personal narrative; we could easily conclude that women do not belong, at least in the starring role. The adventures of the hero of the monomyth would make rather strange sense if he were a woman. If He is the subject of the story, She must be the object. In the System opposites cannot occupy the same position. The woman represents the totality of what is to be known. The hero is the knower. She is life; he is the master of life. He is the main character; she is a supporting actress. He is the actor; she is acted upon.

'Although theroretically the hero was meant generically to stand for individuals of both sexes, actually, like so-called 'generic man,' the hero is a thoroughly androcentric construction' (Kathryn Rabuzzi, 1988, 10).

In general, the cultural repertoire of heroic stories requires different qualities for each gender. The contrast of the ideal narrative line pits the autonomous ego-enhancing hero single-handedly and single-heartedly progressing toward a goal versus the long-suffering, selfless, socially embedded heroine, being moved in many directions, lacking the tenacious loyalty demanded of a quest.

'Culture is male, our literary myths are for heroes, not heroines' (Joanna Russ, 1972, 18).

The differences in our stories are not generally recognized in our culture. In a democratic society, with equal opportunity for all, we do not consider the absence of narrative lines as relevant to unequal representation of people in public positions of power. We do not turn to our biographies to help explain, for example, why so few women are the heads of organizations, climb mountains, or teach math classes, or why so few men are primary caretakers of children? Even when women are leaders in their professions, or exceptional in some arena of life, they find it difficult to tell their personal narratives in the forms that would be suitable to their male colleagues. They are in a cultural hiatus, with a paucity of stories to tell. (How does one become when no story can be found?)

'The emphasis by women on the personal, especially on other people, rather than on their work life, their professional success, or their connectedness to current political or intellectual history clearly contradicts the established criterion about the content of autobiography' (Estelle Jelinek, 1980, 10).

FEMINIST THEORIES AND GENDER DIFFERENCES

Various feminist theorists have emphasized the underlying family dynamics that may sustain our gendered stories. As Nancy Chodorow (1978), Dorothy Dinnerstein (1976),

Jane Flax (1983), Carol Gilligan (1982), Evelyn Fox Keller (1983), and others have suggested, boys and girls are raised to regard their life trajectories differently. All children have as their first love object their mothering figure. However, boys are reared to separate from their mothers, and they learn to replace their attachment to mother with pride in masculine achievements and to derogate women and their relationships with them. Girls are not cut away from their mothers and forced to reidentify themselves. They remain embedded in their relations and do not learn the solitary hero role. But they must bear the burden of shame that the androcentered culture assigns to their gender.

This, then, is my theme: each gender acquires for personal use a repertoire of potential life stories relevant to their own gender. Understanding one's past, interpreting one's actions, evaluating future possibilities – each is filtered through these stories. Events 'make sense' as they are placed in the correct story form. If certain story forms are absent, events cannot take on the same meaning.

> 'We assume that life produces the autobiography, as an act produces its consequence, but can we not suggest, with equal justice, that the autobiography project may itself produce and determine life' (Paul de Man, 1979, 920).

AUTOBIOGRAPHIES AS THE GENDERED STORIES OF LIVES

I have been studying the popular autobiographies of men and women. Of interest to me is not what is there, in the story lines, but what is missing. What is it that each gender cannot talk about – and thus cannot integrate into life stories and life plans? What can a manstory tell that a womanstory cannot and vice versa?

> 'What appears as "real" in history, the social sciences, the arts, even in common sense, is always analyzable as a restrictive and expressive set of social codes and conventions' (James Clifford, 1986, 10).

In critical works concerning autobiography, women's narratives have been almost totally neglected (cf. Sayre, 1980; Olney, 1980; Smith, 1974). Women's writings have usually been exempted because they did not fit the proper formal mold. Their work has been more fragmentary, multidimensional, understated, and temporally disjunctive. 'Insignificant' has been the predominant critical judgment toward women's autobiographies (and their lives) (Estelle Jelinek, 1980).

> 'When a woman writes or speaks herself into existence, she is forced to speak in something like a foreign tongue' (Carolyn Burke, 1978, 844).

INTERPRETING THE STORIES

I look into autobiographies to discover the forms we use to tell a manstory, a womanstory. What story can I tell?

'Autobiography reveals the impossibility of its own dream: what begins on the presumption of self-knowledge ends in the creation of a fiction that covers over the premises of its construction' (Shari Benstock, 1988, 11).

My materials are taken from many biographies. This chapter concentrates on but a few. In this way a sense of life may perhaps be felt. The quotations I have drawn from these texts are hardly proof of my conclusions; they are better viewed as illustrations to vivify my interpretations. Other interpretations can and should be made.

SEEKING THE QUEST

Traditional narratives demand an end point, a goal. Certain rhetorical moves are required by custom – concentrating on the goal, moving toward the point, putting events in a sequence, building the case (no tangents, please). Classical autobiographies delineate the life of cultural heroes – those who have achieved greatness through their accomplishments. We expect those who write their biographies must be such heroes.

'Men tend to idealize their lives or to cast them into heroic molds to project their universal import' (Estelle Jelinek, 1980, 14).

How single-minded are these heroes in pursuit of their goals? How committed are the women who write their biographies? Does their story also fit the classic mold?

Listen to some of their voices.

Lee Iacocca's best-selling autobiography focused on his automotive career. His family life, in contrast, received scant attention. Iacocca's wife, Mary, was a diabetic. Her condition worsened over the years; after two heart attacks, one in 1978 and the other in 1980, she died in 1983 at the age of fifty-seven. According to Iacocca, each heart attack came after a crisis period in his career at Ford or Chrysler.

Iacocca wrote: 'Above all, a person with diabetes has to avoid stress. Unfortunately, with the path I had chosen to follow, this was virtually impossible' (Lee Iacocca, 301).

Iacocca's description of his wife's death was not intended to expose his cruelty. It is a conventional narrative report – appropriate to his gender. The book (and his life) are dedicated to his career. Iacocca seems to have found it unimaginable that he could have ended his career in order to reduce his wife's ill health. As a manstory, the passage is not condemning; however, if we reverse the sexes, as a wife's description of the death of her husband or child, the story would appear callous, to say the least. Unlike Iacocca, a woman who would do such a thing would not be considered an outstanding folk hero.

Yeager is the autobiography of the quintessential American hero, the man with the 'right stuff.' His story is intensively focused on his career as a pilot in the air force. He was the father of four children born in quick succession and his wife became gravely ill during her last pregnancy. Nothing, however, stopped him from flying. Constantly moving around the globe, always seeking the most dangerous missions, he openly states: 'Whenever Glennis needed me over the years. I was usually off in the wild blue yonder' (Chuck Yeager and Leo James, 103).

America's favorite hero would be considered an abusive parent were his story regendered.

Richard Feynman, autobiographer and Nobel prize-winning physicist, was married to a woman who had been stricken with tuberculosis for seven years. During World War II, he moved to Los Alamos to work on the Manhattan Project developing the atomic bomb, and she was several hours away in a hospital in Albuquerque. The day she was dying he borrowed a car to go to her bedside.

He reports: 'When I got back (yet another tire went flat on the way), they asked me what happened? "She's dead. And how's the program going?" They caught on right away that I didn't want to moon over it' (Richard Feynman, 113).

Manstories tend to follow the traditional narrative pattern: becoming their own heroes, facing crises, following their quests, and ultimately achieving victory. Their careers provide them their central lines of narrative structuring, and personal commitments, external to their careers, are relegated to insignificant sub-plots.

What does one find among women authors?

'There is virtually only one occupation for a female protagonist – love, of course – which our culture uses to absorb all possible Bildung, success/failure, learning, education, and transition to adulthood' (Rachel DuPlessis, 1985, 182).

Beverly Sills, who became a star at the New York City Opera, all but gave up her singing career for two years to live in Cleveland because this was where her husband worked. She describes her thoughts: 'Peter had spent all of his professional life working for the *Plain Dealer*, and he had every intention of eventually becoming the newspaper's editor-in-chief. I was just going to have to get used to Cleveland. My only alternative was to ask Peter to scuttle the goal he'd been working toward for almost twenty-five years. If I did that, I didn't deserve to be his wife. Not coincidentally, I began re-evaluating whether or not I truly wanted a career as an opera singer. I decided I didn't. ... I was twenty-eight years old, and I wanted to have a baby' (Beverly Sills and Lawrence Linderman, 120).

The only businesswoman in my sample, Sydney Biddle Barrows, also known by the title of her autobiography, *Mayflower Madam*, shows second thoughts about maintaining a then extremely successful business when it clashed with private goals:

'By early 1984.... I realized that I couldn't spend the rest of my life in the escort business. I was now in my early thirties and starting to think more practically about my future – which would, I hoped, include marriage. As much as I loved my job, I had to acknowledge that the kind of man I was likely to fall in love with would never marry the owner of an escort service.... If I didn't want to remain single forever, I would sooner or later have to return to a more conventional line work' (Sydney Biddle Barrows, 205).

Martina Navratilova discusses her feelings about going skiing after many years of foregoing this dangerous sport: 'I made a decision in my teens to not risk my tennis career on the slopes, but in recent years I've wanted to feel the wind on my face again.... I wasn't willing to wait God-knows-how-many-years to stop playing and start living' (Martina Navratilova, 320).

Nien Cheng's *Life and Death in Shanghai* details her survival during years of imprisonment in China. Although her own survival might be seen as the major goal of her story, this focus is deeply compromised by her concerns with her daughter's welfare. 'I hoped my removal to the detention house would free her from any further pressure to denounce me. If that were indeed the case.... I would be prepared to put up with anything' (Nien Cheng, 132).

Discovering that her daughter is dead greatly disturbs her own will to go on. 'Now there was nothing left. It would have been less painful if I had died in prison and never known that Meiping was dead. My struggle to keep alive ... suddenly seemed meaningless' (ibid., 360).

For the women, the career line was important, but it was not an ultimate end point. Whereas men seemed to sacrifice their lives to careers, women seemed to tell the story in reverse. This is not to say that women avoided achieving goals. They, too, yearn for the joy of success. But men and women do not describe their feelings in the same way. Let us listen.

Lee Iacocca: 'My years as general manager of the Ford Division were the happiest period of my life. For my colleagues and me, this was fire-in-the-belly time. We were high from smoking our own brand – a combination of hard work and big dreams' (Lee Iacocca, 65).

Chuck Yeager: 'I don't recommend going to war as a way of testing character, but by the time ours ended we felt damned good about ourselves and what we had accomplished. Whatever the future held, we knew our skills as pilots, our ability to handle stress and danger, and our reliability in tight spots. It was the difference between thinking you're pretty good, and proving it' (Chuck Yeager and Leo James, 88).

Edward Koch: 'I am the Mayor of a city that has more Jews than live in Jerusalem, more Italians than live in Rome ... and more Puerto Ricans than live in San Juan.... It is a tremendous responsibility, but there is no other job in the world that compares with it ... Every day has the possibility of accomplishing some major success' (Edward Koch, 359).

When John Paul Getty drilled his first great oil well, he was overjoyed: 'The sense of elation and triumph was-and-is always there. It stems from knowing that one has beaten nature's incalculable odds by finding and capturing a most elusive (and often a dangerous and malevolent) prey' (John Paul Getty, 28).

Male voices often have a tone of hostility, aggression, or domination. Their celebration of achievement seems to be the result of what is fundamentally an antagonistic encounter.

The ways that women's voices speak of achievements take a rather different slant.

Martina Navratilova: 'For the first time I was a Wimbledon champion, fulfilling the dream of my father many years before.... I could feel Chris patting me on the back, smiling and congratulating me.... Four days later, the Women's Tennis Association computer ranked me number 1 in the world, breaking Chris's four-year domination. I felt I was on top of the world' (Martina Navratilova, 190).

Beverly Sills: 'I think "se pieta" was the single most extraordinary piece of singing I ever did. I know I had never heard myself sing that way before ... the curtain began coming down very slowly ... and then a roar went through that house the likes of which I'd never heard. I was a little stunned by it: the audience wouldn't stop applauding' (Beverly Sills and Lawrence Linderman, 172).

Sydney Biddle Barrows: 'I was motivated by the challenge of doing something better than everyone else ... I was determined to create a business that would appeal to ... men, who constituted the high end of the market ... I was sure we could turn our agency into one hell of an operation – successful, elegant, honest, and fun' (Sydney Biddle Barrows, 48–49).

In the womanstories, the love of the audience response, the affection of the opponent, and the satisfaction of customers are the significant factors in their descriptions. The womanstory emphasizes continuity with others' goals, not opposition to them. In fact, one's opponent can be seen as a necessary part of one's success:

'You're totally out for yourself, to win a match, yet you're dependent on your opponent to some degree for the type of match it is and how well you play. You need the opponent; without her you do not exist' (Martina Navratilova, 162).

EMOTIONAL INTERDEPENDENCY

What do these stories say about emotion interdependency – being with others and needing reciprocal affections? Here the manstory may be rather thin. Sticking to the narrative line may cut short their emotional lives, at least in print. But this is too black and white a message. Men have their buddies, their sidekicks, their intimate rivals, and compatriots. Perhaps the difference is that together they look outward, rather than at one another.

Let us look at how manstories allowed for the expression of relatedness and emotionality.

Ed Koch, reporting a conversation: 'I've been Mayor for close to three years ... I get involved in a lot of controversies and I make a lot of people mad at me, and so maybe at the end of these four years they'll say, "he's too controversial and we don't want him!" And maybe they'll throw me out. That's okay with me. I'll get a better job, and you won't get a better Mayor' (Edward Koch, 227).

Chuck Yeager: 'Often at the end of a hard day, the choice was going home to a wife who really didn't understand what you were talking about ... or gathering around the bar with guys who had also spent the day in a cockpit. Talking flying was the next best thing to flying itself. And after we had a few drinks in us, we'd get happy or belligerent and raise some hell. Flying and hell-raising – one fueled the other' (Chuck Yeager and Leo James, 173).

John Paul Getty: 'For some reason, I have always been much freer in recording my emotions and feelings in my diaries.... Taken as a whole, they might serve to provide insight into a father's true feeling about his sons. 1939.

Los Angeles, California:
May 20: Saw George, a remarkable boy rapidly becoming a man. He is 5'9" tall and weighs 145 pounds.

Genève, Switzerland:
July 9: Drove to Ronny's school ... Ronny is well, happy, and likes his school. His teachers give him a good report. He is intelligent and has good character, they say. Took Ronny and Fini to the Bergues Hotel for lunch and then to Chamonix...

Los Angeles:
December 10: Went to Ann's house (Ann Rork, my fourth wife who divorced me in 1935) and saw Pabby and Gordon, bless them. They are both fine boys (John Paul Getty, 11).

Manstories seem to celebrate the song of the self. Emotional ties are mentioned as 'facts' where necessary, but the author does not try to re-create in the reader empathic emotional responses. The willingness to play the role of the 'bastard' is seen in man-stories, for example in Koch's remarks above, but women do not take this stance in their stories.

And about our heroines? What do their stories tell about their emotional inter-dependencies? How important are relationships to their life courses? Is there a womanstory, too?

Let us listen.

Beverly Sills: 'One of the things I always loved best about being an opera singer was the chance to make new friends every time I went into a new production' (Beverly Sills and Lawrence Linderman, 229).

She wrote about how she and Carol Burnett had cried after finishing a television show together. 'We knew we'd have nobody to play with the next day. After that we telephoned each other three times a day' (ibid., 280).

Martina Navratilova: 'I've never been able to treat my opponent as the enemy, particularly Pam Shriver, my doubles partner and one of my best friends' (Martina Navratilova, 167).

Sydney Biddle Barrows emphasized in her book her ladylike upbringing, sensitive manners, and appreciation of the finer things of life. Her style of living was obviously challenged when she was arrested and thrown in jail.

On leaving a group of street-walking prostitutes with whom she had been jailed she wrote: 'As I left the cell, everybody started shouting and cheering me on. "Go get em, girlfren!" I left with mixed emotions. These girls had been so nice to me, and so open and interesting, that my brief experience in jail was far more positive than I could have imagined' (Sydney Biddle Barrows, 284).

The necessity of relating to others in a womanstory is especially crucial in Nien Cheng's narrative about solitary confinement. To avoid the bitter loneliness she adopted a small spider as a friend. She describes her concern for this spider: 'My small friend seemed rather weak. It stumbled and stopped every few steps. Could a spider get sick, or was it merely cold?… It made a tiny web … forming something rather like a cocoon … when I had to use the toilet, I carefully sat well to one side so that I did not disturb it' (Nien Cheng, 155).

Though many other examples might be given, these illustrate the major differences I have found between the relatively more profound emotional interdependency and intimacy requirement of women, in the telling of their stories, and those of men. The important aspects of women's autobiographies depend heavily on their affiliative rela-tionships with others. They seem to focus on these ties without drawing strong demar-cations between their public world and 'private' life. Their stories highlight the interdependent nature of their involvements and the centrality of emotional well-being to all facets of life much more vividly than men's stories do.

AUTOBIOGRAPHICAL REFERENCES

Barrows, Sydney Biddle, with William Novak. 1986. *Mayflower Madam*. New York: Arbor House.

Cheng, Nien. 1986. *Life and Death in Shanghai*. New York: Penguin.

Feynman, Richard P. 1986. *'Surely You're Joking, Mr. Feynman!'* New York: Bantam Books.

Getty, J. Paul. [1976] 1986. *As I See It: An Autobiography of J. Paul Getty*. New York: Bantam Berkley.

Iacocca, Lee, with William Novak. 1984. *Iacocca: An Autobiography*. New York: Bantam Books.

Koch, Edward I., with William Rauch. 1986. *Mayor*. New York: Warner Books.

Navratilova, Martina, with George Vecsey. 1985. *Martina*: New York: Fawcett Crest.

Sills, Beverly, and Lawrence Linderman. 1987. *Beverly*. New York: Bantam Books,

Yeager, General Chuck, and Leo James. 1985. *Yeager: An Autobiography*. New York: Bantam Books.

GENERAL REFERENCES

Benstock, Shari. 1988. 'Authorizing the Autobiography.' In *The Private Self: Theory and Practice in Women's Autobiographical Writings*. Edited by S. Benstock. London: Routledge.

Burke, Carolyn G. 1978. 'Report from Paris: Women's Writing and the Women's Movement.' *Signs, Journal of Women in Culture and Society* 3:844.

Campbell, Joseph. 1956. *The Hero with One Thousand Faces*. New York: Bollingen.

Chodorow, Nancy. 1978. *The Reproduction of Mothering: Psychoanalysis and the Sociology of Gender*. Berkeley: University of California Press.

Clifford, James. 1986. 'Introduction: Partial Truths.' In *Writing Culture*. Edited by J. Clifford and G. Marcus. Berkeley: University of California Press.

de Man, Paul. 1979. 'Autobiography as De-Facement.' *Modern Language Notes* 94:920.

Dinnerstein, Dorothy. 1976. *The Mermaid and the Minotaur: Sexual Arrangements and the Human Malaise*. New York: Harper and Row.

DuPlessis, Rachel Blau. 1985. *Writing Beyond the Ending*. Bloomington: Indiana University Press.

Eliot, T.S. 1963. 'The Love Song of J. Alfred Prufrock.' In *Collected Poems, 1909–1962*. London: Faber and Faber.

Emerson, Caryl. 1983. 'The Outer Word and Inner Speech: Bakhtin, Vygotsky, and the Internalization of Language.' *Critical Inquiry* 10:245–264.

———. 1983. 'Political Philosophy and the Patriarchal Unconsious: A Psychoanalytic Perspective on Epistemology and Metaphysics.' In *Discovering Reality: Feminist Perspectives on Epistemology, Metaphysics, Methodology, and Philosophy of Science*. Edited by S. Harding and M.B. Hintikka. Dordrecht, Holland: D. Reidel.

Flax, Jane. 1987. 'Postmodernism and Gender Relations in Feminist Theory.' *Signs, Journal of Women in Culture and Society* 12:621–643.

Gergen, Kenneth J., and Mary M. Gergen. 1983. 'Narrative of the Self.' In *Studies in Social Identity*. Edited by K. Schiebe and T. Sarbin. New York: Praeger.

Gergen, Kenneth J., and Mary M. Gergen. 1988. 'Narrative and the Self as Relationship.' In *Advances in Experimental Social Psychology*, vol. 21. Edited by L. Berkowitz San Diego: Academic Press.

Gergen, Mary M. 1990. 'A Feminist Psychologist's Postmod Critique of Postmodernism.' *Humanistic Psychologist* 18:95–104.

Gergen, Mary M., and Kenneth J. Gergen. 1984. 'Narrative Structures and Their Social Construction,' In *Historical Social Psychology*. Edited by K. Gergen and M. Gergen, Hillsdale, N.J.: Erlbaum.

Gilligan, Carol. 1982. *In a Different Voice*. Cambridge, Mass.: Harvard University Press.

Harding, Sandra. 1986. 'The Instability of the Analytical Categories of Feminist Theory.' *Signs, Journal of Women in Culture and Society* 11:645–664.

Janet, Pierre. 1928. *L'Evolution de la memoire et la notion du temps*. Paris: L. Alcan.

Jelinek, Estelle C. 1980. *Women's Autobiography: Essays in Criticism*. Bloomington: Indiana University Press.

Kauffman, Linda S. 1986. *Discourses of Desire: Gender, Genre, and Epistolary Fictions*. Ithaca, N.Y.: Cornell University Press.

Keller, Evelyn Fox. 1983. 'Gender and Science.' In *Discovering Reality: Feminist Perspectives on Epistemology, Metaphysics, Methodology, and Philosophy of Science*. Edited by S. Harding and M.B. Hintikka. Dordrecht, Holland: D. Reidel.

Mason, Mary G. 1980. 'Autobiographies of Women Writers.' In *Autobiography, Essays Theoretical and Critical*. Edited by J. Olney. Princeton, N.J.: Princeton University Press.

Olney, James. 1980. *Autobiography: Essays Theoretical and Critical*. Princeton, N.J.: Princeton University Press.

Rabuzzi, Kathryn Allen. 1988. *Motherself: A Mythic Analysis of Motherhood*. Bloomington: Indiana University Press.

Russ, Joanna. 1972. 'What Can a Heroine Do? Or Why Women Can't Write.' In *Images of Women in Fiction*. Edited by S. Koppelman Cornillon. Bowling Green, Ohio: University Popular Press.

Sayre, Robert F. 1980. 'Autobiography and the Making of America.' In *Autobiography, Essays Theoretical and Critical*. Edited by J. Olney. Princeton, N.J.: Princeton University Press.

Smith, Sidonie A. 1974. *Where I'm Bound: Patterns of Slavery and Freedom in Black American Autobiography*. Westport, Conn.: Greenwood Press.

———. 1987. *A Poetics of Women's Autobiography. Marginally and the Functions of Self-Representation*. Bloomington: Indiana University Press.

Sprinker, Michael. 1980. 'Fictions of the Self: The End of *Autobiography*.' In *Autobiography: Essays Theoretical and Critical*. Edited by J. Olney. Princeton, N.J.: Princeton University Press.

Tyler, Stephen. 1986. 'Post-Modern Ethnography: From Document of the Occult to Occult Documents.' In *Writing Culture*. Edited by J. Clifford and G. Marcus. Berkeley: University of California Press.

Woolf, Virginia. [1929] 1957. *A Room of One's Own*. New York: Harcourt, Brace, Jovanovich.

———. 1958. *Granite and Rainbow*. New York: Harcourt, Brace, Jovanovich.

13

a secret life in a culture of thinness

lisa m. tillmann-healy

Physicians and therapists focus mainly on medical and psychological aspects of bulimia. The bulimic's home environment, psychological traits, behavioral tendencies, physical health, and treatment options have been thoroughly discussed in the literature.

Many studies suggest that an 'unhealthy' home predisposes one to bulimia. Researchers believe that circumstances such as abuse (Pitts and Waller, 1993), high parental conflict (Lacey, Coker, and Birtchnell 1986), and alcohol misuse (Chandy et al. 1995) occur more frequently in bulimics' families than in families of non-bulimics.

In addition to common environmental factors, therapists indicate that bulimics share psychological characteristics. Those mentioned most often include: body dissatisfaction (Thompson, Berg, and Shatford 1987), low self-esteem (Pertschuk et al. 1986), self-directed hostility (Williams et al. 1993), and attachment and separation problems (Armstrong and Roth 1989). Some research even links bulimia to depression (Greenberg 1986) and borderline personality disorder (Skodol et al. 1993).

Therapists also associate bulimia with certain behavioral tendencies. They suggest that bulimics demonstrate overall impulsivity (Heilbrun and Bloomfield 1986) and perfectionism (Thompson et al. 1987) as well as problems with drinking (Striegel-Moore and Huydic 1993) and drugs (Bulik et al. 1992).

Physicians claim that bulimia threatens physical health. They connect binging and purging to insufficient levels of vitamins (Philipp et al. 1988), enamel erosion (Philipp et al. 1991), migraine headaches (Brewerton and George 1993), ulcers (Neil 1980), pregnancy complications (Franko and Walton 1993), bowel disorders (Neil 1980), spontaneous stomach rupture (Breslow, Yates, and Shisslak 1986), frontal lobe lesions (Erb et al. 1989), heart failure (Kohn 1987), and even death (Neil 1980).

In response to the apparent consequences of bulimia, several treatments have been developed. Health care professionals have experimented with self-help (Huon 1985);

drugs – particularly anticonvulsants (Mitchell 1988) and antidepressants (Crane et al. 1987); progessive relaxation (Mizes and Fleece 1986); hypnotherapy (Vanderlinden and Vandereycken 1988), behavior therapy (Cooper, Cooper, and Hill 1989); cognitive-behavior therapy (Lee and Rush 1986); nutritional counseling (O'Conner, Touyz, and Beumont 1988); and group therapy (Stuber and Strober 1987).

In the medical and psychological literature on bulimia, the voices of physicians and therapists speak. First they tell me about my 'troubled childhood.'
    'Wait a minute,' I say. 'I grew up in a stable and loving home.'
    Then they tell me about my 'psychological and behavioral problems.'
    'But I'm a functioning, well-adjusted adult,' I insist.
    I want their story to help me understand my participation in the dark, secret world of bulimia. But it doesn't. According to the story they tell, I have no reason (indeed no *right*) to be bulimic. But I am, and I know I'm not alone.
    For almost a decade, I have moved through this covert culture of young women, and I can take you there. I am not an 'authority' on bulimia, but I can show you a view no physician or therapist can, because, in the midst of an otherwise 'normal' life, I experience how a bulimic *lives* and *feels*.
    This renders my account different from theirs in a number of ways. Physicians and therapists study bulimia with laboratory experiments, surveys, and patient interviews. I examine bulimia through systematic introspection (Ellis 1991), treating my own lived experience as the 'primary data' (Jackson 1989). They move toward general conclusions. I move *through* what Baumeister and Newman (1994, 676) call 'experiential particularity.' Physicians and therapists use terms such as *causes*, *effects*, and *associations* to try to explain, predict, and control bulimia. I use evocative narratives to try to understand bulimia and to help others see and sense it more fully. They write from a dispassionate third-person stance that preserves their position as 'experts.' I write from an emotional first-person stance that highlights my multiple interpretive positions. Physicians and therapists keep readers at a distance. I invite you to come close and experience this world for yourself.
    You won't find such an account anywhere else – not in the case studies in which the lives of women (hidden behind guises such as 'Miss A' and 'Patient 2') count for little more than 'evidence' in support of the author's hypothesis; not on the talk shows, where women's 'disordered' experiences become public spectacles; not in popular magazines, where most of the attention focuses on celebrities who have 'overcome' bulimia; and not on TV dramas (such as *Days of Our Lives* and *Beverly Hills 90210*), where bulimia becomes a storyline for a few episodes, then magically disappears.
    I don't doubt the good intentions of physicians, therapists, and even producers of popular culture. But these sources focus on 'deviant' behavior, medical diagnosis, and treatment directed toward the ultimate end: 'cure' of the 'disease.' While stopping bulimic behaviors is an admirable goal, directing our attention there obscures the emotional intensity of bulimic experiences and fails to help us understand what bulimia *means* to those who live with it every day and what it *says* about our culture.
    Unlike most accounts, my story reveals the irony of living simultaneously in a culture of abundance and a culture of thinness – a culture in which 80% of fourth-grade girls are on self-imposed diets, a culture in which the same percentage of women believe they are overweight, a culture in which between 3 and 8 million of those women turn to bulimia (Bernstein 1986).

In short, my story implicates the family and cultural stories (see Yerby, Buerkel-Rothfuss, and Bochner 1995) that encourage young women (and, increasingly, young men as well) to relate pathologically to food and to their own bodies. I take the emotional/ professional risk of sharing the darkest, most painful secret of my life in order to expose some of the lived, felt consequences of these stories and to open dialogues aimed at writing new and better ones [...]

TEACH YOUR CHILDREN WELL

I lie on my stomach across the patchwork quilt that covers my parents' bed. Wearing only a cream lace bra and panties, my mother styles the chestnut locks that fall freely across her shoulders and down her back. The brush whooshes softly as it rolls off the ends. She stands in front of the mirror attached to the pine dresser her father made. I look up at Mom's reflection, and she smiles at me.

When her gaze returns to her own image, a different expression washes over my mother's face. She sets the brush down. Turning to the side, she squeezes the skin beneath her rib cage.

Back to center, Mom's hand sweeps over her slightly rounded middle. Her eyebrows curl and her lips purse as she watches herself intently.

Mom turns away and dresses hurriedly. While she dons baggy sweatpants and a long shirt, I reach underneath my sweater and feel for excess flesh.

I am 4 years old.

SIXTY POUNDS

I enter the upstairs bathroom and flick on the light. The door closes behind me, and I turn to push the lock.

I slide the digital scale back from the peach-papered wall. Stepping on, I watch the glowing numbers roll. I imagine myself to be a contestant on *The Price Is Right*. Today, the 'big wheel' stops on ... 60. 'That can't be right,' I think to myself as I step off.

'I'd like to spin again, Bob,' I say to my imaginary host.

Once more, the whirling digits come to rest on 60. I kick off my sandals – no change. I shed my long-sleeved T-shirt – nope. My corduroy pants and underwear – still 60 pounds. I dress quickly and bolt out of the bathroom.

'Grilled cheese and tomato soup okay for lunch?' my mother asks as I pass her in the hall.

'I don't want any lunch, Mom,' I say, exiting through the back door.

I run laps around the house until I can no longer breathe.

I am 7 years old.

CELLULITE

'You have cellulite,' Samantha tells me.

'What?' I ask, trying to negotiate last year's bathing suit over my hips.

'Cell-yoo-lite,' she repeats.

'What's that?'

'Those fatty dimples on the back of your legs.'

'Where?' I ask, turning my butt toward the mirror.

'*There*,' Samantha says, pointing.

'I don't see anything.'

'Look,' she orders, moving me closer to the mirror. 'See how your skin back here is bumpy.'

'I guess so.'

'That's cellulite,' Samantha says.

'Yuck. What can I do?'

'Diet and exercise,' she suggests. 'For now, you might want to wear a towel around your waist.'

'Yeah. I wouldn't want anyone else to see my cellulite.'

'My sister says it makes a woman's things look like cottage cheese,' Samantha tells me.

'Great, and I'm not even a woman yet.'

I am 10 years old.

WEIGHING IN

'Who's first?' my sixth-grade gym teacher calls.

Nobody steps forward, so Mr. Turner checks his roster. 'Collins!'

'Lucky me,' Kelly says, dropping her chin.

Mr. Turner instructs the rest of us to form a line in alphabetical order, then turns to his assistant, who records the results.' Collins ... 99 pounds!'

This is met with some hushed 'oohs' and 'aahs.'

'Dankins,' he says as the next girl steps on, '87 pounds!'

I sneak off to the locker room. Once inside, I enter the far stall and close the door. Hoping a miracle of nature will send 10 pounds of liquid weight rushing out of my body, I push on my stomach and bear down. Only a few ounces spill into the toilet.

Through several concrete walls, I can still hear the gym teacher booming. 'Frank ... 84 pounds!'

I flush and wash my hands.

As I exit the locker room, Becky shoots me a pained look from the front of the line. She crosses her fingers behind her back.

'Kirkland ... 97 pounds!' I can hear her groan.

I pass Sharon, who is running in place.

'What are you doing?' I ask her.

'Burning calories,' she answers matter-of-factly.

'You have to burn 3,500 to lose a pound,' I tell her. With a disappointed look, she stops.

'Mason ... 103 pounds!'

'I wish he'd shut up!' someone behind me shouts. I wish the same thing.

The line's moving quickly now. One after the other, names and numbers echo off the walls. 'Nichols ... 86 pounds!' 'O'Reiley ... 89 pounds!' [...]

He turns to me. 'Ah, Tillmann. Get on the scale, please.'

'Can I take off my shoes?' I ask him.

'Just get on it, will you?'

'Tillmann ...' he begins. It seems like an eternity. I can't look. I can't breathe. '94 pounds!'

I cringe.

I am 12 years old.

A SYMBOLIC PURGE

I read these stories aloud and feel conflicted. As a feminist, I'm embarrassed by the amount of attention I've paid to my body. As a daughter, I worry that these revelations will hurt my parents. As a scholar, I'm concerned that fellow academics will dismiss my work as self-absorbed.

One after the other, over and over, I take these in. I swallow the words and feel them waddle down my throat. More voices, new doubts, I ingest them all.

At last, my stomach tumbles and churns, twisting, sloshing. In a mass eruption, the words rush out of my mouth – a symbolic purge. On the page, my insides lay bare for everyone to read. Perhaps I should be ashamed, but somehow, I feel only relief.

THE FIRST TIME

I kneel in front of the toilet bowl, afraid yet strangely fascinated. As I stare at my rippling reflection in the pool of Saniflush-blue water, my thoughts turn to an article in the latest *Teen Magazine* about a young woman who induced vomiting to control her weight. It sounds repulsive in light of my experiences with the flu and hangovers. Still, I want to try it, to see if I can do it.

I place the shaking index finger of my right hand to the back of my throat. I hold it there for five or six seconds, but nothing happens. I push it down further. Still nothing. Further. Nothing. Frustrated, I move it around in circular motions. At last, I feel my stomach contract, and this encourages me to continue, Just then, I gag loudly.

Shhh.

Footsteps clonk on the linoleum outside the bathroom door, and I immediately pull my finger out of my mouth.

'Lis?' my father calls. 'You OK?'

'I'm fine, Dad,' I answer. 'Playing basketball tonight?'

'Yeah, and I'm late.'

I hear him pass through the dining room and ascend the stairs.

Listening closely for other intruders, I gaze into the commode, determined to see this through. The front door slams as my father exits, and I return to my crude technique. Again my stomach contracts. When I feel my body rejecting the food, I move my hand aside to allow the smooth, still-cold liquid to pour out of me – a once perfect Dairy Queen turtle sundae emerges as a brown swirl of soft-serve ice cream, hot fudge and butterscotch, and minute fragments of chopped pecans.

Again and again, 20 times or more, I repeat this until I know by pushing on my stomach that it is satisfactorily empty. My pulse races.

I am 15 years old.

THE LAST TIME

I pull out the drain stopper and set it atop the sink. As I'm turning the faucet, I notice the skin just above my first knuckle. A small, purplish patch there reminds me of the wounds I used to incur playing soccer the yard with our beagle, Sparky. Of course, I didn't get this bite from a dog.

I start to put that finger in my mouth, but I worry that the mark will become too visible. I know that my friend, Patti, uses a toothbrush to induce vomiting, so I decide to try that. It works well enough, but I hate how it feels. I then switch to the index finger of my left hand, but the angle seems so foreign that I can't relax enough to release the food.

I decide to do it the usual way. I vomit in four sets of five. A set happens like this: I slip my right index finger down my throat, wiggle it around, move my hand, and vomit; down, wiggle, move, vomit; down, wiggle, move, vomit; down, wiggle, move, vomit; down, wiggle, move, vomit. The further along in the set, the easier the food comes up.

After the first set, I meet my gaze in the mirror above the sink. As if touching my face, I run wet, sticky fingers over the place in my reflection where mascara and eyeliner run in murky brown streaks and fresh lipstick swirls with foundation. From my mouth flow orange saliva, bile and tiny remnants of macaroni.

I cup my hand under the tap and splash my mouth and cheeks with warm water, taking some in to rinse my teeth. I worry about them a lot, these four-years-of-braces, three-thousand-dollar teeth. They've already turned a bit yellow, and I've seen pictures of bulimic women whose enamel wore off. Disgusting!

Seeing that I'm short on time, I decide to do one long set of 15 to save the in-between clean-up time. I'm counting off in my head – one, two, three, four, five, six ... Oh, god!

What is this? Rocked by the crescendo of a wrenching, stabbing pain in my chest, I feel my stomach tighten, and my lungs seem to cave in. Struggling to breathe, I lower myself to the floor. With the same hand I used to vomit just moments before, I pound violently on my breast bone. *Make it stop.*

Laying my forehead on the cool tiles, I clutch my heart. I start to cry but the contractions only intensify the pain.

I imagine the headlines: 'Local Girl Dead at 17,' or worse, 'Bulimic Dies of Heart Attack.' *No, god. Please no.*

What a way to go – crumpled here with vomit dripping from my mouth, running down my arm. Who will find my body? My mom should be home from work in an hour. She'll have to call my father at the office. Will she tell him over the phone or wait until he can see for himself what has become of this only daughter? Perhaps my 10-year-old brother will find me first.

How did I get here? How could I become so out of control?

The pain begins to taper off, and I'm able to sit up. After a minute or so, it's over.

I'll never do it again. I swear I'll never do it again.

Promises, Promises.

I am 17 years old.

[...]

MY FIRST CONFESSION

My cheek presses against his chest. His breathing shifts over from consciousness to sleep.

Do it, Lisa. Don't wait.

'Douglas?' my strained voice calls out.

'Umhmm ...'

'There's something I need to tell you.'

Probably not a good opening line.

'What's that?' he asks.

'I know I should have told you this before, and I hope you won't be upset that I didn't.' Deep breath. swallow.

It's okay. You're doing fine.

'What is it?' he asks, more insistent this time.

Loooong pause. 'Lisa, What is it?'

He's getting nervous. Spit it out.

'Oh, god, Douglas, I don't ... I ... shit!'

You've come too far. Don't fall apart. Just say it, Lisa. Say the words.

'To one degree or another ... I have been ... bulimic ...

Fuck! I hate the sound of that word.

... since I was 15.'

It's out there. You said it.

He pulls me closer. 'Who knows about this?'

A few old friends and some people I go to school with.'

'Your family?'

Oh god. Here we go.

'No ... I haven't told them.'
Boom!
'Jesus,' he says.
No kidding.
'Well, how bad is it now?'
'It has been much worse.'
'That's not what I asked.'
'It's not that bad.'
Liar.
'Have you done it since you met me?'
If you only knew.
'A couple of times, but I don't want you to be concerned.'
Oh, please. Please be concerned.
'You must know what that does to your body.'
Believe me, I know. I know everything.
'I'm really glad you told me,' he says as I start to cry.
'I love you, Lisa. Tell me how I can help you. Please.'
You just did. You can't imagine how much.
He pulls me close, stroking my hair until I go to sleep.
I am 22 years old.

A PRIVATE CELEBRATION

I sit down to Christmas dinner at Andy's apartment. It feels strange to be here, among colleagues, instead of at my parents' house in Minnesota, surrounded by quirky relatives.

The food covers Andy's small table and kitchen counter. Pretty much the usual – a roasted turkey, mashed potatoes, candied yams, two salads, homemade bread, relishes, and, of course, pumpkin and pecan pies. I wait for the feeling of alarm to come over me, the sweat to bead at the base of my neck. To my surprise, it doesn't.

I take a little of everything onto my plate. I pepper my turkey, dress my salad, and butter my potatoes and bread. It all tastes very familiar – delicious – and scary.

After the meal, we laugh, drink, and assemble a puzzle. An hour passes, and Andy serves the pie.

'Pecan or pumpkin?' he asks me.

'A little of both please,' I request.

Ten minutes later, I get up from the table. When I excuse myself, Doug looks at me with narrowing eyes. 'Don't do it,' they seem to plead.

I close the bathroom door and move toward the toilet. Automatically, I put my finger in my mouth. I hold it there for several seconds, then slowly slide it out. I turn to my reflection in the mirror above the sink and watch myself for a long time. Washing my hands, I can't believe what I'm about to do – walk away.

When I rejoin the men at the table, I smile at Doug. With what might be relief, he smiles back. Maybe later I'll tell him that this is the first holiday dinner I haven't purged since 1986.

I am 23 years old.

EPILOGUE

If my paper were a medical or psychological report, this section would contain the author's definitive conclusions aimed at explaining, predicting, and controlling bulimia. If it were a TV drama, the 'cured' protagonist would be moving on to a normal life. But this is my story, and it is a story without resolution. Unlike popular culture depictions, mine isn't a tale of fighting my eating disorder, overcoming it, and living happily, healthily ever after. Bulimia is not a one-time battle I have won; it is an ongoing struggle with food, body, self, and meaning.

It may frustrate some that I close without revealing 'what it all means.' But, as Robert Coles (1989, 47) tells us, 'the beauty of a good story is its openness – the way you or I or anyone reading it can take it in, and use it for ourselves.'

At the same time, I purposefully told my story *this way*. I wrote a sensual text to pull you away from the abstractions and categories that fill traditional research on eating disorders and into the *experience* (Parry 1991, 42), to help you engage how bulimia *feels*. I used multiple forms to mimic the complex and multilayered nature of food addiction. Wanting the action to unfold before your eyes, I wrote most episodes in present tense. Later (with the exception of the opening piece) I arranged these chronologically to guide you along my nine-year journey. I then interjected three experiences I had *as a reader* of my own work to show you that I continue to 'experience the experiences' (Ellis and Bochner 1992) in new and different ways. [...]

Before I began this project, I couldn't understand why 'someone like me' – bright, educated, feminist – would binge and purge. I have since looked long and hard at the family and cultural stories that surround(ed) me. In the context of those stories – stories that teach all of us to relate pathologically to food and to our bodies, stories told and repeated at home, at school, and in the media – bulimia no longer seems an illogical 'choice.'

Often, I'll admit, the personal and professional risks of writing about my relationship with bulimia have overwhelmed me. Did I really want you to know this? What would you think of my work? How would you feel about *me*?

Still, I knew I had something to say that wasn't being said. I knew I could show you in detail how a bulimic *lives*, and I wanted you to know. Perhaps you already knew; if so, I offer this account as comfort and companionship. If you didn't, I offer it as instruction. I hope that my lived experience helps maintain a critical attitude many of our culture's stories of body and food and helps create new and better stories that direct us toward healthier bodies and more contented hearts.

REFERENCES

Armstrong, J. G., and D. M. Roth. 1989. 'Attachment and Separation Difficulties in Eating Disorders: A Preliminary Investigation.' *International Journal of Eating Disorders* 8: 141–155.

Baumeister, R. F., and L. S. Newman. 1994. 'How Stories Make Sense of Personal Experiences: Motives that Shape Autobiographical Narratives.' *Personality and Social Psychology Bulletin* 20: 676–690.

Bernstein, F. 1986. 'Bulimia: A Woman's Terror.' *People Weekly* 26: 36–41.

Breslow, M., A. Yates, and C. Shisslak. 1986. 'Spontaneous Rupture of the Stomach: A Complication of Bulimia." *International Journal of Eating Disorders* 5: 137–142.

Brewerton, T. D., and M. S. George. 1993. 'Is Migraine Related to the Eating Disorders?' *International Journal of Eating Disorders* 14: 75–79.

Bulik, C. M., P. F. Sullivan, L. H. Epstein, M. McKee, W. H. Kaye, R. E. DahI, and T. E. Weltzin. 1992. 'Drug Use in Women with Anorexia and Bulimia Nervosa.' *International Journal of Eating Disorders* 11: 213–225.

Chandy, J. M., L. Harris, R. W. Blum, and M. D. Resnick. 1995. 'Female Adolescents of Alcohol Misusers: Disordered Eating Features.' *International Journal of Eating Disorders* 17: 283–289.

Coles, R. 1989. *The Call of Stories: Teaching and the Moral Imagination*. Boston: Houghton Mifflin.

Cooper, P. J., Z. Cooper, and C. Hill. 1989. 'Behavioral Treatment of Bulimia Nervosa,' *International Journal of Eating Disorders* 8: 87–92.

Crane, R. A., V. Raskin, M. Weiler, J. Perri, T. H. Jobe, J. Anderson, and B. Burg. 1987. 'Nomifensine Treatment of Bulimia: Results of an Open Trial.' *International Journal of Eating Disorders* 6: 427–430.

Ellis, C. 1991. 'Sociological Introspection and Emotional Experiences.' *Symbolic Interaction* 14: 23–50.

Erb, J. L., H. E. Gwirtsman, J. M. Fuster, and S. H. Richeimer. 1989. 'Bulimia Associated with Frontal Lobe Lesions.' *International Journal of Eating Disorders* 8: 117–121.

Franko, D. L., and B. E. Walton. 1993. 'Pregnancy and Eating Disorders: A Review and Clinical Implications.' *International Journal of Eating Disorders* 13: 41–48.

Greenberg, B. R. 1986. 'Predictors of Binge Eating in Bulimic and Nonbulimic Women.' *International Journal of Eating Disorders* 5: 269–284.

Heilbrun, A. B., and D. L. Bloomfield. 1986. 'Cognitive Differences Between Bulimic and Anorexic Females: Self-Control Deficits in Bulimia." *International Journal of Eating Disorders* 5: 209–222.

Huon, G. F. 1985. 'An Initial Validation of a Self-Help Program for Bulimia.' *International Journal of Eating Disorders* 4: 573–588.

Jackson, M. 1989. *Paths Toward a Clearing: Radical Empiricism and Ethnographic Inquiry*. Bloomington: Indiana University Press.

Kohn, V. 1987. 'The Body Prison: A Bulimic's Compulsion to Eat More, Eat Less, Add Muscle, Get Thinner.' *Life* 10: 44.

Lacey, J. H., S. Coker, and S. A. Birtchnell. 1986. 'Bulimia: Factors Associated with its Etiology and Maintenance.' *International Journal of Eating Disorders* 5: 475–487.

Lee, N, F., and A. J. Rush. 1986. 'Cognitive-Behavioral Group Therapy For Bulimia.' *International Journal of Eating Disorders* 5: 599–615.

Mitchell, P. B. 1988. 'The Pharmacological Management of Bulimia Nervosa: A Critical Review.' *International Journal of Eating Disorders* 7: 29–41.

Mizes, J. S., and E. L. Fleece. 1986. 'On the Use of Progressive Relaxation in the Treatment of Bulimia: A Single-Subject Design Study.' *International Journal of Eating Disorders* 5: 169–176.

Neil, J. 1980. 'Eating Their Cake and Heaving it Too.' *MacLean's* 93: 51–52.

O'Conner, M., S. Touyz, and P. Beumont. 1988. 'Nutritional Management and Dietary Counselling in Bulimia Nervosa: Some Preliminary Observations.' *International Journal of Eating Disorders* 7: 657–662.

Pertschuk, M., Collins, M., Kreisberg, J. and Fager, S.S. (1986) 'Psychiatric Symptoms Associated with Eating Disorder in a College Population' *International Journal of Eating Disorders*, 5, 563–8.

Philipp, E., K. M. Pirke, M. Seidl, R. J. Tuschl, M. M. Fichter, M. Eckert, and G. Wolfram. 1988. 'Vitamin Status in Patients with Anorexia Nervosa and Bulimia Nervosa.' *International Journal of Eating Disorders* 8: 209–218.

Philipp, E., B. Willershausen-Zonnchen, G. Hamm, and K. M. Pirke. 1991. 'Oral and Dental Characteristics in Bulimic and Anorexic Patients.' *International Journal of Eating Disorders* 10: 423–431.

Pitts, C., and G. Waller. 1993. 'Self-Denigratory Beliefs Following Sexual Abuse: Association with the Symptomology of Bulimic Disorders. *International Journal of Eating Disorders* 13: 407–410.

Skodol, A. E., J. M. Oldham, S. E. Hyler, H. D. Kellman, N. Doidge, and M. Davies. 1993. 'Comorbidity of DSM-III-R Eating Disorders and Personality Disorders.' *International Journal of Eating Disorders* 14: 403–416.

Striegel-Moore, R. H., and E. S. Huydic. 1993. 'Problem Drinking and Symptoms of Disordered Eating in Female High School Students.' *International Journal of Eating Disorders* 14: 417–425.

Stuber, M., and M. Strober. 1987. 'Group Therapy in the Treatment of Adolescents with Bulimia: Some Preliminary Observations.' *International Journal of Eating Disorders* 6: 125–131.

Thompson, D. A., K. M. Berg, and L. A. Shatford. 1987. 'The Heterogeneity of Bulimic Symptomology: Cognitive and Behavioral Dimensions.' *International Journal of Eating Disorders* 6: 215–234.

Vanderlinden. J., and W. Vandereycken. 1988. 'The Use of Hynother the Treatment of Eating Disorders.' *International Journal of Eating Disorders* 7: 673–679.

Williams, G. J., K. G. Power, H. R. Millar, C. P. Freeman, A. Yellowlees Dowds, M. Walker, L. Campsie, F. MacPherson, and M. A. Jack 1993. 'Comparison of Eating Disorders and Other Dietary/Weigh Groups on Measures of Perceived Control, Assertiveness, Self-Esteem and Self-Directed Hostility.' *International Journal of Eating Disorder* 27–32.

Yerby, J., N. Buerkel-Rothfuss, and A. P. Bochner. 1995. *Understanding Communication* Scottsdale, AZ: Gorsuch Scarisbrick, Publishers.

14

troubling the angels

patti lather & chris smithies

'Statistics Are Human Beings
with the Tears Wiped Off' (Linda B)

Twenty-five women with HIV/AIDS, ages 23–49, have participated in this project. Four are Hispanic, five are African-American, and sixteen are white. Thirteen are mothers and six are grandmothers. At the time of the support group interviews, in 1992, seventeen held jobs across varying professional and service sectors and eight were not employed. Twenty-three women have completed high school, and sixteen have some post secondary education. One is pursuing doctoral study, and another is preparing to take the MCAT examination for entry into medical school.

Dates of HIV+ diagnosis range from 1987–1992. By September 1996, over half of the women are living with an AIDS diagnosis and four are dead. Demographic charts are included in the Appendix, including a summary table that allows the reader to track individual women across their comments in the book.

Why are these women willing to open up their lives to strangers? No other disease is associated with so many stigmas. To identify as HIV+ is to invite the most personal of questions, spoken and unspoken. It also risks loss of relationships with family and friends, sexual intimacy, jobs and, with that, insurance and financial security, housing, identity and self-esteem. Illness and mortality may assume center stage in one's life. Denial makes sense in such a scenario, but it often results in a high price being paid in terms of attending to healthcare needs and changing risk-related behaviors. The following presents some of what these women intend by their participation in this project. It is assembled across various support groups at various times and places.

According to current diagnostic criteria, adopted in 1993, the line between HIV+ and AIDS is determined by a T cell count of less than 200 or the onset of two or more of the numerous opportunistic infections that characterize AIDS, e.g., thrush, kaposi sarcoma (rare in women), herpes simplex with an ulcer that lasts more than a month, diarrhea that lasts more than a month, PML (affects nervous system), lymphoma, and, specific to women, vaginal candidiasis that is recurring and resistant to treatment and/or invasive cervical cancer. The criteria themselves have shifted over the fifteen plus years of the pandemic, representing the changing nature of knowledge about AIDS.

'IT'S OK TO BE A POSITIVE WOMAN'

Chris: Winding down our interview, is there any feedback on what this evening has been like?

Melody: It was like after the retreat weekend. Tonight I feel is one of the times I can say I feel lucky that I am HIV+. I feel blessed with something special, that I can be bonded with so many special women. I feel special to be involved, with the women and the love.

Linda B: How else do we get the people who are afraid of us to hear this stuff?

Lori: I'm really excited about you guys writing this book and I want you to get it published right away. That's just where I'm at right now. I want to do something. I think we've all had this feeling, why did this happen to me? And I keep thinking that there's something there, there's some message, there's something that I need to be doing. Maybe it's connected with going public, and that's a struggle I'm going through and then this book is coming up at the same time. And maybe this is the sign that I've been waiting for, that things are going to change, we have to make them change, and I think the book is really good. Going through the interviews and hearing everyone's story, a lot of this stuff, we don't talk about in group, we don't talk about like how do you really feel about that stuff? I think it's good that these interviews let us do that.

CR: I'm glad about our meetings and the book because if the interviewers would have been doctors, especially men, I would have felt exploited. But I know there are women just like us all over, and hopefully other women and some doctors will read this.

Rita: I go to the library a lot. There is not one book about women. The closest it comes is a woman writing about her husband with AIDS. Everything I've found out about me and what I can expect comes from the women in this group.

Sandy: The one thing I wanted to stress whether in the book or not, is how important it is for them to give more to research on women, to help women get tested earlier, to find out earlier.

Chris: Any other comments on the process, how it's felt being here and doing this?

Diane:	I think it's good to have a forum, to be able to talk about it. And to know that what we're talking about is really going to go out and maybe make a difference somehow.
Patti:	Why did you participate?
Danielle:	Well, I think, if at all possible, I would like to reach certain people like government people and say 'help us.' And to reach other women or other people who are infected and say 'don't give up.'
Alisha:	Also, try to reach out to the few deaf women who are HIV+. I don't think that they have really stepped our and I would like to reach them. Maybe deaf people are very afraid of it, and they are hiding from it. The deaf community is very, very small. And they wouldn't want to step out because everybody would know. It is like one big family. And I want to encourage deaf women to do that and for them to know that there is nothing wrong with it. It is OK to take those steps. I want to help them, but who they are exactly, I don't know. I feel like at this point that I am the only one in the world who is deaf and has HIV although I know that I am not. I want encourage them to come out so that we can help each other.
Joanna:	I want this book to get in the right hands so that people will do something about it, take some kind of action, get more people involved, to open the door for other people, let them know that it is OK to say that I am HIV+. It's OK to be a positive woman.

On July 1, 1994, Being Alive in Los Angeles became the first HIV/AIDS organization to comply with the Americans with Disabilities Act of 1990 by opening its programs to the deaf community. Services include an ongoing deaf support group, a phone line for deaf callers, sign language interpreters at all social and program events and the formation of a Deaf/HIV Issues Advisory Board. *Being Alive*, 3626 Sunset Blvd., LA CA 90026. *Listen to the Hands of Our People* is a documentary film about seven deaf people living with AIDS, directed by Ann Marie 'Jade' Bryan, 1990.

Positive Attitude: Keep in Mind the Following Things

1. New treatments are becoming more rapidly available.
2. Support networks are available at no or little cost.
3. Quality of life can be maintained and enhanced.
4. Developing and maintaining a positive attitude can have a strong beneficial impact on your health.
5. Remember that most people who test positive remain symptom-free and healthy for many years (*The Positive Woman* newsletter, see Resources).

15

silent voices: a subversive
reading of child sexual abuse

karen v. fox

THE CASE STUDY

The account that follows is written in an unorthodox manner to capture the experiences of a survivor (Sherry)[1] and her offender (Ben) as well as my subjectivity as a survivor and researcher of child sexual abuse. The text is displayed in three columns representing our three voices. By following the text, the reader moves among the voices in a weaving pattern so that a single perspective is not privileged. This three-column narrative style draws the reader into divergent perspectives of abuse.

The account is based on interviews, participant-observation, and phone conversations with Ben, a convicted sex offender, over a six-month period, including my attendance at one of his group therapy sessions. Ben was arrested for abusing his 12-year-old step-granddaughter, Mary, on two occasions. He also admitted to abusing Sherry, his step-daughter, when she was a child. In an interview, Sherry contributed her perspective on Ben's abuse toward her and niece Mary, her ongoing familial relationship with Ben, and the process of dealing with the public attention resulting from Ben's arrest. Contact with Sherry was limited after this because she found reading the field notes of our session a painful reminder of her abuse, and she felt incapable of discussing her experiences further.

I used an unstructured, informal interview style, asking open-ended questions to encourage Ben and Sherry to feel comfortable about discussing this sensitive topic. In Ben's case, our contact extended from private conversations about the abuse to having dinner with his wife and discussing other life experiences, such as retirement. Initially, I asked informants to describe their abuse experiences and later asked follow-up questions for elaboration on specific issues. For example, I asked Ben to tell me about the 16 years during which he claimed not to have engaged in sexual contact with children, whether or not he had sexual desire for children throughout that time, and how he now felt after being arrested and receiving therapy? I also asked Sherry to explain the feelings of love toward Ben that she expressed.

I took notes during the interviews and after participant-observation and gave them to each interviewee for review. Ben commented on field notes that contained not only the substance of our sessions but also my reactions to his abuse experiences. I wanted Ben and Sherry to read the entire three-person account and give me their feedback. This was not possible, however, because Sherry did not want Ben to read her interview notes, and she did not want to comment on his notes. I subsequently took excerpts from the field notes that focused on the experiences of Ben, Sherry, and me, as well as parts I recalled from my own abuse story. These excerpts are juxtaposed in columns to show the range of emotions and interconnections among the three of us.

Although the words presented in this text are Sherry's and Ben's I chose how to present them. At first I attempted to get their stories 'right,' but then I realized that we are always in the process of revising ourselves (Bochner, 1994; Crites, 1986; Ellis, 1995; Linden, 1993). The telling of my own abuse story has changed over time until now I question whether I ever had the story 'right.' Rightness is 'situated in relation to the present in which it is re-collected' (Crites, 1986, 158) and is based on my current understanding of the 'flashbacks, after-images, dream sequences, faces merging into one another, masks dropping, and new masks being put on' (Denzin, 1992, 27) that I experience as I move through my life. There is not just one version of abuse, but there are many stories that are 'differently contoured and nuanced' (Richardson, 1994, 521). In the end, I was less concerned with 'rightness' and more interested in the 'practical value' (Bochner, 1994, 23) of how the account contributes to current understandings and prevention of abuse.

Parts of the account are graphic in nature, and I am concerned that readers may view this as pornographic. But exposing these graphic stories may open up the 'unexpected, shadow places' (Richardson, 1992, 131) that can stimulate discussions about what is going on behind the closed doors of child sexual abuse. The silent voices in abuse research have an opportunity to speak in the three-person account and challenge us to go beyond seeing the issue exclusively in terms of offender/victim dichotomies.

A THREE-PERSON ACCOUNT

Ben – Sex Offender

I was watching TV in the living room, and the bathroom was around the corner. I had the TV turned up loud the way I like it. I heard Mary screaming, 'Poppop, Poppop.' I thought maybe something had happened, that she was hurt or something. She was screaming so loud. So I went to the door. It was closed. And I didn't go in. I yelled, 'What's the

Sherry – Victim

She was 13. It's not the same impact on a 13-year old as a younger child. You're out of the 'I love you unconditionally' stage. And he wasn't her parent. He was a step-grandfather. More damage is done when it is the parents doing it.

Ben – Sex Offender (cont.)

matter?' She told me to come in, and I did. There she was in the tub filled with bubbles. She was in it up her neck. She said, 'Look.' I asked her where she got the bubbles, and she said she got into my wife's stuff. Well I saw her there. And I had felt things towards her before. I just took advantage of the situation. I went over to the tub and bent down and fondled her breasts. She sunk deeper into the tub. Then I put my hand in between her thighs, and she clamped them shut and said, 'No!' So I left.

Ben – Sex Offender

Later, she would still sit on my lap and hug me. She was starving for affection.

Karen – Researcher

I had that starving for affection when I was a child. I had that affection for my abuser. One day, he took me to the bathroom with the other children in my Sunday school class. He wiped me and stayed too long. It felt good. I liked this man. I was only 5.

Ben – Sex Offender

I admitted to molesting Mark and Sherry. I didn't want to admit to abusing Mary when I was arrested, for legal reasons. You know, the sentence might have been worse.

Karen – Researcher

(I wonder, did he pay enough for what he did?)

Ben – Sex Offender

I plea-bargained. One thousand hours of community service, 5 years probation.

Sherry – Victim

He paid some fines. And he lost the right to vote. And he had to go to counseling.

Karen – Researcher
(Why did he get off?) (He tells me later about a man in his therapy group. This man was having sex with his 17-year-old girlfriend. He was 21. The girl's mother got him arrested. He served two years in prison. He was black.)

Sherry – Victim
The punishment fit the crime.

Karen – Researcher
(What?!)

Ben – Sex Offender
The only reason the case did not got to court was because Sherry decided not to testify against me.

Karen – Researcher
(What's wrong with this woman!?)

Ben – Sex Offender
I love her, you know. You see we really had a good relationship. And I think this is the reason she couldn't testify against me.

Sherry – Victim
I didn't testify against him because of the statute of limitations. They would have ripped me up one side and down the other for the details of my abuse. What was the sense? I could have been put through that, and the judge could have thrown it out. Mary didn't want to testify either. Both of us were embarrassed.

Karen – Researcher
(How can they have a good relationship? I feel sick.)

Ben – Sex Offender

The district attorney wanted to take the case to court, but Sherry threatened to give testimony that would find her not credible.

You know, I love her. And she loves me.

Karen – Researcher

My mother told me that this man who abused me loved children, 'especially you four girls,' my mother said (my sister and me). 'Why, he always had one of you on his lap,' my mother said. Yeah, I just bet he did.

Ben – Sex Offender

I know what I did was wrong. I hurt her. But more than that, I hurt many more people. I didn't realize that at the time, when I was doing it. Then one day I was at a counselor's office in a hospital, and he just said, 'Do you realize how many people you have hurt?' This comment got to me like nothing had ever gotten to me before. It was then that I realized that I could never do this again.

Ben – Sex Offender

The arrest hit the papers, and it became the talk of the town. Some friends stood by me, and others couldn't believe I did this because of the positions I'd held in the community. I was on the Board of Health for four years and president for one of those years. I was a member of a civic organization for five years and was president for one of those years. This group had doctors, lawyers, and businessmen in it.

Sherry – Victim

The prosecuting attorney didn't think my testimony would be considered. I think he would have gotten a lighter sentence if we had gone to a jury trial. The prosecuting attorney and I sat down and discussed it. Ben got the maximum sentence for that crime. Remember he was only arrested for molesting Mary, not me. He did it to her two times.

Sherry – Victim

He's sorry for what he's done. Sorry he got caught. Anyone would be. I am sure that he is sorry.

Karen – Researcher

My mother tells me that this man, this deacon who sexually violated me was one of the pillars of the church. I found a booklet on the history of the southern Baptist church where my father was the minister. This man was the chairman of a major committee.

Sherry – Victim
It's scary. He's a big person. He looked like a giant. I used to think of him as a drill sergeant. He thinks he is perfect. His philosophy is – I may not be right all the time, but I'm never wrong.

Karen – Researcher
He was a big, fat man. He held me down on the cold, cement floor. The big, fat man's breathing gets louder and quicker. I can feel this. He gets rushed with excitement in his body. And so do I. I feel I am inside his body. My body moves with his. What sensation. Someone is unlocking the door. 'Shut up! Stop that crying. I'm telling you, you better shut up!' He quickly pulls up my underwear, brushes me off, and wipes my tears. 'If you say anything, I will get you! I will get your father fired! And you won't have a house to live in, and you won't have any food to eat! And I will kill your father if you say one word!'

I feel the agony of his words, but the separation of his body and his power are more traumatic. He is mad at me. I must have done something bad. He doesn't like me anymore. What did I do? I am sorry.

This was the last time I was with this man, this big, fat man, this deacon, this pillar, this man who gave me candy and a silver dollar.

I no longer had his affection. I was no longer special to him.

Ben – Sex Offender
I love her, you know. You see we really have a good relationship. She loves me, she told me that.

Karen – Researcher
I want to believe Ben. I guess I've always hoped that I meant something to my abuser; that he really did love me; that he really did feel I was special.

Ben – Sex Offender
When they first came to live with me, they never had much before. They were eating pancakes most of the time. They ate better with us. And I took them places. Their father never did that. So I was around more, and they liked that

Sherry – Victim
He gave us a life we didn't have. I didn't eat meat until I was 7. We lived on pancakes and eggs.

He gave us a home. He gave us discipline. We kids were out of control.

There is no way, shape, and form that the good he did out-weighs the bad. This doesn't excuse what he did.

I've had feelings of love for him, like for a father.

> **Karen – Researcher**
> Betty Anne, his wife, says Ben and Sherry were very close. They talked about everything together. She talked with him about her period, his wife tells me. She said, 'The kind of things you would think she would talk about with me, her mother.'

Ben – Sex Offender
Others have said that too, that I must have something to attract women. Of course this made me feel real good about myself.

We couldn't stay in Minnesota. Every time we went out to the store, people would stare. It's a small town.

Ben – Sex Offender
I didn't know that when I moved here that I would have to go to more counseling. And I didn't really want to go at first. But now, I am glad I did. In this group, there are 30 people. They don't let you get by with lying. They know when you are lying. And the spouses can come. Betty Anne comes every time. It's saved our relationship.

Ben – Sex Offender
As long as we sex offenders are in denial, we can't get help. We have to admit to what we did. What I did was wrong. I know that now.

Sherry – Victim
It must be nice to just pack your bags and leave your past behind you.

I had people corner me in the store and want to discuss the abuse and the arrest with me. They would ask explicit details. I spent three months not going out of the house.

People accused me of letting him off, and I say, 'Here's my shoes. Put yourself in them. Take a walk on the wild side.' Then I got mad, and I wiped the word 'victim' off my forehead!

Sherry – Victim
I think it is sinking in. He's getting help he needed. You take responsibility.

Sherry – Victim
Nobody gets well in two years.

Ben – Sex offender
I will always be a sex offender.

Ben – Sex Offender
I don't ever want to offend again. So I have to remember that this is in me and to keep it in check. [...]

Sherry – Victim
It doesn't happen that quickly. Who knows if he won't do it again?

Karen – Researcher
[...] Part of my healing is to get past my identification as a survivor. I have other things to do in life.

Sometimes I think the ideas about psychotherapy keep us in the very prison they claim to release us from. Could it be that alcoholics, sex offenders, and others are sentenced by psychotherapy for life? ... this is not for me ... aren't there other ways to view this issue? [...]

Ben – Sex Offender
I have 13 weeks left of therapy. The group decides when you are finished though. They have to approve it. I plan to continue with the group even when the group says I am finished. It helps to have offenders in the group who have gone through the program because we can see the denial in the new members. We've been there.

I have hurt a lot of people. You know, it will never be over ... the effect. This is something I will have to deal with forever.

DISCUSSION

Ben and Sherry have contradictory perspectives of the abuse experience. Ben expresses a view that is not conventionally acceptable. Several times he states that he loved Sherry and that they had a good relationship. Individuals who have read the three-person account view Ben as a 'con-artist, a manipulator,' and a person who 'exhibited distorted thinking.' In the offender position, Ben can only be seen as an aggressor, and his love for Sherry is considered a lie. Sherry interprets herself through the lens of a victim, expressing the canonical story of child sexual abuse. Respondents typically express empathy for her, 'realizing how vulnerable and powerless the child was – like all children are.' But what perspective, we might wonder, would Sherry have provided at an earlier age about the experience?

The use of the multivocal narrative and my sociological introspection (Ellis, 1991) facilitate a subversive reading of abuse that attempts to move closer to the perspective of a child's agency. By juxtaposing conflicting experiences in the three columns with myself in the center position, I found myself within the culturally mediated territory between adults' and children's bodies. As a survivor of abuse, I cannot help but be actively engaged in my research on Ben and Sherry [...]

In the three-person account, I attempt to get at the child's perspective through the telling of my own story of abuse. I placed myself inside the characters of my abuse story and asked questions about how they might have experienced the storyline? I subsequently had bodily and emotional experiences that led me to ask questions about agency and child sexuality. I wanted to explore further Ben's 'love' for Sherry, my recollection of sexual response and affection toward my abuser, and the moments when both Sherry and her niece exerted their agency in relation to Ben. I did not want to contextualize these marginal experiences exclusively within the master narrative and, thereby, dismiss feelings of love and sexual response on the part of both the offender and the victim as originating completely from the offender's manipulation.

The arbitrary boundary that society places between the sexual nature of adults and children remains intact in most studies of abuse. Research on child sexual behavior is taboo and is based on 'the presupposition that children do not (or should not) have sharable or credible knowledge of their own sexuality' (McKenna and Kessler, 1985, 254). Traversing this *forbidden zone* gave me an opportunity to move beyond the socially constructed positions of Ben and Sherry to consider the perspective of children's bodies and agency [...]

When we bring children's agency, choice, and sexuality into discussions of adult sex with children, we capture the *outsider* voice that can produce a more open dialogue about the complexities of this issue. It is, as bell hooks says, 'the silence and taboo that make coercion and exploitation more possible' (hooks, 1995, 38). I think we can no longer silence children's bodies when researching child sexual abuse – to do so leads to simplistic solutions that perpetuate the objectification and exploitation of children. By including children's agency and bodies in research on sexual abuse, change can be created that reroutes 'knowledge in new directions' (Graham, 1994, 634) and, thereby, sustains new perspectives on understanding relationships between adults and children.

NOTE

1. All names are pseudonyms.

REFERENCES

Bochner, A. 1994. 'Perspectives on Inquiry II: Theories and Stories.' In *Handbook of Interpersonal Communication*, edited by M. Knapp and G. R. Miller. (Thousand Oaks: Sage): 21–41.

Crites, S. 1986. 'Storytime: Recollecting the Past and Projecting the Future.' In *Narrative Psychology: The Storied Nature of Human Conduct*, edited by T. Sarbin. (New York: Praeger): 152–173.

Denzin, N. 1992. 'The Many Faces of Emotionality: Reading Persona.' In *Investigating Subjectivity: Research on Lived Experience*, edited by C. Ellis and M. G. Flaherty. (Newbury Park: Sage): 17–30.

Ellis, C. 1991. 'Sociological Introspection and Emotional Experience.' *Symbolic Interaction* 14: 23–50.

———. 1995. *Final Negotiations: A Story of Love, Loss, and Chronic Illness.* Philadelphia: Temple University Press.

Graham, L. 1994. 'Critical Biography without Subjects and Objects: An Encounter with Dr. Lillian Moller Gilbreth.' *The Sociological Quarterly* 35: 621–643.

hooks, b. 1995. 'In Praise of Student/Teacher Romances.' *Utne Reader* (March–April): 37–38.

Linden, R. 1993. *Making Stories, Making Selves: Feminist Reflections on the Holocaust.* Columbus: Ohio State University Press.

McKenna W., and S. Kessler. 1985. 'Asking Taboo Questions and Doing Taboo Deeds.' In *The Social Construction of the Person*, edited by K. Gergen and K. Davis. (New York: Springer-Verlag): 241–257.

Richardson, L. 1992. 'The Consequences of Poetic Representation: Writing the Other, Rewriting the Self.' In *Investigating Subjectivity: Research on Lived Experience*, edited by C. Ellis and M. G. Flaherty. (Newbury Park: Sage): 125–137.

———. 1994. 'Writing: A Method of Inquiry.' In *Handbook of Qualitative Research*, edited by N. K. Denzin and Y. S. Lincoln. (Thousand Oaks: Sage): 516–529.

16

together against the computer

gustavo i. de roux

The following account describes an experience in participatory action-research that was undertaken by Afro-Colombian communities at the southern end of the Cauca river valley in Colombia, with the cooperation of outside agents from two 'self-reliance promoting organizations' – Empresa de Cooperación al Desarrollo (EMCODES) and Fundación El Planeque – interested in promoting popular education and strengthening grassroots organizations. This essay is limited to describing the ways in which information to support a collective bargaining effort was gathered and organized, and strategies for action developed by community organizations known as Public Service Users Committees (Comités de Usuarios de Servicios Públicos) to improve their negotiating ability with the state electric company that operated in the area. Other grassroots organizations in the region have had similar experiences related to other issues; they have defended their interests, changed situations that adversely affected them and reaffirmed their role in the effort to effect social change.

THE RESEARCH CONTEXT

Villarrica is a community of some 9,000 inhabitants, located in the southern Cauca river valley in southwestern Colombia. Like neighboring communities, it is populated primarily by Afro-Colombians, descendants of slaves brought to the region mainly in the seventeenth and eighteenth centuries to work as laborers on haciendas and in gold mines.

The community of Villarrica has had problems with the electric service, practically, since it was installed in the early 1960s. At first the people tolerated the shortcomings, figuring that after all they had benefited from access to electric lighting. But little by little, and as electricity became increasingly important to their daily lives and essential to small businesses, individual members of the community began to complain from time to time about the poor quality of the service. The first massive protests in Villarrica in the early 1970s were geared mainly toward improved electric service; at the time, there were power outages 'every time it rained' due to defective power lines and lack of sufficient transformers. In 1972 an engineer from the electric company was detained until service was restored after an extended interruption due to defects in the high voltage lines. There were sporadic protests throughout the 1970s to demand that something be done about electricity supply problems. The most insistent demands were for quality and continuity in the service.

The availability of electricity created new needs. People had begun purchasing home appliances, taking advantage of what appeared to be good deals at commercial outlets in relatively nearby cities – Cali, Santander, Jamundi and Puerto Tejada. These stores sent salesmen door-to-door to promote sales of household goods on credit, quite alluring in low-income communities. Many woodstoves were replaced by electric stoves, among other reasons because it was much harder to obtain firewood for fuel as sugar cane cultivation spread. Refrigerators, irons and television sets also began to appear, all of which led to a rapid increase in per capita electricity consumption; there were also bills to pay resulting from the purchase of appliances.

In the early 1980s the international economic crisis, relating to the foreign debt burden and the subsequent need to make debt service payments, pressured the state institutions (especially in the energy sector) to adjust their rate schedules upward, thus forcing the consumers to bear the burden of fulfilling the country's commitments to the international banking community. Low-income communities where most incomes were spent meeting such basic needs as food were the hardest hit, and inhabitants faced the possibility of having to halt or drastically reduce their electricity consumptions, which by then had become a daily need.

The situation was dramatic in many small communities of the region because the electric company, as a result of the crisis, also stopped underwriting the cost of installing power lines and transformers. Thus the inhabitants of these communities had to assume the overall cost of installation, including putting up power lines over distances of five kilometers or more. The Agrarian Bank (Caja de Crédito Agrario) agreed to extend loans to the peasants so that they would be able to assume these costs. Purchasing equipment with borrowed capital led to being faced with loan amortization and interest payments, all of which added to the already high cost of electricity. If to this we also add the debts that many semi-proletarian peasants already had incurred with the Agrarian Bank for production loans for farms affected by the expansion of the sugar cane plantations, we see a clearly risky and indeed dangerous situation. The peasants could have easily found themselves forced to sell off their lands at an accelerated pace.

Concurrent with these difficulties, people also began to notice that their monthly electric statements included many irregularities. First, they showed month-to-month changes in consumption figures that in many cases could not have been real. Also, similar consumption totals were being charged at different rates per kilowatt-hour. Finally, in some communities people noted that the bills were higher in June and December when the company had to pay employee benefits.

Individual complaints began to proliferate. They were communicated to a company official based in the area, who took charge of passing them on to the main office in the departmental capital, Popayan. In some isolated cases the claims were accepted, but in most cases the company simply accumulated the debt when it was to paid, threatened to cut off service and charged interest on the amount each user accumulated. On one occasion when several people went together to the main office to speak with the engineer in charge of their area, he answered that the calculations were done on a computer and that 'the computer does not make mistakes.'

Convinced that however distinguished and respectable the 'computer,' it was erring in the company's favor and doing consumers a disservice – and that efforts and pressures brought to bear up to that moment had only resulted in minimal changes in the company's practices – a group of approximately twenty people, mostly women, decided to form a Public Service Users Committee. As such, they would lead the struggle for the right to quality electric service at reasonable and consistent rates. They added several variations to the previous years' demands: an end to irregularities in billing, cancellation of accumulated debts and the right to electricity at prices in line with the population's means.

The Committee felt the people had to strengthen their negotiating capacity. Two things were needed. First, evidence in support of the people's points of view had to be gathered and organized into sufficiently tight arguments to defeat the computer. That is, more research had to be done on the electricity problem to discover its roots and determine how it was manifested in specific cases. In other words, a more comprehensive understanding of the situation and its causes was needed, as were solid, watertight arguments. Second, community participation and organization had to be encouraged. Previous experience had shown that short-term and unorganized participation would not be sufficient in maintaining continuous pressure on the state institutions, and that the organized involvement of the people was the only guarantee that the company would fulfill its commitments if some agreement were reached. This led the Committee to attempt to involve several of the already existing grassroots organizations in the region in the electricity issue. To this end they drew on and promoted community events and other forums for discussion and made use of small community-based newspapers published in the area. Meetings and assemblies for the discussion and generation of new knowledge were also promoted.

THE METHODOLOGY: SOME CONSIDERATIONS

In contrast to conventional research exercises, which use different theoretical frameworks to generate knowledge that reflects as faithfully as possible the reality to be interpreted, the participatory action-research exercise undertaken by the Villarrica Users Committee (with the support of some outside collaborators) was aimed at generating knowledge that would also point to the proper course of action. Developing this knowledge would also per force involve personal and social changes. This, in and of itself, had to have profound implications for the method, as it assumed that the ways in which knowledge would be generated would have an immediate impact on the dynamics of community life.

In other words, it was not only a matter of generating knowledge on the electricity problem; both the process of generating knowledge and the knowledge itself would have a liberating effect. This meant using a methodology that met two criteria. First, at the rational level it must be capable of unleashing the people's pent-up knowledge, and in so doing liberate their hitherto stifled thoughts and voices, thus stimulating their creativity and developing their analytical and critical capacities. That is, a research experience had to be set in motion which would develop the participants' potential so that they would not only see reality for what it is but do so with a view to changing their place and role within it. If in suffering the reality, participants also discovered what made it tick, it would be possible to experience it differently.

Second, at the emotional level, the process had to be capable of releasing feelings, of tearing down the participants' internal walls in order to free up energy for action. A methodology was needed that would stir up both levels – the rational and the emotional – so that the people would link their rational conclusions to profound emotions.

But the process of generating knowledge also must have a mobilizing effect, reaffirming the people as actors capable of transforming reality. In this regard their emergence should result in the erosion of the power structure, at least locally. It was thus necessary for the people's word to take on an assertive power in order to improve their ability to negotiate. Further, the process of generating knowledge must contribute to broadening the exercise of grassroots democracy and to strengthening the people's organizations.

These conditions meant that priority would be placed on generating and collectively processing knowledge within two main social contexts, the first occurring in various types of community and regional events. The Users Committee promoted several activities aimed at involving people in discussing the problem and designing strategies for solving it. One night in late 1982, for example, the Committee organized a 'march of lights' in Villarrica, in which the schoolchildren, women's groups and members of different grassroots organizations marched while carrying lit candles and torches to symbolize the right to electric illumination. This activity helped sensitize the entire town to the electricity issue through stimulating discussion within each family and in the community organizations on the importance of collectively participating in the electricity struggle. The Committee also promoted participation of the population in several cultural activities in Villarrica and throughout the region, in which different groups wrote and presented poems, plays and songs that reflected their perceptions of the electricity problem. The cultural events proved to be excellent opportunities for the people to organize and disseminate their knowledge; this knowledge was creatively expressed through the population's particular forms and codes. But above all, since this process contributed to affirming their own culture, it moved people to become involved.

Meetings and assemblies, which periodically brought the community together, represented another context for generating knowledge. In addition to reporting on how the effort was unfolding, people used these activities as a time for reflection. Many told about their own experiences or discussed past struggles. This information was processed collectively at such gatherings, pulling together the pertinent aspects of past experiences resulted in a common narrative. The Villarrica Users Committee and the outside agents played an important role in organizing the information, promoting reflection, choosing and articulating key aspects to be integrated into a synthesis and selecting strategic codes to be used in designing the actions to be taken.

Language ceased to serve simply as a vehicle for conveying isolated opinions – often the case when people respond in an isolated fashion in surveys or interviews – becoming instead the springboard for a new process of collective reasoning. The knowledge produced socially, and heard and legitimized collectively, was added to the people's ideological arsenal.

There were at least three 'moments' in the research process related to the collective production of (1) a mirror-like narrative, (2) strategic codes and (3) the community's *pensamiento propio* – that is, their own ideological outlook. These 'moments' do not correspond to rigidly defined stages, nor did the process involve moving from one to the next. The initiative did not stick to a timeline or a research plan; instead, it was largely conditioned by the pace of events. Receiving the monthly bill, for example, always led to much excitement and greater participation in the discussions. On such occasions reflection obviously centered on the content of the bills. On other occasions it focused on evaluating the actions. On the whole, however, discussion tended to progress through the above-mentioned levels.

PRODUCING A MIRROR-LIKE NARRATIVE

Such a narrative, which yielded codes for designing strategies for action, was a central aspect of the process. It involved the collective production of a shared discourse that reflected the majority of the people's individual electricity problems; it was thus a discourse with which the people could identify. There were two main aspects to this process:

(1) *Socialization of individual experiences in collective contexts (meetings, assemblies, forums and events), usually presented in the form of denunciations.* At these gatherings, the participants illustrated their particular situations through anecdotes; they often interspersed their opinions of the company and suggestions for action. Sometimes small groups used skits, poetry or song to communicate their perceptions of the problem. Organizing the perceptions and interpretations, and drawing initial conclusions, enabled the Committee to come up with an initial definition of the problem.
(2) *Expanding knowledge of the electricity issue.* The Villarrica Public Service Users Committee organized a campaign to collect bills, and promoted it through the region's grassroots organizations. This was done to ensure that the community would have a solid collective sense of its problem and solid evidence that could not be questioned either by company officials or the computer.

[...]

The knowledge generated in this process added to the people's original narrations, rounding them out with data and extending them so as to be representative of the problem in several communities. The initial discourse, fundamentally emotive and reflecting an ethical criticism, became a social criticism; yet it maintained its language and forcefulness. Part of the collectively processed information was translated into a list of demands, supported by the evidence gathered. This was the ammunition with which the people later entered into negotiations with the company representatives.

STRATEGIC CODES

Detecting and reworking strategic codes for action was another important aspect of the research process. The collective narrative no doubt contributed a great deal to helping the people decide what to do, which was largely reflected in the text of the 'list of demands.' They requested, for example, that the company cancel the accumulated debts, adopt procedures whereby the meters would be read only when someone from the household was present and recognize the Public Service Users Committee as the representative of the community's interests in electricity-related matters. In terms of how to approach the negotiations, simultaneously mobilizing the population, there were valuable lessons on:

(a) *Collectively reviewing the history of the black population's struggles in the region and earlier organizational experiences, and analyzing previous successes and failures.* Drawing lessons for action implied not only a reflection on the electricity problem but an enrichment of their knowledge by drawing on the legacy of common memories of the struggles in which blacks had participated. Picking up on the long-standing liberation tradition meant reaffirming the capacity of the people and their ethnic group to defend their constitutional and civil rights.

(b) *Evaluation of how the tasks were being implemented through periodical assemblies and meetings.* This exercise, carried out on an ongoing basis, enabled people to learn more about the dynamics of their communities, the existing mechanisms for political control and the limitations and obstacles affecting popular participation on an extended scale. Reflection on the action made it possible to accumulate knowledge on the day-to-day process, problems, fears and limitations involved in taking collective action. But more importantly, reflection revealed the key role of culture in its different manifestations as a factor of resistance to oppression and as a tool for strengthening forms of struggle. This kind of reflection made it possible for each experience to yield lessons on participation. On this level of analysis, priority was given to knowledge that, going beyond the facts and beyond the problem at hand, placed emphasis on the collective discovery of the best courses of action. This was the dimension that contributed most to the people's ability to learn more about themselves as a community, to characterize themselves collectively and to discover the possibilities that would be opened up by continuing their struggle through organized efforts.

DEVELOPING A *PENSAMIENTO PROPIO*

A *pensamiento propio*, or own alternative ideology, was also a significant part of the process. This *pensamiento propio* represented a consolidation of the knowledge that was generated in the popular consciousness. It was important, first, because development of an ideology would make it possible to go beyond the immediate problem of electricity, placing it in the context of basic rights. It was also important because a *pensamiento propio*, an ideology generated at the grassroots, could provide a common grounding for different grievances, while at the same time serving as a cementing factor in bringing together different sectors and groups in the region interested in taking action to obtain redress for their grievances. Finally, developing a *pensamiento propio* was significant insofar as it required asserting concepts and values that the people themselves had helped forge in order to have the process become a building block in a broader social movement. Without popular participation in defining these concepts and values, they would not have taken root in their own consciousness.

SOME OF THE RESULTS

The participatory action-research process described here yielded results at several levels. First, it made it possible to gather knowledge about an electricity problem, facilitating a successful negotiation process with the company. The arguments, collectively designed and appropriated, were incontestable. Defeating the computer was a triumph for the people, who demonstrated that 'yes, it did make mistakes' when at the service of policies geared to resolving the company's problems at the expense of the poor users. It was only by making major advances in popular participation that pressure was successfully brought to bear on the company to bring it to the negotiating table. These pressures included dispatching letters with demands and requests from hundreds of people, periodically sending delegations to the main office, denouncing the situation in communiqués and articles published in small local newspapers and bringing the electricity problem before town councils. Yet, it was the collective decision to withhold payments of electric bills unit the company agreed to negotiate, and to promote a regional civic strike, that tipped the scales in favor of the users.

Given the impossibility of negotiating individually with each of them, and wanting to avoid a worsening of the conflict that would lead to even greater losses, the company's directors decided to negotiate with the people's organizations.

The negotiations were held in Villarrica at a public meeting house with hundreds of users present. For the first time the people's spaces became the stage for negotiations. After several meetings – also attended by municipal authorities and some politicians, high-level company officials (including the manager) and community spokespeople – an agreement was signed which was beneficial to the people and which outlined procedures for the redress of their grievances.

A second result of the process was that it re-created civil society and broadened grassroots democracy. The process stimulated the rise and strengthening of popular organizations and the networking among them, providing methodologies for promoting popular participation. The Users Committees, for example, have supported the indigenous peoples' struggles for recovering their territory, and the protest marches of peasants from the Cordillera Occidental whose farms were flooded by construction of a dam. They have also promoted discussions among the peasants, encouraging them to refuse to sell their lands to the expanding sugar interests and to insist on access to the land. Likewise, they have stimulated reflection and action to confront educational problems and housing shortages.

glimpses of street children: through short stories

marcelo diversi

'You see, they don't want to be helped. There's a bunch of institutions and shelters in town trying to help them, but they are here on the streets, terrorizing old ladies and scaring our clients away,' he said calmly, rubbing his beard.

'And how is killing the kids going to help?' I asked, trying to keep my cool.

'The old folks will be able to come to the square in peace and read the paper without having to worry nonstop about their watches and wallets. The corners of the square wouldn't smell like pee and the ground wouldn't be covered with crumbs of food they throw everywhere.'

'Killing is not right,' Nancy said.

'It's the only solution though…. These kids were born bad and there is nothing you can do to help them. Look at all the shelters that close down because they don't have enough kids. In the meantime, downtown is full of them. I grew up very poor and knew a lot of kids like that. I worked hard and got out of the slums. But kids like them don't want to work, don't want to change their lives…. They like to be bad!' The man's voice was calm throughout. (Notes from a conversation with two shop owners in downtown Campinas, Brazil, May 1996).

Like the male shop owner in the passage above, many people in Brazil seem to share the notion that street kids are a social byproduct that needs to be eliminated. Communities and all levels of government show little concern with these kids' social condition. The population's perception of street kids as lesser beings can be felt in the eerie silence that follows aggressions such as the Candelaria massacre in July of 1993, when eight street kids sleeping by a church in Rio de Janeiro were shot by hired guns. To be sure, the dominant discourse on street kids is not monolithic and, thus, is also composed of narratives of resistance. Nevertheless, the demonizing narratives about street kids must be overwhelmingly prevalent among the population. How else could I make sense of, for instance, the open support for the killing of these kids that I have heard so often in Brazil? Or the public silence that has followed reported violence against street kids?

I have been doing fieldwork with kids living on the streets of Campinas, a large urban center in the southeast of Brazil, since 1994. In brief, the main goal of my research has been to give voice to street kids, to offer fuller representations of their lived experiences – representations that show the depth of their humanness and that transcend the limited, stereotypical image of 'little criminals' prevalent in the national and local dominant narratives.

Many times during my fieldwork, I wondered how I was going to be able to represent the kids without losing their voices, the three-dimensionality of their humanness, and the mystery that surrounds their lived experiences. Early on, I decided that I did not want to represent these street kids' experiences from a theoretical perspective, for that would inevitably bury their voices beneath layers of analysis (Denison, 1996, p. 352). Therefore, subscribing to current epistemological and methodological debates, I decided to transgress the boundaries of traditional forms of writing in the social sciences to build one more bridge between the social sciences and the humanities (Denzin, 1997; Ellis & Bochner, 1996, pp. 13–42; Freeman, 1993), by representing the kids I met in my fieldwork through the short story genre. Based on my field notes and on reconstructions of lived experiences I shared with the kids, I employed short story techniques such as alternative points of view, dialogue, unfolding action, and flashback to attempt to create the tension, suspense, delay, and voice that compose a good short story and that are inseparable from lived experience.

The short story genre has the potential to render lived experience with more verisimilitude than does the traditional realist text, for it enables the reader to feel that interpretation is never finished or complete. Short stories that show, instead of tell, are less author centered, which, in turn, invites interpretation and meaning making (Denzin, 1997). This invitation is crucial to avoid authorial omnipotence, the view from 'everywhere' (Richardson, 1994) and to avoid 'closing off or nailing down an interpretation without allowing alternative views to creep into view' (Van Maanen, 1988, p. 53).

In my view, short stories as a writing genre have a unique potential to bring lived experiences unknown to the reader closer to his or her own struggles for humanization, to touch the feelings and emotions of people whose only channel of access to street kids' lives is the slanderous representations of the printed and televised media. Dialogues and descriptions (of places, smells, looks), which are integral parts of short stories, have the power to move readers from abstract, sterile notions to the lively imagery of otherwise distant social realities. Well-written short stories, which create tensions and voices that sound real, have the power to allow readers to see themselves in the human dramas being represented, even if the specific circumstances shaping these human dramas are different from the circumstances shaping the readers' own dramas (Polkinghorne, 1988). My most optimistic goal, then, is that these stories will connect, at least initially, in an emotional realm, human beings living in extremely different social contexts.

To be sure, I am the author of these stories and, as such, have made important choices in the writing process that both carry my own interpretations of the lived experiences and define the possibilities of the reader's interpretations. The view from 'nowhere' is impossible from an epistemological standpoint that is founded on the social construction of reality (i.e., reality can only be understood through consciousness, through symbolic systems created and inscribed by historically situated humans), and therefore, the view from 'somewhere' is the closest an author can get to a text that gives voice to the people she or he writes about.

Although I am the one who spent time and shared lived experiences with kids living in downtown Campinas, I wanted to represent them in ways that allowed interpretations of their realities beyond – in addition to, in contrast to – my own. I am the one, through these short stories, opening up windows into a word of lived experience currently unrepresented in the academic and public debates about street kids, but the gaze that interprets and makes sense of the narratives must also be yours as reader. My own interpretations and deconstructions, as a researcher and writer, are already all over the stories, starting from the writing genre I chose. They are also present in my descriptions, in my positions as a character in the stories, and in my questions and silences. Nevertheless, I hope the windows I have tried to open are big enough for you to gaze into some of the kids' lived experiences and to make interpretations of your own.

STREET LIFE

I saw Dalva[1] crossing the street as I got off the bus. She was carrying a brown bag in one hand and a can of Coke in the other. Dalva, 16 or 17 years old, was one of the first kids living on the streets that I met and I'd become really fond of her. She was walking toward Rosario Plaza, and I rushed through the crowd to catch up with her. 'Hey Dalva, wait up!'

'Tio! You are lucky.... I just got some food.... Are you hungry?' she said between gulps of Coke.

Kids say 'tio,' which means uncle, to anyone visibly older than them, and I was already getting used to it.

'No thanks Dalva, I just ate lunch'. We walked together until she found some shade under the trees on the quiet side of the plaza. She sat down and took a plate of commercial food out of the brown bag. 'It looks good.... Where did you get it?' I asked, looking at the small mountain of rice and beans on her plate.

'You know that new self-service restaurant they just opened next to that big book-store?' she pointed.

I followed her finger, imagining a line shooting from it through the busy-looking passersby, through the luxurious bank building on the corner, through all the shops on that block, until I saw in my mind the 'big book-store.' I had been there the day before trying to find an illustrated book about pregnancy and birth. I had spent almost an hour in the bookstore but didn't find any book with more illustrations than text. Katia couldn't read much, and Marga, a female street educator, thought that a book with illustrations showing how a baby develops inside the womb would catch her interest. Katia, who had just turned 15, was well advanced in her pregnancy but hadn't seen a doctor yet. She had moved in with her boyfriend's parents when she found out she was pregnant. Her boyfriend had been taken to a juvenile reformatory, and she didn't feel safe on the streets of downtown. But she was now back on the streets, and last time I'd seen her, after dark in front of Orly Bakery, she was sweet-talking another girl, Kleo, into giving her 50 cents.

'Come on Kleo, you selfish girl, just 50 cents. I already have 4.50, and I know where to buy a stone for 5 bucks.' *Stone* is slang for a small portion of crack. 'I'll let you smoke some with me,' Katia said, getting closer, trying to grab the coins in Kleo's hands.

'No way, Katia!' said Kleo, putting the coins in her pocket. 'I'm gonna buy myself some bread with this money.... All I ate today was an ice cream.... I'm hungry!'

'One more reason why you should take a few hits, girl,' Katia said, smiling and putting her arm around Kleo's shoulders.

'No! And you shouldn't be smoking with this!' Kleo said, poking Katia's belly and pushing her away.

'Wow! You sure sound just like some of them street educators,' Katia said, laughing and walking away.

Later that night I'd see the two of them from a distance, walking together, teasing and laughing at some taxi drivers standing next to a hot dog stand.

'Yes,' I said looking at Dalva again.

'Well.... I was sitting by the door asking the people coming in and out of the restaurant for money.... Then the manager came and said he would give me a plate of food if I went away, so I did ...' Dalva paused to stuff her mouth with food again, 'But I guess I'm going back there again soon!' We looked at each other and laughed.

'You know, many restaurants now have security guards to keep us away,' Dalva said, still eating. 'Some security guys are nice, they let us stay near the door for a while, but some are real mean. Did you hear what happened to Tate?'

I shook my head no, feeling from the tone of her voice that something bad had happened to him, imagining what it could be while she finished chewing. Tate was a very good-natured boy of about 16, always smiling and ready to tell me some story about his 'other life,' as he used to refer to his life before coming to the streets of Campinas from a small town in a neighboring state. I never understood whether he left home because of an abusive stepfather, or because he got a girl pregnant, or because of other stories he only half told me. But I learned a great deal about farm animals, birds, and plants from his detailed and rich narratives. His travel adventures were told with gaiety and wit, and he had a special talent for making himself look foolish without losing his dignity. People in downtown seemed to be especially fond of him, perhaps because of that. He was so peaceful that I had a hard time imagining that someone had harmed him.

'He got beat up real bad by that security guard working in front of the computer school, you know, near the restaurant where he is always watching customers' cars. He didn't do anything. This lady had just parked her car in front of the restaurant, and he went up to her, asking if he could watch the car for her. You know, that's how he makes money. He doesn't steal or anything. But she must have thought he was gonna rob her and started screaming. You know how these rich people is.... They see a dirty kid coming to talk to them and they already think we are gonna rob 'em. So the security guy started pushing and punching Tate before he could say anything. Celi and I were the only kids around and we were too afraid of getting beat up too. People started coming out of the shops to see what was going on. Some men started laughing at Tate. Nobody did nothing to stop the beating. Poor Tate ... he was all bloody and crying by the time the guy let go of him, and nobody did nothing. Then this man who was talking to the lady started coming towards us shouting that we should be in jail, that we should be ... hmmm ... how do you say ... terminated?'

'Exterminated?'

'Yes, like those kids who were shot dead while sleeping by that church in Rio de Janeiro.'

'What happened to Tate, then? Did he go to the hospital? You said he was bleeding...'

'No, he said they would treat him bad at the hospital too because he was all dirty and smelly. Celi and I walked around to find a street educator to take him to the hospital but didn't find no one. When we came back, Tate had disappeared. I haven't seen him since then.... Nobody knows where he's hiding. Do you know that security guy?'

I shook my head no.

Dalva started eating again. I felt that she wanted me to go talk to him. But I didn't know what to do. We were in silence for a while. Then she wrapped the food left on the plate, some rice and beans and a chicken leg, with a napkin and put it inside the brown bag.

'I'm gonna take this food to Kleo and Grace. They are sleeping behind the post office and will wake up hungry,' she said, getting up.

The post office is a large old building in one of the busiest areas of downtown; the wide sidewalks surrounding it are crowded with food and cheap merchandise stands, and there is a bus stop connecting downtown with the working-class neighborhoods right in front of its main entrance. It's a noisy place in the middle of the afternoon. 'How can they get any sleep there?' I thought out loud.

'We didn't get much sleep last night,' Dalva said, helping me up on my feet.

The post office was only a few blocks from where we were, and as we walked, Dalva began telling me how they had been on the lookout for this woman dealer who was after them. 'She said she's gonna kill us if we don't pay our crack debts, and we don't have no money. It's in the night that things happen, you know? So last night, we kept on going from place to place, trying to stay awake.'

Dalva told me they laid down at the doorstep of a pediatric clinic, but that after a few minutes, a police car stopped by, some policemen came out and got them up, saying they couldn't stay there. I had seen this clinic before. It has caught my attention one afternoon when I was looking for some of the kids. I remembered thinking that it was in an odd place, squeezed between small clothing shops on one side and a crumbling hotel where some young women and men took their clients, on the other side. I had stopped in front of it and read the sign with big yellow letters: WHERE WE CARE FOR THE CHILDREN OF CAMPINAS.

Dalva said they then walked to the church, laid down again, and the same cops came and kicked them out of there. The sun was already rising when they fell asleep in front of a vegetarian restaurant on a tiny street, a little hidden from the busy streets of downtown. But at 10 a.m., the manager came to open it and woke them up.

'We then went to the post office and lay down by the back entrance, you know, where nobody goes. But the sun was cooking us and we couldn't fall asleep. Kleo and Grace rolled under a parked car and fell asleep in no time. I was too scared to fall asleep under the car.... Imagine if they didn't see us and just drove away! So I left and started looking for something to eat.'

I shook my head, imagining. Dalva started to sing a rap tune.

We're 30 million street kids
But you pretend you don't see us
We're tugging at your Armani suit, begging
Still you pretend you don't see us
You drive expensive cars
We knock on your window, begging
But you pretend you don't see us
You see us getting beat up by the police
Still you walk by, you pretend you don't see us
Is a blade on your throat the only way
The only way to get your attention?

Dalva told me the rap is by a new band formed by ex-street kids from Sao Paulo. She said she'd give me their tape. 'Two bucks for a pirate tape at the bus terminal market,' she said, winking.

We got to the post office, walked past food stands, lines of people waiting for buses, and men trying to sell lottery tickets. Going around the building to the back entrance, we saw Kleo and Grace under an old blue van. The blue van's chassis was really close to the ground, and I had to bend down to see the girls. I hadn't known many people who looked under their cars before driving, so I understood exactly why Dalva was too afraid to join her friends. She put the brown bag next to Kleo, under the van, without waking them up, and sat down leaning against the post office wall. I sat next to her, and we watched the van till the kids woke up.

The church bell had just struck 2 p.m. when first Kleo then Grace came out from under their urban tent carrying the brown bag with them. They sat down in front of us and, stretching and yawning, unwrapped the food.

'My hair is a mess, Tio,' Grace said, pulling her black curly hair back with both hands. 'Give me your cap, Tio, I don't want you to see me like this.'

I took my cap off my head and gave it to her, saying that she looked fine. 'Don't bullshit me, Tio, I know I look horrible, I'm all dirty and smelly and haven't washed my hair in days.' She put my cap on and grabbed the cold chicken leg from the plate.

'They don't let us shower at Casa Aberta anymore, Tio,' said Kleo with her mouth full of rice and beans.

'Yeah, but sometimes Tio, Marcio lets us use the shower to clean up and wash our clothes,' Dalva said.

'But only when the other staff members aren't there, those sonuvabitch don't want us there no more,' Grace almost shouted between bites, just as a middle-aged couple walked out of the post office through the back entrance. They first looked at the three girls, their faces sulking, and said something I could not make out. But as they kept on walking away, the woman looked at me and asked, 'What are *you* doing among these moleques de rua?' *Moleques de rua* is a pejorative term for street kids, so I knew she wasn't really asking a question, and I just watched as the couple disappeared in the crowd and hoped that they couldn't hear Dalva and Grace show off their own repertoire of pejorative names for women.

A few weeks before, I had seen Lucio, a 15-year-old boy, almost get into trouble for a similar thing. Another street educator and I were hanging out with several kids near the newspaper stand in Rosario Plaza that day. It was near lunchtime and the plaza was packed with passersby. Celi was standing alone a few yards from where we were, gnawing on an ice cream she'd been given (though not very willingly) by a young girl walking to or from school. Lucio got up and, sneaking behind Celi, took the ice cream from her hand and ran away with a mischievous smile. As Celi started chasing after him, Lucio bumped into a well-dressed man in his late 30s who was walking by, spilling ice cream over his suit. Celi and the other kids began laughing at Lucio, who stepped back from where the man was standing, looking at his spotted suit. The man took a handkerchief out of his pocket to clean the mess and cursed at Lucio as he began to walk away. Lucio stood there staring at the man for a while, then used the same name-calling to offend the man's mom. The man stopped, turned around, took something we couldn't see out of his briefcase, and started trailing after Lucio. Lucio darted across the jammed street, the man after him, and we didn't see him till later that afternoon, when he bragged about knowing his way around downtown like no one else.

'Can you take us to Casa Aberta, Tio? Maybe they will let us take a shower and wash our clothes if you talk to them,' Kleo said after a while.

'Okay,' I said to Kleo. But I knew it'd be difficult to convince the people at Casa Aberta to let the girls use their facilities. I had taken Lara there the week before and heard the whole spiel about Casa Aberta's new policies. Casa Aberta, which means 'open house,' used to be a place where street kids could always go for a meal, a shower, and sometimes, for a session of occupational therapy. But, as I was told by an administrator, feeling that Casa Aberta was serving as a crutch for kids who didn't want to commit to recovery, they decided to change it into a halfway house for adult recovering addicts.

'Kids came here just for the food and shower, not wanting to stick to the hardships of recovery and salvation. We realized we were not helping them get out of the streets but were instead keeping them dependent and unmotivated by being so lenient. We have now adopted the philosophy of tough love, so the kids have to prove they are really willing to stick to the program before they can go to the shelter,' the same administrator told me. Then looking at Lara, who was standing next to me, 'These kids need to know that everything has a price in life.' Lara didn't smile back.

'And how can they prove their willingness if they are no longer allowed to come in here?' I wanted to ask. 'Lara has a doctor's appointment today and wants to clean up before going,' I said instead.

Lara had told another street educator, a woman, that she thought she might be pregnant or have some venereal disease.

'So we were wondering if you could let her use your shower, just today, as a favor ...' I said, being interrupted by Lara.

'I don't have any other place to go, Tia! And I can't go to the doctor like this,' she said, pointing to her dirty bare feet.

The administrator, an older woman with short gray hair and a large wooden cross resting on her breasts, looked at Lara, touched her chin softly, and said that she was sorry but couldn't make an exception, that it wouldn't be fair to the other kids who were coming by for the same reason.

'I won't tell anybody, I promise!' Lara said.

'Sorry honey, but I can't do that...'

Lara's eyes watered. She turned around and started to walk away. I asked her not to leave, saying that we would find another place.

'Where?! In your house?!' She said to me crying. 'All I want is to take a damn shower,' she shouted at the woman with a cross standing next to me and then bolted out of our sight. Lara was gone.

As the administrator talked about the problem of street children and the lack of love in their families, I tuned out and began wondering how I was going to tell the doctor that Lara wasn't going to make the appointment because we couldn't find a place for her to bathe.

Lara had just turned 17 and had lived in foster homes since she was 3 years old, when her mother was sent to jail. She had just come to the streets again, after a quarrel with the young woman coordinating the Baptist female shelter where she had been living. After a night on the streets of downtown, Lara tried to go back to the Baptist shelter and apologize for having left in anger. But the Baptist shelter was also following the tough love philosophy, and Lara was told she'd have to wait a week before being allowed to return. Her punishment was to spend a week on the streets so that she'd learn to appreciate what she had at the shelter.

'And they said I can't hang out with Dalva or Katia or Celi, or any other kids they think are bad, if I want to go back at all!' Lara said to me on the first night I saw her on the streets, with Dalva and Celi, in front of a pizza place. 'But I'm too afraid of being by myself here.... I'm not used to making money on the streets, you know, I don't know how to steal and am too embarrassed to beg. I'm afraid someone I know will see me sleeping out here or dressed in rags.' Here, Lara was interrupted by Dalva.

'But somehow you always have new and clean clothes, nice shoes.... I wonder how you get the money for these things,' Dalva said, affecting an innocent air.

Lara gave a mean look to Dalva, who then made a gesture of ironic apology. 'It's not fair what they did, Tio. I apologized, on my knees, and they didn't believe me. I know I was wrong when I called her names and left the shelter.... I was angry.... All I wanted to do was watch the soap opera, you know, that one that everybody's talking about. It was my birthday, so I though I deserved to watch what I wanted and not that boring religious channel.... I know I have a bad temper... but I apologized.' Lara started to cry softly.

'It's true, Tio, she doesn't know how to live on the streets,' Dalva told me, 'she can't even ask people for food, she gets too embarrassed, so I have to take care of her, right Lara?'

'Yeah, Dalva got me some food tonight.... I was starving.'

'She started to cry, Tio' Dalva said, smiling a little.

'My stomach was hurting!' Lara replied.

'I know, I'm just teasing you, Lara. It's not right what they did to Lara, Tio!' Dalva told me, her face turning somber. 'It's dangerous to be here alone, especially after dark, and I can't take her with me when I go buy crack. You see, the dealers don't like when people that don't smoke come with us. They think you are spying for the police, and that's bad business. So I have to leave her alone sometimes, or she'll have to come along and pretend she smokes too.'

'I'm afraid to do that, Dalva.'

'I know.... It's unfair what they did, you know? They say they want to help us, but they don't even know how! I'd like to see one of them rich goody-goody kids staying in that shelter, see how long they would last there... and I bet that their parents don't send them to the streets for a week when they act like brats,' Dalva burst out.

Celi, who had been standing by the pizza place's door the whole time while we talked, came over where Dalva, Lara, and I were and, laughing and talking at the same time, told us that a couple had just given her a bill worth 5 bucks. It was a lot of money for spare change. 'I think they were too drunk to see the bill they were giving me,' Celi said, pointing to the couple. We looked at them and, from the way they were walking, wondered whether they were seeing two sidewalks where there was one?

'We have enough money for a stone now,' Celi said, looking at Dalva.

'Sorry, Tio… we gotta go,' Dalva said with an impish smile.

'See you later,' I said, wondering where they were going to sleep that night. I watched as they disappeared into the night, Lara going with them.

Grace and Kleo were finishing eating when Dalva pointed to a man opening the blue van's door. He threw a large mail bag in the passenger seat, started the engine, and drove away in a hurry. Kleo and Grace looked at each other and started laughing, stopping only when Dalva began a graphic description of what their smashed bodies would look like had they still been sleeping under the van. 'You are sick, girl,' Grace said to Dalva, and they all began to laugh again.' That's good way to die anyway, in your sleep, you don't feel anything, just like going to sleep, but you'll never wake up,' Grace said.

'I think so too! It's better than getting shot and left in a ditch to die slowly, like Pedro,' Dalva said.

'And Marcy too…' Grace recalled.

'You are so gloomy! I don't wanna die young…' Kleo was beginning to say.

'Get real, girl!' whispered Grace. 'How many street kids do you know live much beyond our age?! Huh?!'

'I'm gonna get out of the streets…' murmured Kleo, gazing past us. 'yeah right! Only if Tio Marcelo here marries you', Grace said, and we all chuckled. Only I blushed.

'Let's go, guys, it's getting late, and I want to shower today!' Dalva got up and we followed her lead.

We were two blocks from Casa Aberta, walking through a street market, inebriated by the smells coming from the third-class steaks barbecuing on dozens of grills all around us and from the countless fruit stands stacked with ripe tangerines and guavas, when Dalva abruptly stopped. I stopped too and looked at where Dalva was looking. I saw a woman with black straight hair in a ponytail, wearing jeans and a loose white shirt, only a few steps ahead, staring right back at us.

'It's Regina! Come on Kleo, hurry up, time to split,' Dalva said pulling Kleo by the hand and running back toward the way we had come. I didn't even see which way Grace had gone, and just stood there. I figured the woman was the dealer Dalva had told me about. She came up to me and asked for a lighter. I lit up her cigarette trying not to shake too much.

'Do you know those little sluts?' the dealer said, looking fiercely into my eyes. I was glad that Dalva had seen her in time to escape and that I was in a place with lots of people around.

'I was trying to help them find a place to shower…'

NOTE

1. All names used in the stories have been changed.

REFERENCES

Denison, J. (1996). Sport narratives. *Qualitative Inquiry, 2*, 351–62.

Denzin, N. (1997). *Interpretive ethnography: Ethnographic practices for the 21st century.* Thousand Oaks, CA: Sage.

Ellis, C., & Bochner, A. (Eds) (1996). *Composing ethnography: Alternative forms of qualitative writing.* Walnut Creek, CA: AltaMira.

Freeman, M. (1993). *Rewriting the self: History, memory, narrative.* New York: Routledge.

Polkinghorne, D. (1988). *Narrative knowing and the human sciences.* Albany: State University of New York Press.

Richardson, L. (1994). Writing-stories: Co-authoring 'The Sea Monster,' a writing-story. *Qualitative Inquiry, 1,* 189–203.

Van Maanen, J. (1988). *Tales of the field.* Chicago: University of Chicago Press.

the relational reconstruction of self

Part four

f asked to describe your family, chances are you would begin to talk about the various individuals in the family. You might describe the differing personalities of a father or mother, perhaps a brother or sister. You might also describe your feelings about each of them, and the impact they have on your life. This common way of describing one's family is revealing: how quickly and unproblematically we assume that the group is made up of independent beings, each with particular characteristics, private feelings, and perceptions of each other. Much the same kind of account would be given of a classroom, a community, or life in an organization. The unspoken and unexamined assumption is that individual actors form the basic atoms of social life. Each of us acts according to internal dictates – of cognition, emotion, motivation, and so on. On this account 'you' and 'I' are distinct and separate beings. Relationships are artificial; they only exist when otherwise independent individuals come together. And, to keep society together, each of us is charged with being responsible for our conduct; irresponsible individuals are punished and individual sacrifice for others applauded.

Yet, it should also be clear from the preceding chapters that the concept of the individual self is a social construction. The vocabulary of individual minds is not required by 'the way things are,' nor is the belief in their fundamental independence. The conception of human beings may vary dramatically across both culture and history, and even in Western culture the preeminent status of the individual self is of relatively recent historical vintage. Prior to the 16th century the ordinary individual was typically identified in terms of the group to which he or she belonged – the family, clan, or craft. That the conception of individual selves is constructed is not in itself a criticism. In fact, many of our most precious traditions – democracy, public education, protection under the law – draw their rationale from the individualist tradition. However, to recognize the historical and cultural contingency of individualist beliefs does open the door to reflection. Should we settle for the status quo?

Such reflection does indeed reveal a substantial dark side to the conception of individual agents. As psychologist Edward E. Sampson (Reading 18) proposes, the self/other distinction contributes to a pervasive alienation and antagonism. Because of the distinction we begin to see others as interferences, adversaries or inferiors. We become defensive and/or exploitative. In Reading 19, feminist theorist Judith Butler extends this line of critique to argue that by positing a self that pre-exists our discursive constructions, we limit the possibilities of transformative politics. Specifically, in identifying oneself as a woman or a man, we acquiesce to a category system that is both conservative ('This is simply how things are and always will be.') and suppressive. For example, the gender distinction slots one's sexual life into two categories (e.g. either heterosexual or homosexual). These critiques are representative of a large body of literature placing the autonomous self into question. The interested reader might also wish to explore Lasch's *Culture of Narcissism*, Sennett's *The Fall of Public Man*, Paul, Miller and Paul's *The Communitarian Challenge to Liberalism*, and the Bellah et al. volume, *Habits of the Heart*. The substantial problems inhering in the individualist tradition also invite an exploration of alternatives. The attempt is not to simply abandon the individualist tradition, but to develop concepts and practices that open new possibilities. We may add to our cultural resources through creative reconstruction.

In this spirit of adventure new dialogues centering on the possibility of 'relational being,' have emerged. In one form or another, theorists and practitioners explore how we can begin to understand ourselves as inherently related to each other. Countering the individualist tendency to understand society as 'all against all,' the attempt is to articulate ways in which we are inextricably interdependent, even in identifying who it is that we are. There are many different approaches to relational reconstruction. For example, in works such as Bruner's *Acts* of *Meaning*, and Shore's *Culture in Mind*, a strong emphasis is placed on the way in which private meanings are given birth within cultural traditions. Miller and Stiver's volume, *The Healing Connection*, reflects the views of many feminists that individual development must be viewed in terms of relationships; it is through relationships, they propose, that we not only grow in understanding but come to know ourselves. Many contemporary psychoanalysts are drawn to a relational view of subjectivity, in which self and other are intertwined. One knows the other through oneself, and oneself through the reactions of others. Stephen Mitchell's *Hope and Dread in Psychoanalysis* is an excellent discussion of this position. And, family therapists add to relational understanding an emphasis on individuals as parts of larger systems; in this case the individual is primarily understood in terms of his or her functioning within the system (see for example, Palazzoli, et al. 1978).

The readings we have selected for the present volume grow more directly out of the social constructionist dialogues. As the preceding readings make clear, these dialogues place a heavy emphasis on the linguistic creation of reality. And too, this creative process is typically traced not to individual minds but to processes of relationship – to the ways in which we coordinate ourselves in language and action. How might this orientation help us to reconceptualize traditional views of individual, mental processes? We consider first the traditional view of memory. We typically speak of memory as a process within the head of the individual. 'I remember,' we say, or 'you fail to remember.' Memory stands or falls within the individual mind. However, as the social theorist, John Shotter, demonstrates in Reading 20, when further examined we find remembering to be an inherently social act. To remember correctly is to give an account that is acceptable to a particular social group. Thus, if a child responds to the question, 'What happened to you today in school?' with the words, 'blue, fast, go, happy,' his or her parents will not treat this as an acceptable memory. If the child talks about a teacher who let him play with a blue car, and he made the car go fast, which made him happy, the child may be credited with proper memory. The success lies not in the mental process, but in the arrangement of words. The reader wishing to explore these issues further should see Middleton and Edwards' *Collective Remembering*, and Pennebaker, Paez and Rime's *Collective Memory of Political Events*.

In Reading 21, psychologist Michael Billig extends this line of reasoning to reconstruct the Freudian conception of repression. In the psychoanalytic tradition repression is a pivotal conception. As it is said, individuals have the capacity to force from consciousness unwanted or painful materials. In effect, our states of normal consciousness fail to acknowledge unwanted desires and memories. However, theorists have never been content with the idea of an internal censor (presumably unconscious) that permits some content into consciousness while distorting or destroying the remainder. And too, the concept of repression functions culturally in such a way that the individual loses credibility in accounting for him/herself. It is the therapist who is credited for the 'true insight' into the client. Using constructionist conceptions of language, Billig offers an alternative view of repression. He argues that as people negotiate reality together they create effects that are repressive in consequence. Certain content is simply 'pressed to the margins of the page' upon which 'reality' is inscribed. According to Billig's view, one need not dig deeply into 'the unconscious' to reveal unrecognized truths. Rather, by exploring what is created and hidden in our common speech practices, we may all expand the domain of awareness.

In Reading 22, philosopher Rom Harré takes up the topic of the emotions (see also Lutz' discussion in Reading 8). Traditionally the emotions are viewed as biologically based mechanisms of universal standing. From this viewpoint, every biologically normal human being should have the capacity for certain basic emotions (e.g. anger, fear, sadness). Challenging this individualist view of the emotions, Harré proposes that when we take into account the way emotion words are used in relationships, there is a strong moral or normative component. How, when and where one can shriek, 'I am angry' are all dictated by cultural convention. To perform anger in the wrong place at the wrong time will be treated as bad manners, stupid, or pathological. Not only does this argument lend itself to thinking of emotions as culturally specific (as opposed to universal), but as fully embedded in social process. In effect, one learns within specific cultural traditions how to perform actions that we call emotional. Here the interested reader may wish to examine Lutz' *Unnatural Emotions*, Hacking's *Rewriting the Soul*, and Harré's edited volume, *The Social Construction of Emotions*.

We complete this section with Kenneth Gergen's relational reconstruction of meaning (Reading 23). Within the individualist tradition, meaning occurs within the mind of the individual. 'Let me tell you what I mean,' we say, or 'I want to know what this means to you? Meaning is private, and sometimes we give our private meaning expression in words. However, this conception of meaning presents us with a riddle that no one has yet solved: if meanings are private, how can we ever know what others mean; how can we know the 'meaning behind the words' or actions? In this reading, Gergen extends Wittgenstein's (Reading 4) view of meaning as emergent from social practice. Here we find that one's words cannot mean anything by themselves; their meaning requires supplementation by another person. By focusing on the way in which meaning is created through relational efforts, we can also begin to see how all reasoning or rationality is inherently social. For more on meaning in dialogue the reader should explore the literary theories of Mikhail Bakhtin, a good introduction to which is contained in Bell and Gardiner's *Bakhtin and the Human Sciences*.

REFERENCES

Bell, M. M., & Gardiner, M. (Eds) (1998) *Bakhtin and the human sciences*. London: Sage.

Bellah, R. N., et al. (1985). *Habits of the heart*. Berkeley: University of CA Press.

Bruner, J. (1990). *Acts of meaning*. Cambridge, MA: Harvard University Press.

Hacking, I. (1995). *Rewriting the soul*. Princeton, NJ: Princeton University Press.

Harré, R. (Ed.). (1986). *The social construction of emotions*. Oxford, New York: Blackwell.

Lasch, C. (1979). *Culture of narcissism*. New York: Norton.

Lutz, C. A. (1998). *Unnatural emotions*. Chicago: University of Chicago Press.

Middleton, D., & Edwards, D. (1990). *Collective remembering*. London: Sage.

Miller, J. B., & Stiver, I. P., (1997). *The healing connection: How women form relationships in therapy and in life*. Boston, MA: Beacon Press.

Mitchell, S. (1993). *Hope and dread in psychoanalysis*. New York: Basic Books.

Palazzoli, S., Boscolo, L., Cecchin, G., and Prata, G. (1978). *Paradox and counterparadox*. New York: Jason Aronson.

Paul, E. F., Miller, F. D., and Paul, J. (Eds) (1996). *The communitarian challenge to liberalism*. New York: Cambridge University Press.

Pennebaker, J., Paez, D., & Rime, B. (1997). *Collective memory of political events*. Hillsdale, NJ: Erlbaum Press.

Sennett, R. (1977). *The fall of public man*. New York: Knopf.

Shore, B. (1996). *Culture in mind*. New York: Oxford University Press.

18

possessive individualism and the self-contained ideal

edward e. sampson

In order to celebrate the self we first need to think of the self as a kind of bounded container, separate from other similarly bounded containers and in possession or ownership of its own capacities and abilities. In order to ensure this container's integrity, we need to think of whatever lies outside its boundaries as potentially threatening and dangerous, and whatever lies inside as sufficiently worthy to protect. These beliefs establish a possessively individualistic view of the person and the assumption of a negative relation between self and other, both of which understandings permeate much of Western civilization.

Regardless of how life was once experienced, or how life may still be experienced in other societies, or even how much we may complain and protest:

> There is an individualist mode of thought, distinctive of modern Western cultures, which, though we may criticize it in part or in whole, we cannot escape. It indelibly marks every interpretation we give of other modes of thought and every attempt we make to revise our own. (Lukes, 1985, p. 298)

This inescapable cultural vise has given us – or, least, the dominant social groups in the West – a sense of themselves as distinctive, independent agents who own themselves and have relatively clear boundaries to protect in order to ensure their integrity and permit them to function more effectively in the world. This describes the self-contained ideal. This ideal is supported by the twin pillars of a possessively individualistic understanding of the person (primarily, the male person) and the sense of the self as being like a container.

The hallmark of a democratic system involves its citizens' right to vote. For this reason, among all the world's nations, the United States is usually considered to be one of the prime bastions of democracy. Some assume that voting is a natural right of

US citizenship, forgetting the long history of political battles that eventually enfranchised increasingly more people. It was not until 1870 that enfranchisement was granted regardless of race, color or previous condition of servitude; not until 1920 that women were given these rights; not until 1971 that these rights were granted to all those aged 18 and over rather than the previous age of 21. If we regard citizenship as an essential aspect of what it means to be a person within modern society, we can view each of these constitutional amendments as enlarging the definition of 'persons' to be more inclusive than it was previously.

But what do citizenship, personhood and voting rights have to do with the self-contained ideal? An examination of several debates held in seventeenth-century England, pitting the Levellers on one side and Cromwell on the other, will lead us to this connection and, in so doing, enrich our understanding. The central issue in the debates involved who should be entrusted with the right to vote. Should everyone living in England have this right, or only certain people? And, if the latter, then which people were entitled, and which were not?

According to Macpherson's (1962) examination of the various sides in these debates, the issue boiled down to a question of personhood, while personhood itself involved the capacity to operate in a self-determining, autonomous manner. Did the mere fact of birth grant the individual the status of personhood, with its attendant right to vote? The Levellers argued:

> The birthright, we may presume, was not only forfeitable for acts against society, but was also forfeited, or not even entered upon, by those whose age or whose status as servants or beggars was deemed inconsistent with the free exercise of rational will. (Macpherson, 1962, p. 124)

In the Levellers' view, all people whose 'living was not directly dependent on the will of others, were entitled to the franchise' (p. 128). The key point in their argument centered around independence from the will of others, considering criminals, servants and beggars either to have forfeited this quality of their character or not even to have possessed it in the first place.

It would make no sense, for example, to give the vote to someone who was held in servitude to another, for the master would then have more votes than he deserved: that is, his own plus those of people in servitude to him. Similar arguments suggested that it would be inappropriate to include wage-earners (who might simply cast their vote to protect their employment), beggars and people on welfare: after all, these people were not autonomous – that is, free from the will of others.

Cromwell's cynical view of the Leveller position argued that 'The Leveller franchise proposals "must end in anarchy" ... because they refer to "men that have no interest but the interest in breathing"' (p. 126). He favored restricting the vote to property-owners whose freedom from others' will was clear, and whose interest in protecting their property rights warranted their self-determination through voting.

These themes from America's English heritage were involved in the later debates concerning voting as well as other individual rights. The US Constitution, for example, was initially interpreted to mean that white, male property-owners should not only have the right to vote, but should in addition be free from governmental interference in their affairs. Only later were both voting rights and other individual rights extended to larger classes of people. In all cases, the decision to grant an individual the vote or other individual rights was sculpted by the cultural understanding of personhood. This understanding, in turn, was defined by what Macpherson terms *possessive individualism*: being the owner of one's own capacities and self.

Possessive individualism first tells us that in order to vote, one must be free; and second, that in order to be free – that is, independent from another's will – one must be the owner of oneself. Any conditions thought to impinge upon the individual's personal ownership over himself would infringe on freedom, and thus deny such a person the right to vote.

Those who were still too young to be free from dependence on another should not vote, nor should women (then subjected to their husband's will or, if unmarried, to their father's); nor persons in servitude who were required to submit to another to sustain themselves. All these people were not in possession of themselves; thus they were not free, and thereby did not deserve the vote. In so far as voting plays a vital role in setting forth the conditions under which a person lives, to be denied the right to vote is effectively to be considered not quite a person.

It is clear that the possessively individualistic formulation defines the self-contained ideal and simultaneously establishes the negative self-other relationship that is at the root of the self-celebratory world-view. In order to be one's own person, one cannot be beholden to anyone else. In other words, possessive individualism posits a negative relationship between self and other: the more the other is involved in the life of the person, the less the person is involved in his or her own life. To be capable of voting means to be capable of making one's decisions without being subjected to the will of others. Others are posited as potential thieves of one's personhood. The more others take priority, the less priority exists for the individual.

The second pillar on which the self-contained ideal rests involves a view of the self as a kind of container.

THE SELF AS A CONTAINER

Most of us in the West today would subscribe to three relatively simple and seemingly 'natural' ideas: (1) the boundary of the individual is coincident with the boundary of the body; (2) the body is a container that houses the individual; (3) the individual is best understood as a self-contained entity. The self-celebratory quality of our cultural understanding of human nature is built upon this tripartite foundation, with its container view of the individual.

Point (1) clearly connects the notion of the individual with the idea of a skin-encased body. It tells us that individuals begin and end at the limits of their body. Some might say, 'of course this so', noting that because we all have bodies, our understanding of individuals must be based on this simple fact of nature. Since people everywhere have always had bodies and always will have bodies, this natural fact sets the terms for all people's understanding of what an individual is, where they are located, and so forth. In short, point (1) has a natural ring about it – at least *to us*. This idea is found today primarily in the Western world, and is by no means a universal understanding.

Point (2) observes that bodies are very much like containers which house everything that is vital about the person. Housed inside the body-as-container, then, are both the physiological qualities that comprise a person and the psychological characteristics they possess. If we want to know where the stomach, liver and heart are located, we looked *inside* the body-as-container. If it is the mind we seek, once again, we know we must look inside the body-as-container. Where are feelings? Inside the body-as-container, of course. What about opinions, attitudes, beliefs, values? Once again, seek them inside the body-as-container. Where are the will, motivation, drive? Inside the body-as-container, of course.

Point (3) simply completes the picture, telling us that if the individual is a body and the body is a container, then it would seem to follow that the individual must be a self-contained entity.

Although they came at this matter from a somewhat different place and arrived at a conclusion somewhat at variance with my own, the analyses suggested by the linguist George Lakoff (1987) and the philosopher Mark Johnson (1987) offer us a helpful examination of what they refer to as *the container metaphor*. Listen first to Johnson (1987):

> Our encounter with containment and boundedness is one of the most pervasive features of our bodily experience. We are intimately aware of our bodies as three-dimensional containers into which we put certain things (food, water, air) and out of which other things emerge (food and water wastes, air, blood, etc.). From the beginning, we experience constant physical containment in our surroundings (those things that envelop us). We move in and out of rooms, clothes, vehicles, and numerous kinds of bounded spaces. We manipulate objects, placing them in containers (cups, boxes, cans, bags, etc.). In each of these cases there are repeated spatial and temporal organizations. (p. 21)

Johnson argues that our everyday, repeated experience is of our selves as bodies and our bodies as containers. A collection of cultural sayings convey this meaning: 'I've had a *full* life. Life is *empty* for him. There's *not much left* for him *in* life. Her life is *crammed* with activities. *Get the most out of* life. His life *contained* a great deal of sorrow. Live your life *to the fullest*' (Lakoff and Johnson, 1980, p. 51). We speak of ourselves and others as *filled* with anger; as unable *to contain* our joy; as *brimming* with rage; as trying to get anger *out of our system* (Lakoff, 1987, p. 383; original emphasis).

Even our mind is said to reason in terms of this container metaphor. For example, Johnson argues that the logical meaning of *transitivity* and of set membership is based on generalizing our experiences based on our body as a container. If our liver is inside our body and our body is in the living-room, then our liver is in the living-room. Johnson suggests that several other logical principles likewise derive from this sense of the body as a container.

In other words, thinking of the person as a container is a rather commonplace feature of our everyday livers. [. . .] Two ideas are central: (a) Containers have an inside and an outside; what is not inside must clearly be outside, and vice versa. In other words, there is a rather clear-cut in–out distinction. (b) Containers have boundaries that separate their inside from the outside, and offer a kind of protective shield.

Let us now apply these features of containers to our understanding of the individual. First, we believe that an individual has an inside that contains all the important features that comprise the person – everything that the person owns – and that this inside is distinct, separate and cut off from all that is not part of the person, located outside the container. The person's essence, whatever we believe this to be, is housed within the individual and is distinguished from everything that is outside. Because we draw the in–out line at the edges of the body, we insist that the human core lies within those edges, period, end of sentence. And so, when I describe our current conception of the person as the *self-contained individual*, I am referring to this container whose boundaries lie at the edge of the skin within which is housed the essence possessed by the person.

Secondly, we see the boundaries of the person-as-container to be vital in the defense of the human core, and in sustaining the individual's integrity as a viable entity in the world. Boundary maintenance and boundary defense are key features of being a person and in maintaining individual sovereignty. We believe that a loss of boundaries – for example, when the individual is not certain where she ends and her children begin – threatens the individuality that requires boundary maintenance in order to be sustained.

I remember a moment in my own family in which our son, who was quite young at the time, came home from school carrying his report card. Seeing it, we asked him about his grades. Somewhat defiantly, he showed us an 'F' in one of his subjects (comportment would be my guess). Suddenly, my wife broke down in tears. After quieting down, we all three talked about it, discovering that 'his F' had become 'her F'. In other words, at that moment, her boundaries fused to include his: she experienced his F as though it were her F, as though she had received the failing grade, not he. We tend to view such fusions negatively and believe that she should learn how to separate herself from him.

In my own somewhat unconventional young adulthood I wore a full beard, shed with advancing years and, if not maturity, at least a greater need not to look quite so old and worn out. Seeing me for the first time with my beard, my mother proclaimed, 'My face [and she meant *her* face] doesn't look good with a beard', all the while stroking her own face. Again, the boundaries between self and other broke down. We even have a professional term to describe families in which these boundary-busting events appear: *enmeshed*. This term is never used to connote anything healthful or good! [...] In other words, I do not simply protect my integrity by erecting a firm boundary to separate me from the other. I also work to construct an other whose qualities ensure that my own integrity will remain unscathed and intact.

Needless to say, those who occupy dominant positions in society have this avenue more available to them than those who become their serviceable others, who most often learn simply to live with the hands that they have been dealt. Whether we erect a firm line separating self from other or construct a safely serviceable other, the message about the self-other relationship remains much the same: the other is a potentially dangerous threat. We do not embrace or celebrate the other as she is, but approach her with caution or with abandon – but only when she has been placed under our control.

REFERENCES

Johnson, M. (1987). *The body in the mind: The bodily basis of meaning, imagination, and reason*. Chicago: University of Chicago Press.

Lakoff, G. (1987). *Women, fires, and dangerous things: What categories reveal about the mind*. Chicago: University of Chicago Press.

Lakoff, G., & Johnson, M. (1980). *Metaphors we live by*. Chicago: University of Chicago Press.

Lukes, S. (1985). *Individualism*. Oxford, England: Blackwell.

Macpherson, C. B. (1962). *The political theory of possessive individualism: Hobbes to Locke*. Oxford: Clarendon Press.

19

identity, deconstruction, & politics

judith butler

The foundationalist reasoning of identify politics tends to assume that an identity must first be in place in order for political interests to be elaborated and, subsequently, political action to be taken. My argument is that there need not be a 'doer behind the deed,' but that the 'doer' is variably constructed in and through the deed.

The question of locating 'agency' is usually associated with the viability of the 'subject,' where the 'subject' is understood to have some stable existence prior to the cultural field that it negotiates. Or, if the subject is culturally constructed, it is nevertheless vested with an agency, usually figured as the capacity for reflexive mediation, that remains intact regardless of its cultural embeddedness. On such a model, 'culture' and 'discourse' *mire* the subject, but do not constitute that subject. This move to qualify and enmire the pre-existing subject has appeared necessary to establish a point of agency that is not fully *determined* by that culture and discourse. And yet, this kind of reasoning falsely presumes (a) agency can only be established through recourse to a prediscursive 'I,' even if that 'I' is found in the midst of a discursive convergence, and (b) that to be *constituted* by discourse is to be *determined* by discourse, where determination forecloses the possibility of agency.

[...]

If identity is asserted through a process of signification, if identity is always already signified, and yet continues to signify as it circulates within various interlocking discourses, then the question of agency is not to be answered through recourse to an 'I' that pre-exists signification. In other words, the enabling conditions for an assertion of 'I' are provided by the structure of signification, the rules that regulate the legitimate and illegitimate invocation of that pronoun, the practices that establish the terms of intelligibility by which that pronoun can circulate. Language is not an *exterior medium or instrument* into which I pour a self and from which I glean a reflection of that self.

[...]

The substantive 'I' only appears as such through a signifying practice that seeks to conceal its own workings and to naturalize its effects. Further, to qualify as a substantive identity is an arduous task, for such appearances are rule-generated identities, ones which rely on the consistent and repeated invocation of rules that condition and restrict culturally intelligible practices of identity. Indeed, to understand identity as a *practice*, and as a signifying practice, is to understand culturally intelligible subjects as the resulting effects of a rule-bound discourse that inserts itself in the pervasive and mundane signifying acts of linguistic life.

[...]

I suggest that the identity categories often presumed to be foundational to feminist politics, that is, deemed necessary in order to mobilize feminism as an identity politics, simultaneously work to limit and constrain in advance the very cultural possibilities that feminism is supposed to open up. The tacit constraints that produce culturally intelligible 'sex' ought to be understood as generative political structures rather than naturalized foundations. Paradoxically, the reconceptualization of identity as an *effect*, that is, as *produced* or *generated*, opens up possibilities of 'agency' that are insidiously foreclosed by positions that take identity categories as foundational and fixed. For an identity to be an effect means that it is neither fatally determined nor fully artificial and arbitrary. That the *constituted* status of identity is misconstrued along these two con-flicting lines suggests the ways in which the feminist discourse on cultural construction remains trapped within the unnecessary binarism of free will and determinism. Construction is not opposed to agency; it is the necessary scene of agency, the very terms in which agency is articulated and becomes culturally intelligible. The critical task for feminism is not to establish a point of view outside of constructed identities; that conceit is the construction of an epistemological model that would disavow its own cultural location and, hence, promote itself as a global subject, a position that deploys precisely the imperialist strategies that feminism ought to criticize.

This theoretical inquiry has attempted to locate the political in the very signifying practices that establish, regulate, and deregulate identity. This effort, however, can only be accomplished through the introduction of a set of questions that extend the very notion of the political. How to disrupt the foundations that cover over alternative cultural configurations of gender? How to destabilize and render in their phantasmatic dimension the 'premises' of identity politics?

This task has required a critical genealogy of the naturalization of sex and of bodies in general. It has also demanded a reconsideration of the figure of the body as mute, prior to culture, awaiting signification, a figure that cross-checks with the figure of the feminine, awaiting the inscription-as-incision of the masculine signifier for entrance into language and culture.

There is no ontology of gender on which we might construct a politics, for gender ontologies always operate within established political contexts as normative injunctions, determining what qualifies as intelligible sex, invoking and consolidating the reproductive constraints on sexuality, setting the prescriptive requirements whereby sexed or gendered bodies come into cultural intelligibility. Ontology is, thus, not a foundation, but a normative injunction that operates insidiously by installing itself into political discourse as its necessary ground.

The deconstruction of identity is not the deconstruction of politics; rather, it establishes as political the very terms through which identity is articulated. This kind of critique brings into question the foundationalist frame in which feminism as an identity politics has been articulated. The internal paradox of this foundationalism is that it presumes, fixes, and constrains the very 'subjects' that it hopes to represent and liberate. The task here is not to celebrate each and every new possibility *qua* possibility, but to redescribe those possibilities that *already* exist, but which exist within cultural domains designated as culturally unintelligible and impossible. If identities were no longer fixed as the premises of a political syllogism, and politics no longer understood as a set of practices derived from the alleged interests that belong to a set of ready-made subjects, a new configuration of politics would surely emerge from the ruins of the old. Cultural configurations of sex and gender might then proliferate or, rather, their present proliferation might then become articulable within the discourses that establish intelligible cultural life, confounding the very binarism of sex, and exposing its fundamental unnaturalness. What other local strategies for engaging the 'unnatural' might lead to the denaturalization of gender as such?

20

the social construction of remembering and forgetting

john shotter

In this chapter I want to discuss a non-cognitive, social-constructionist approach to forgetting and remembering. It is an approach in which not so much language as such, but our ways of speaking, and in particular their *rhetorical* (and contested) nature are our initial (but not necessarily our final) concern. Bartlett's early work (Bartlett, 1923) will occupy a prominent place in the account below. Although Neisser (1967) saw Bartlett's later work (Bartlett, 1932) as inaugurating the current 'cognitive' revolution in psychology – concerned as it is with systematic processes – Bartlett's earlier work is clearly both social constructionist, *and* concerned with practices for dealing with non-systematic, conflicting processes. He said:

> We shall see that the attempt to find the beginning of social customs and institutions in purely individual experience may be essentially a mistaken one. In general terms our problem is to account for a response made by an individual to a given set of circumstances *of which the group itself may always be one.* (Bartlett, 1923: 11, his emphasis)

Bartlett thought of such responses as being initially manifested as *tendencies* to act in certain ways under certain conditions, which are influenced in a *formative* manner in the course of their expression by individuals having to fit them into the circumstances of the group. One such major human tendency is that towards construction itself, and, 'as result, largely, of the operation of the tendencies toward construction and conservation, characteristic institutions arise within a group and are perpetuated' (Bartlett, 1923: 45). But:

> None of the tendencies which have been considered operates entirely by itself in determining the behaviour of man in society. We must therefore discuss what happens when, in reference to the same situation, more than one tendency is called into activity, and must deal in particular with the conflict of tendencies, and their mutual reinforcement. (1923: 105)

It is towards the recovery, the 'remembering' of this early 1923 stance of Bartlett's – towards the social and institutional determinants not just of remembering, but also of forgetting – that this chapter is directed. For, as we shall see, current *cognitive* accounts of memory, which 'forget' or repress the social processes involved in forgetting, fail, because of that, also properly to account for remembering: the tendencies determining people's behaviour are all conflicting tendencies, in which one is usually dominated and repressed by its polar opposite. In this, ironically, Bartlett proved himself right. As Mary Douglas (1980: 25) puts it, 'The author of the best book on remembering forgot his own first convictions. He became absorbed into the institutional framework of Cambridge University psychology, and restricted by the conditions of the experimental laboratory.' And in such circumstances, he came to treat remembering as that tradition demanded: as wholly an inner process. Both he and others forgot his original emphasis upon social institutions.

THE CENTRALITY OF OUR 'ACCOUNTING PRACTICES'

In the non-cognitive approach adopted here, our ways of speaking become central, because it is assumed that the primary function of our speech is to 'give shape' to and to co-ordinate diverse social action. We speak in order to create, maintain, reproduce and transform certain modes of social and societal relationships. Such an approach takes it that it is *not* the primary function of all our talk to represent the world; words do not primarily stand for things. If, in our experience, if seems undeniable that at least some words do in fact denote things, they do so only from within a form of social life *already constituted* by ways of talking in which these words are used. Thus, the entities they denote are known, not for what they are in themselves, but in terms of their 'currency' or significance in our different modes of social life – that is, in terms of what it is deemed sensible for us to do with them in the everyday, linguistically structured circumstances of their use.

This approach implies that we cannot take our 'lived' experience as in any way basic. Indeed, from this point of view it becomes a problem as to why, at this moment in history, we account for our experience of ourselves as we do – as if we all existed from birth as separate, isolated individuals, containing wholly within ourselves 'minds' or 'mentalities', set over against a material world itself devoid of any mental processes. This goes for our remembering also: for, although in our experiences of remembering – or at least, in what we talk of as our experiences of remembering – it seems as if we always make reference to something within us such as a picture or impression, like an *object* of some kind. We forget the many everyday occasions in which no such experience of referring to an 'inner' image in order to remember occurs. For example, in remembering how to spell and to type the words of this paper, for the most part, no such consultation of memory images occurred. Or did it? … One perhaps wants to say: 'I *must* have made such a reference, perhaps unconsciously. How else could the remembering have been done if not by the consultation of a copy, image, trace, or representation of some kind of what one remembers?' What alternative is there?

In Bartlett's (1932) account of remembering, he suggests that, initially, remembering is very largely a matter of feeling or affect; something like a vague, unformulated attitude first emerges: 'Very little of his [a subject's] construction is literally observed and often, as was easily demonstrated experimentally, a lot of it is distorted or wrong so far as the actual facts are concerned. But it is the sort of construction which serves to *justify* his general impression' (1932: 206, my emphasis). Indeed, as will be explored later in more detail, even if it were conceded that reference to some 'inner' already well formed object *must* have occurred, there still remains the problem of how such a reference could exert in any way a formative or informative influence upon our behaviour. Clearly, in remembering, we have the power to 'get in touch with', so to speak, something sensuous, with certain original, unformulated 'feelings of tendency' as William James (1890) called them, and these are what inform our actions and our judgements, not any well formed picture-like 'images'. These are the feelings in terms of which we judge the adequacy of our more explicit formulations and expressions, and, on finding them inadequate, call for their reformulation. And yet we feel driven to forget or ignore this.

Why? What do we remember from our own experience of remembering, and what do we forget, and for what reason? By what warrant *do* we take certain of our clear experiences as basic – those experiences when it is as if we clearly *do* make reference to an 'inner' picture – and extrapolate from them as models or paradigms to determine the character of those less clear to us? My argument is that it is because our ways of talking about our experiences work, not primarily to represent the nature of those experiences in themselves, but to represent them in such a way as to constitute and sustain one or another kind of social order.

Now although the view of language I am putting forward is very obviously a Wittgensteinian (1953) one, C.W. Mills also put forward a similar view in the following words:

> The major reorientation of recent theory and observation in sociology of language emerged with the overthrow of the Wundtian notion that language has as its function the 'expression' of prior elements within the individual. The postulate underlying modern study of language is the simple one that we must approach linguistic behaviour, not by referring it to private states in individuals, but by observing its social function of co-ordinating diverse actions. Rather than expressing something which is prior and in the person, language is taken by other persons as an indicator of future actions. (1940: 439)

Mills discussed this view of language within the context of people's *accounting practices* – that is, within the context of how people render what is otherwise a puzzling, senseless or indeterminate activity visible as a familiar, sensible, determinate and *justified* commonplace occurrence.

An *account* is not a description, which by the provision of evidence could be proved true or false, but it works as an aid to perception, literally instructing one both in how to see something as a commonplace event, and, in so seeing it, appreciating the opportunities it offers for one's own further action. As Mills put it, in describing the function of 'motive-accounts' in explaining people's conduct: 'Motives are imputed or avowed as answers to questions interrupting acts or programs. Motives are words. Generically, to what do they refer? They do not denote any elements "in" individuals. They stand for anticipated situational consequences of questioned conduct' (1940: 440). In other words, they serve to keep in good repair and to progress a certain kind of social action, to offer opportunities for one rather than another form of social relationship. And this also is what our talk of memories, of remembering and forgetting, must do. In other words, primarily vague, but not wholly amorphous, tendencies are linguistically specified further in this or that particular way, within a medium of communication – according to the particular requirements of that medium of communication, which is the reproduction of a certain established social order (Shotter, 1984). For example, this can be illustrated in terms of what it is to produce accounts as psychologists. The issue here is not just to do with how we must talk about ourselves as ordinary individuals in everyday life, but also with how as *professional* psychologists we must talk about how, as-ordinary-people, we must talk about ourselves – if, that is, we are to meet the requirements mentioned above. For our talk must be perceived by the other professionals around us as intelligible and legitimate, as authoritative, if they are to find what we say acceptable. It is thus in this way that our talk works to reproduce the professional social order of social scientists.

THE TWO-SIDED RHETORICAL NATURE OF LANGUAGE

The social constructionist privileging of the formative nature of language over its referential aspect (re)emphasizes its primarily rhetorical (and poetic) character – something taken for granted in the past, but gradually forgotten as the scientific revolution took its hold (Ong, 1958; Vico, 1948). There are two aspects to this emphasis, one familiar, the other less so. First, the familiar aspect of rhetoric is to do with the *persuasive* function of language. I want to emphasize here the capacity of speech bodily to 'move' people, its power to affect their behaviour and perceptions in some mysterious (and dangerous), non-cognitive way. It is its capacity to affect people's 'feelings' which we shall find below to be of great importance. Secondly, the other more unfamiliar aspect of rhetoric is to do with the poetic powers of language to 'give' or to 'lend' a *first form* to what are in fact only vaguely or partially ordered feelings and activities, to give a shared *sense* to already shared circumstances.

Elsewhere (Shotter, 1986) I have traced discussions of this aspect of rhetoric back to Vico. Current writers on rhetoric, however, often see themselves as influenced by Nietzsche. De Man (1979: 105–6), for instance, in claiming that the figurative (formative) aspect of language is not just one linguistic mode among many, but characterizes all language as such, quotes Nietzsche as follows:

> It is not difficult to demonstrate that what is called 'rhetorical' as the devices of a conscious art, is present as a device of unconscious art in language and its development ... No such thing as unrhetorical 'natural' language exists that could be used as a point of reference ... Tropes are not something that can be added or subtracted from a language at will; they are its truest nature.

Among the many implications of this, as De Man points out, is a whole set of seeming *reversals* (and instabilities) of a surprising kind; a revealing of linguistically created illusions of experience to which we have fallen victim. We have already met one such illusion: The fact that by means of our *immersion* in an intralinguistically constructed reality (which 'has us', so to speak), we come to experience ourselves as possessing our language *within* ourselves (as 'having it'), as if we could exist as who we are, independently of any of our linguistic involvements with others. To this we can add another reversal, one which De Man (1979: 106) notes: linguistically formulated claims gain their authority from being adequate to an already intralinguistically constructed reality, rather than to the nature of an extralinguistic world. But we have already met this reversal too in the claim above that, no matter what else may influence the structure of our ways of talking, they *must* reproduce in their use certain social orders (else they will be considered unintelligible, or illegitimate).

Now my purpose in discussing such 'reversals' is also to make clear their 'instability': the fact that to an extent one *can* say that *both* ways of talking are true. We could say that our ways of talking *depend* upon the world, to the extent that what we say is rooted, or grounded in, what the facts of the world will permit or allow us to say. On the other hand, it is equally true to say that what we take to be the nature of the world *depends* upon our ways of talking about it. In fact, it is not just that one can say that both are true, but that one *must* assert both; for they owe their distinct existences to their *interdependency*. In other words, although one must say about circumstances only what the facts will permit, the nature of the facts above are such that two equal and opposite truths can be asserted. And indeed, this two-sided nature of all such linguistically structured circumstances is general.

JUSTIFYING MEMORIES

Because we have no difficulty in making intelligible use of such ordinary words as 'know', 'think', 'imagine', 'remember' and so on, it is assumed in mainstream cognitive psychology that we all know what such words mean, that we all already know what phenomena these words signify and what states of affairs are described by sentences incorporating them. Hence, our interest must be in the phenomena themselves, in the 'real' nature of thought and memory and so on, the 'inner processes' said to be underlying them. Thus, the right method of investigation is surely the direct experimental study of the real phenomena – the actual 'memory traces', the nature of the actual 'memories' containing them: the 'sensory registers', the actual 'retrieval processes' and so on. Social constructionists are in total disagreement with such an approach. As they see it, such an interest is both misdirected and mistaken. If C.W. Mills and Wittgenstein are right, there are no such *things* underlying and making remembering possible, and our initial assumption – that we already know what kind of activity remembering is – must be questioned. The fact is, we lack a clear view as to what remembering is – and evidence of that failure is manifested in the puzzles and problems we raise and in the confused manner in which we try to solve them.

To clarify what is at issue here, let us explore the nature of the question – 'What enables people to 'recall' or 'remember' something from the past? At the moment, instead of probing some of the dubious presuppositions underlying our current answers to this question – (a) that there is some 'thing' or 'trace' of a thing past 'inside' the person to which reference is made, and (b) that there is such a 'how' for every 'doing' (action) a person does – we straightaway embark upon the formulation of theories about the nature of such inner entities, and the search for evidence in their support. We fail to notice the ambiguity of the question ; we could be asking either: 'What "in" us enables us to act in such a way?', or 'What socially are the enabling conditions?' The importance of the second way of formulating the question becomes crucial when we realize that, socially, we face a problem when, after having claimed to remember something, someone asks us 'How do you know?' How do we in fact check that our claim to have remembered something is correct?

One thing is clear: one does not check out whether one is correctly remembering (or imagining) something by referring in one's activity to a copy or an image of what is required. As Wittgenstein (1965: 3) argues, not only is such a process unnecessary, in many instances, it is impossible.

The correctness of an inner process cannot be tested by comparison with yet another inner process – for how could the correctness of that process be tested? At some point, reference to activities in daily life at large is necessary, for that is where judgements as to what is right and wrong take place. Such judgements as to their own correctness are not made for one by one's biology or neurology; for they operate just as effectively whether one is acting correctly or mistakenly. It is not their job to make correct judgements for one; that is one's own responsibility, and it is a part of the nature of social life that people can take such responsibilities upon themselves.

REFERENCES

Bartlett, F.C. (1923). *Psychology and primitive culture*. Cambridge: Cambridge University Press.

Bartlett, F.C. (1932). *Remembering: A study in experimental and social psychology*. London: Cambridge University Press.

De Man, P. (1979). *Allegories of reading*. New Haven: Yale University Press.

Douglas, M. (1980). *Evans-Pritchard*. London: Fontana.

James, W. (1890). *Principles of psychology*. London: Macmillan.

Mills, C.W. (1940). Situated actions and vocabularies of motive. *American Sociological Review*, 5, 439–52.

Neisser, U. (1967). *Cognitive psychology*. New York: Appleton-Century-Crofts.

Ong, W.J. (1958). *Ramus: Method and the decay of dialogue*. Cambridge, MA: Harvard University Press.

Shotter, J. (1984). *Social accountability and selfhood*. Oxford: Blackwell.

Shotter, J. (1986). A sense of place: Vico and the social production of social identities. *British journal of Social Psychology*, 25, 199–211.

Vico, G. (1948). *The new science of Giambattista Vico*. (Ed and Tr. by T.G. Gergin & M.H. Fisch.) Ithaca, NY: Cornell University Press.

Wittgenstein, L. (1953). *Philosophical investigations*. Oxford: Blackwell.

Wittgenstein, L. (1965). *The blue and the brown books*. New York: Harper & Row.

the relational reconstruction of repression

michael billig

'Freudian repression' – the very phrase is ambiguous. At first glance, it indicates quite simply Freud's theory of repression. Freud believed that people repress, or drive from their conscious minds, shameful thoughts that, then, become unconscious. This was his key idea. ... More obliquely, the phrase 'Freudian repression' suggests something else: maybe Freud, himself, was engaging in a bit of repression, forgetting things that were inconveniently embarrassing. The ambiguity is deliberate, for both meanings are intended. Freud's idea of repression remains vital for understanding human behaviour. Yet, right at the center of Freud's central idea is a gap: Freud does not say exactly how repression takes place? It is as if Freudian theory, which promises to reveal what has been hidden, itself has hidden secrets. However, if we want to understand repression, we must try to see what Freud was leaving unsaid.

The present work aims to reformulate the idea of repression in order to fill the central gap. Repression is not a mysterious inner process, regulated by an internal structure such as the 'ego'. It is much more straightforward. Repression depends on the skills of language. To become proficient speakers, we need to repress. The business of everyday conversation provides the skills for repressing, while, at the same, time; it demands that we practise those skills. In this respect, language is inherently expressive and repressive. ...

PROBLEMS WITH FREUD'S METAPSYCHOLOGICAL MODEL

Freud's metapsychological model of the mind has a number of problems, preventing it from providing a suitable psychology for understanding thinking. Certainly, some of the terminology is old-fashioned, not sharing the computing and information-processing metaphors of today's cognitive science. Yet, curiously, the underlying model of mental activity is not that out-of-date. Several psychologists have pointed out the resemblance between some of the models in contemporary cognitive psychology and Freud's metapsychology. When Freud writes about preconscious ideas becoming conscious, he is, it is said, talking about the same issues as cognitive psychologists, discussing how information is accessed from 'memory-stores'. Sympathizers of psychoanalysis have been pleased to note such similarities. They claim that the parallels demonstrate the continuing relevance of Freud's ideas.

This is not the position taken here. Quite the reverse, the parallels with today's cognitive psychology are sufficient to raise doubts about the adequacy of Freud's meta-psychology. In fact, the sort of criticisms, which can be raised against much cognitive psychology can equally be addressed to Freud's theory of consciousness. Particularly, both Freud and cognitive psychologists tend to concentrate on depicting hypothetical internal processes; and, most crucially, both ignore the centrality of language in human thinking.

Certainly, Freud's metapsychological writings, despite the precision of their techni-cal terms, have an abstract quality, positing hypothetical structures of the mind. Freud took what he called 'a topographical point of view', talking of the structures of the mind as if they were located in space. Thus, the 'preconscious' is spoken of as if it were an entity, which exists somewhere in the brain. And similarly 'the unconscious' appears as a structure which has its place. The same is true of the 'memory organization packets' and 'information-stores' of contemporary cognitive science.

The problem for both Freud and today's cognitive theorists is that these mental structures are not actually mapped onto a neurophysiological basis. Freud cautioned against presuming that the preconscious and unconscious could be identified with an actual anatomical structure in the brain. As he wrote, 'every endeavour to think of ideas, as stored up in nerve-cells and of excitations as migrating along nerve fibres, has miscarried completely'. Yet his writings do not exclude the possibility of discovering the neurophysiological location of thinking. In 'The ego and the id', he drew a diagram, suspiciously resembling the human brain, to depict the relations between ego and id. The ego, with its links to the perceptual apparatus, is on the surface of the system, while the id is diagrammatically located well below. Similarly, the diagrams of cognitive science today share a similar ambiguity. Authors might specifically deny that they are depicting actual physiological processes, but they use a terminology which implies that the depicted processes may link up with neurophysiological structures.

This all matters for a simple reason. Freud's metapsychology, like contemporary cognitive science, suggests that the real psychological action is going on within the head. Moreover, the action is being carried on by the unseen structures of the mind. Outwardly in daily life, we hear people acting, talking, going about their daily busi-ness. But this is only the outward manifestation of their interior mental processes. To use Freud's terminology, the person is able to talk, because unconscious ideas in the preconscious have been associated with word-presentations and reached a sufficient level of excitation, in order to reach the system of consciousness (a modern cognitive psychologist may say that the appropriate 'mental model' has been accessed from the 'memory-store' and been given semantic form).

Once psychologists talk of the person in this way they are breaching the principle that we should attribute actions to people rather than to hypothetical mental structures.

This relates to a major problem with Freud's metapsychology (which again is paralleled in cognitive psychology). Although Freud claims that most human thinking is verbal, language is of secondary importance in his model of consciousness. Words are seen to be attached to thoughts, rather than forming thoughts. Perception and the unconscious are, in his scheme of things, essentially non-verbal. Language becomes, as it were, a means of moving the non-verbal impulses of the unconscious into the outer surface of conscious awareness. In consequence, depth psychology is committed to looking beyond language, stripping away the 'mere' words, in order to find the 'real' thoughts or impulses.

Freud called his metapsychology 'dynamic' as well as 'topographical'. By this he meant that the structures of the mind not only had a location with respect to each other (for instance, the ego being the outer layer and the id being deeper); but also that the structures were in dynamic relations to each other. Once the metapsychology is taken seriously, then thinking is to be seen in terms of the relations between preconscious, unconscious and conscious etc., as if these structures are doing the thinking. But, of course, none of these regions, however, can be identified as an actual entity, just as cognitive scientists cannot actually produce an 'attitudinal schema' or 'frame of reference' for inspection. The existence, operation and mutual interaction of these inner structures must all be inferred from the outer actions of the person.

In this regard, Freud's metapsychology fits a dominant trend in western theorizing about thinking during the past three hundred years. His theory is 'Cartesian' in that it treats thinking as a series of unseen processes occurring within the individual thinker's mind. A good visual illustration of this view is provided by Rodin's famous stature, *Le Penseur*. Rodin depicts the thinker (of course, a man) sitting naked on a rock. His head rests on his hand. He is not looking at anything, nor is he speaking. All his attention is focused inwards. There he sits alone and silent, lost in his own thoughts, abstracted from social life. By his nakedness, he carries nothing that can link him to a particular cultural group or historical period. We don't know what he is thinking about, but, from the state of his body, we might presume it's not a sexual fantasy. There's serious business going on inside Le Penseur's skull. But we're not privy to the secret.

There is a very important difficulty with the Cartesian model of thinking, whether it appears in the form of Freud's metapsychology of consciousness or in cognitive psychology's account of mental processing. Because thinking is a hidden process, which unfolds in the head of the individual and which can never be directly observed by others, it is difficult to see how children could ever learn to think. One cannot copy Le Penseur, except by taking off one's clothes and sitting quietly on a rock.

Furthermore, and crucial to psychoanalytic theorizing, it is difficult to see how children could learn to repress. Perhaps Le Penseur, has been struck by a shameful thought, against which his whole moral being rebels. We might imagine that he is driving the thought away. But what are these skills of repression and where did they come from? If they are hidden, internal processes, operated by the unseen ego, then we cannot acquire them by observing others. We may watch Le Penseur repressing his disturbing thoughts. Even if we study him for hours, all we see is his outer form. We glimpse no repression, which we might be able to copy.

So where does one acquire the ability to repress thoughts, when the need arises? Freud's metapsychology gives few clues, especially since it is constantly examining the passage to conscious awareness rather the activity of pushing ideas from consciousness.

SPEECH AND THOUGHT

What is required is a psychological approach, which, in contrast to Freud's meta-psychology, does not distinguish sharply between language and thought. There is an important psychological consequence from taking such a position. Thinking, as Wittgenstein stressed in his later philosophy, is not to be considered as a hidden, unobservable and silent process, occurring within the head of the individual. In contrast to what Cartesian philosophers have assumed, thinking can be outwardly observed in conversation. This is something taken seriously by the new movements in social constructionist and discursive psychology.

For social constructionists, language is primary. It does not merely provide labels attached to our perceptual impressions. Language permits us to enter into the life of culture. Nor is language merely to be conceived as a system of grammar. As the Russian thinker Mikhail Bakhtin and his *alter ego* Vološinov argued, language is based on the practical tasks of conversation. The project for discursive psychology, then, is to examine how we use language in social life. In so doing, this psychology seeks to show our thinking is constituted through language.

Every day, in conversation we hear and formulate utterances, which, in their detail, have never been made before. Linguistic creativity depends, above all, on the rhetorical skills of argumentation, most principally, on the practices of justification and criticism. If speakers merely were to agree with one another, there would be little thinking within language. Our use of language would resemble the communication-systems of other species. The bee, who communicates to other bees where pollen might be, receives no disagreement from its audience. Bees cannot challenge communicators critically, forcing them to justify their statements. No bee can say 'You say there's pollen over to the west, but surely there's better pollen to the east.' Nor can the challenged bee reply in self-justification: 'No, the pollen to the east is not so flavorsome, as you imagine', and then open up a buzzing discussion about pollen, directions and flavour.

For all this, more is required than the bee can hope to provide. Only humans have the necessary skills. A discussion, which pushes a dialogue into new directions, depends upon speakers' possessing the syntax of negation – they must be able to say 'no', as well as 'yes'. In addition, reasons must be given to justify the 'no' and to criticize the previous speaker's 'yes'. The ability to justify and criticize does not mean accessing a store of ready-made formulations. New utterances have to be spontaneously created for each new discursive situation, so that the justifications and criticisms fit the present context.

In the continually creative activity of justification and criticism, we can hear the activity of thinking. As people discuss issues, even in banal, seemingly boring conversations, they are engaging in complex, co-ordinated creation. Even those who like to ride verbal hobby-horses, pontificating on familiar subjects, will be producing novel utterances with subtle changes of emphasis, wording or intonation. It is wrong to suppose that each utterance is only an outward sign of the thought processes, which must be occurring silently and internally within the speaker's head. In discussions, turn and counter-turn can occur too quickly to assume the spoken words to be merely the surface manifestation of the 'real' thought, which has to be formulated before the utterance is made. Often we hear ourselves saying something in response, only discovering what our thoughts are as we speak. The thinking is not hidden, but is happening out there in the conversation.

If the Cartesian position has difficulty explaining how children might learn to think, the discursive position faces no such problem. From an early age, children hear conversations. By living in worlds filled with dialogue, they acquire the rhetorical skills to justify and criticize. In this, they learn how to participate in the collective thinking of conversation. Thus, they learn to think.

But what about silent thought? Surely not all thinking is to be located in the burble of dialogue. It might be suggested that *real* thinking goes on when everyone stops talking. However, it would be a mistake to overestimate the difference between the thinking, which occurs outwardly in dialogue, and the thinking which occurs in isolated silence.

We can imagine Le Penseur having an internal debate. Perhaps his voice of conscience is debating with his voice of desire. He wants to get off the rock to buy an icecream, but he tells himself, repeating the words of his doctor, that he should cut down his fat-intake. 'But I worked hard this morning, I deserve a treat' says the internal voice of desire. 'But that would be weakness, which would threaten the whole diet' replies the critical voice of conscience. Round and round the voices go. Were there no debate, Le Penseur would already be on his way to the ice-cream parlour. The point is that Le Penseur, even if he is seated alone, is not abstracted from social life and the world of dialogue. Because Le Penseur is a member of the dialogic species, he is 'the thinker'. Chickens or guinea-pigs, seen at rest with downcast head, would not be recognized as thinkers.

[...]

OPENING UP AND CLOSING DOWN DIALOGUE

It has been suggested that human thinking should not be considered in terms of hidden processes, but should be examined in relation to the outward skills of rhetoric. These skills are continually on display in conversation. This psychology does not appear to delve into the hidden psychological hinterland, which forms the basis of the Freudian vision. Quite the reverse, the person, as it were, has been turned inside-out: what was considered to be individual, internal and hidden is shown to be social, external and observable.

Generally, it must be admitted that discursive psychologists are uncomfortable with the notion of consciousness. They prefer to talk about the structure of conversation, rather than the speakers' interior life. Certainly, discursive psychologists do not explain conversational interventions in terms of the speakers' motives, let alone their inner egos. If consciousness is not a topic for discursive psychology, then unconsciousness is doubly out of bounds. It is as if this psychology is declaring that there is no secret mental life: all can be heard, if one listens closely enough. Moreover, speakers know what they are doing: they do not have secrets hidden from themselves.

The detour into discursive psychology seems to have taken us to a terrain, which is not only flatter than the Freudian hinterland, but which has a more cheerful, welcoming aspect than the gloomy crags and crevices of the psychoanalytic landscape. Rhetorical skills enable us to open up topics, whether in social debate or in private conversation. Because we can do more than merely say 'yes', or express a preference for agreement, we can, and do, go forward dialogically. Matters, which were unspoken and unthought, become objects of speech and, thereby, of thought. Thus, we have an image of people as Socratic debaters, pushing the limits of conversation back with their probing conversational gambits. In this celebration of argumentative skills, there is no hint of Freudian cynicism to tell why people may not take advantage of their skills of intellectual exploration and why they may be crippled by secrets, which they dare not admit to themselves.

There is another side – a side, which tends to be ignored by psychologists who admire the creativity of argumentative rhetoric. If we humans possess the rhetorical skills to open up matters for discussion, then so we are equipped with the abilities to close down matters discursively. For every rhetorical gambit to push debate forward, so there must be analogous rhetorical devices which permit discursive exploration to be curtailed. Routinely, we are able to change the subject, pushing conversations away from embarrassing or troubling topics.

We might assume that, for everything which is said, other things are not being said. This is not to say that the other things are necessarily being hidden, nor that speakers are deliberately stopping themselves saying certain things. The point is simpler. No speaker can be making two utterances at once. Every utterance, which fills a moment of conversational space, is occupying a moment which might have been filled by an infinity of other utterances. These potential utterances will now never be said, at least in that specific context. ...

The idea of the 'unsaid' provides a clue about the rhetorical nature of repression. 'The said' and 'the unsaid' are intimately linked: to say one thing implies that other things are not being said. If language provides the rhetorical skills for opening up lines of talk, then it also provides the skills for creating the unsaid. More than this, language provides the means for closing down areas of talk. The opening up and closing down must proceed simultaneously, so that dialogic creativity and avoidance, far from being polar opposites, might be closely linked in practice.

From this, there is a short step which takes us back into Freudian terrain. When listening to certain dialogues we might entertain suspicions about the speakers' patterns of opening up and closing down topics. In particular, we might suspect that avoidances are occurring. Traces of the avoidance should be audible, even in long silences between uttered words. As the conversation seems to lurch towards a topic, which will disturb the speakers, so the speakers might steer around the unspoken obstacle, putting the dialogue safely back on course.

Analysts of conversation have shown how speakers use particular linguistic devices for opening up topics for discussion. Little words can be so important for the task. For instance, the speaker who wishes to disagree, but also to keep the conversation going, may be faced with a dilemma. Too forceful a disagreement may be heard as aggressive or rude and, in consequence, may threaten the continuation of the dialogue. On the other hand, too ready an agreement will fail to move the conversation to a discussion. Often speakers will resolve the dilemma by prefacing comments of disagreement with markers of agreement. If one speaker feels the other has missed the point, they can use the rhetorical device of starting their critical reply with 'Yes, but ...' In this way, the speaker expresses agreement in order to dismiss the previous speaker's argument, thereby moving the point of conversation towards the topic, which the speaker claims to the 'real' issue.

This rhetorical device simultaneously moves the discussion *towards* a particular topic, while redirecting the conversation *away* from another. This is not accidental, for a conversational move *towards* is simultaneously a conversational move *away from*. Conversation analysts have shown that speakers have conventional ways of signalling changes of topic. 'Anyway' or 'but' can function in this way. Such markers alert conversationalists 'not to try to look for any connection between what they have just been talking about, and what he or she is about to say'. Without the marker, listeners would assume that the present utterance is in some way connected with the previous one: the assumption of relevance has been called one of the basic maxims for conversation, which conversationalists tend to take for granted. 'Yes, but ...' can be used as a discontinuity marker. The previous speaker's remark is acknowledged by agreement ('yes'), and then the topic is redirected ('but, what about...').

Changing the topic of conversation is not necessarily a sign of repression, but further signs might be suggestive. An observer might suspect that the movement *away* is dominating the movement *toward*, especially if the speaker continually changes the subject when a particular topic is mentioned. The observer might surmise that the speaker is not fully aware of what they are doing, so that the avoidance appears automatic rather than deliberate. Perhaps, the speaker shows outward signs of resisting any invitations to talk on the avoided topic. And, maybe, what the speaker actually talks about betrays tell-tale signs of the topic they seem to be avoiding.

[...]

REPLACEMENT AND REPRESSION

At its simplest, repression might be considered as a form of changing the subject. It is a way of saying to oneself 'talk, or think, of this, not that'. One then becomes engrossed in 'this' topic, so 'that' topic becomes forgotten, as do the words one has said to oneself in order to produce the shift or topic. This forgetting is helped by the fact that the discontinuity markers are themselves small, eminently forgettable words.

It can be presumed that thinkers can only accomplish shifts in their 'inner speech' because they have been speakers, successfully accomplishing topic-shifts in dialogue. On the other hand, the shifting of topic need not be confined to the words that one says to oneself. Actual conversations with other speakers can be brought into play, so that the repression, rather than being confined to the inner dialogues of the isolated individual, is part of outward social life. Two rhetorical elements are required for successful shifting – whether in external or internal dialogue. First there are the small words of the discontinuity markers, which indicate that such shifting is occurring. The second requirement is another topic to move towards. 'Anyway' should not be followed by silence. A replacement topic is needed, if attention is to be shifted.

It would a mistake to think that 'real' repression is internal, or even that there is a sharp distinction between internal mental life and external social life. The topic, which is used as a replacement, need not be confined to the interior dialogue: it can become part of an external conversation. Repression stands a better chance of success if it involves outer dialogue. That way, other people can be enrolled into its accomplishment. It is even better still if the repression becomes sedimented into habits of life, so that repression becomes a repeated, habitual dialogic activity.

22

the social construction of emotion

rom harré

Psychologists have always had to struggle against a persistent illusion that in such studies as those of the emotions there is something *there*, the emotion, of which the emotion word is a mere representation. This ontological illusion, that there is an abstract and detachable 'it' upon which research can be directed, probably lies behind the defectiveness of much emotion research. But what there is are angry people, upsetting scenes, sentimental episodes, grieving families and funerals, anxious parents pacing at midnight, and so on. There is a concrete world or contexts and activities. We reify and abstract from that concreteness at our peril.

With that caution in mind, we have to rethink the question, 'What is anger?' or love, mawkish sentimentality, spleen and so on, to which the research process must, among other questions, provide an answer, and without a try at which it cannot start. Our answers are, as likely as not, liable to reflect the *unexamined* commonsense assumptions of our local culture. These assumptions can best be brought to light by a preliminary study of how this or that culture or subculture uses that section of its emotional vocabulary and other relevant linguistic resources, with which we, from our more or less distant standpoint, can roughly pick out episodes in their emotional lives. But it is not that these differences should then be deleted to reveal what say anger really is. Anger can be only what this or that folk use the word 'anger', or something roughly approximating it in their culture, to pick out. We must be careful to suspend any assumptions we may have about the viability of cross-cultural translations of vocabularies and interpretations of practices, upon which any nativist theory of universal emotions must depend, to wait upon proper and careful empirical research. Instead of asking the question, 'What is anger?' we would do well to begin by asking, 'How is the word "anger", and other expressions that cluster around it, actually used in this or that cultural milieu and type of episode?'

The first step to a more sophisticated theory will be to show how, in research, priority must be given to obtaining a proper understanding of how various emotion vocabularies are used. Recent work has shown that the very idea of an emotion as a response suffered by a passive participant in some emotive event is itself part of the social strategies by which emotions and emotion declarations are used by people in certain interactions. This is not to deny that there are 'leakages' into consciousness from raised heartbeat, increased sweating, swollen tear ducts and so on. But these effects are incidental to what it is to be in this or that emotional state. It turns out that the dominant contribution to the way that aspect of our lives unfolds comes from the local social world, by way of its linguistic practices and the moral judgements in the course of which the emotional quality of encounters is defined. Turning our attention away from the physiological states of individuals to the unfolding of social practices opens up the possibility that many emotions can exist only in the reciprocal exchanges of a social encounter.

What does the analysis of the differential uses of a vocabulary show? It makes abundantly clear that the study of emotions like envy (and jealousy) will require careful attention to the details of local systems of rights and obligations, of criteria of value and so on. In short, these emotions cannot seriously be studied without attention to the local moral order. That moral order is essential to the existence of just those concepts in the cognitive repertoire of the community.

The point can be illustrated in some recent work of Nadja Reissland. She found that the mothers of small children were unable to say whether quarrelling children were envious or jealous of one another? At first she thought this showed that the concepts were not clearly distinguished in the linguistic community of the mothers. She devised a test to see. The mothers were asked to imagine three characters N, M and O. N and M are seated at an out-door café, very jolly together, sipping an aperitif. O sees them from across the street. In the first scenario, M is married to N, while in the second M is married to O. Unhesitatingly, the group thought that O would be envious of N in the first case, but jealous in the second. Here is a very simple example of the role of a moral order in the differential use of a pair of emotion words. What is at issue in differentiating the emotions are the rights, duties and obligations of married people, *in that culture*. How do we explain the mothers' original difficulty? They had no idea what moral order obtained with regard to matters in dispute among their children, the communal toys of a university developmental psychology department.

There are many other language games in which the words 'envy', 'envious', 'jealous' and so on play a part. For example, 'envious' can be used to express congratulations and avow a wish, as in 'I am envious of your trip to Athens'. Then there is the dog-in-the manger use of 'jealous': 'Guard this jealously'; that is , 'Don't let anyone else get at it.' This is close to the pathological sense of jealousy that we ascribe to a woman who makes a scene if her husband 'so much as looks at another women' (and of course vice versa). [...]

The extent to which local moral orders are involved in human emotions suggests that there might be considerable cultural variety in the emotion repertoires of different peoples and epochs.

23

meaning in relationship

kenneth j gergen

The traditional view that meaning originates within the individual mind, is expressed within words (and other actions), and is deciphered within the minds of other agents, is deeply problematic. If meaning were pre-eminently an individual matter, we should be unable to communicate. There appear to be no means of inferentially or intuitively moving past another's words (or actions) to the subjective source, nor of translating another's words (or actions) into a system of understanding that is not already at one's disposal. Or in short, to begin the problem of human meaning with the assumption of individual subjectivity leaves no means by which it can be solved.

Yet, we need not frame the question of meaning within the individualist tradition. There is an alternative way of approaching the issue of social meaning, and by not taking the individual as its starting point, it opens a range of promising possibilities. Rather than commencing with individual subjectivity and working toward an account of human understanding through language, we may begin our analysis at the level of the human relationship as it generates both language and understanding.

In this case one begins not with subjectivity but with the system of language or signs common to a given culture. Social understanding is generated from participation within the common system. In this sense, it is not the individual who pre-exists the relationship and initiates the process of signification, but patterns of relationship and their embedded meanings that pre-exist the individual.

[...]

AN INDIVIDUAL'S UTTERANCES IN THEMSELVES POSSESS NO MEANING

If we begin our account of meaning with individual subjectivity, the mind of the individual serves as an originary source of meaning. Meaning is generated within the mind and transmitted via words or gestures. However, in the relational case, there is no proper beginning, no originary source, no specific region in which meaning takes wing. For we are always already in a relational context, a condition in which we are positioned vis à vis others and the world. Therefore to speak of origins we must generate a hypothetical space in which there is an utterance (marking, gesture, etc.) without relational embedding. Granting this idealized case, we find that the single utterance of an individual in itself fails to possess meaning: This is most obvious in the case of uttering any selected morpheme (e.g., *the, ed, too*). Standing alone, the morpheme fails to be anything but itself. It operates, as in the textual case, as a free-standing signifier, opaque and indeterminate. (One may generate a variety of apparent exceptions to this initial assumption – e.g., a shout of 'help' on a dark night; or more extended word sequences, such as 'Eat at Joe's' – but the communicative value of such exceptions proves, on closer inspection, to depend on an implied context.) Even by placing the morphemic arrangement within a specific environmental setting does not grant meaning to the utterance. Consider the sound 'woo,' issuing from the lips of a damsel in a nearby glade. Although the utterance drips with significatory potential, it remains ultimately opaque. The sounds, even in context, remain 'untranslatable.'

THE POTENTIAL FOR MEANING IS REALIZED THROUGH SUPPLEMENTARY ACTION

Lone utterances begin to acquire meaning when another (or others) coordinate themselves to the utterance, that is, when they add some form of supplementary action (whether linguistic or otherwise). The supplement may be as simple as an affirmation (e.g., 'yes' or 'right') that indeed the initial utterance has succeeded in communicating. It may take the form of an action, for example, shifting the line of gaze upon hearing the word, 'look!' Or it may extend the utterance in some way, for example, when 'the' uttered by one interlocutor is followed by 'end!' uttered by a second. In the case of the damsel, meaning is generated when we hear a voice that responds to 'Woo' with, 'Yes, dear,' now furnishing the sound with its meaning as the calling of a name.

We thus find that an individual alone can never 'mean'; another is required to supplement the action, and thus furnish it with a form of meaning. To communicate is thus to be granted by others a privilege of meaning. If others do not treat one's utterances as communication, if they fail to coordinate themselves around the offering, one's utterance is reduced to nonsense. In this regard, virtually any form of utterance may be granted the privilege of being meaningful, or conversely, serves as a candidate for nonsense. (Jerzey Kozinsky's *Being There* furnishes numerous puckish examples of how the words of an idiot may be turned into profundity by surrounding believers. Garfinkel's (1967) exercises in questioning the routine grounds of everyday conversation – for example, 'what do you mean exactly by "flat tire"?' – demonstrate the possibility of aborting even the most obvious candidates for meaning.)

In semiotic terms, the present attempt is to remove meaning from the impersonal structure of the text and to place it within the structure of relationship. For many semioticians, the fundamental unit of meaning is contained in the relationship between signifier and signified; it is not located within either unit individually, but within the linkage between the two. In the present case, however, this linkage is removed from its textual location and placed within the social realm. Thus, we may view an individual's actions as a primitive 'signified,' whereas the responses of another person may serve the place of the 'signifier.' This 'sign' relationship, signifier-linked-to-signified in semiotic terms, is now replaced by action-and-supplement. It is only by virtue of adding supplementing signifiers that actions gain their capacity as signifieds, and it is only within the relationship of action-and-supplement that meaning is to be located at all.

SUPPLEMENTS ACT BOTH TO CREATE AND CONSTRAIN MEANING

The initial action (utterance, gesture, etc.) of the individual does not, in the hypothetical space developed thus far, demand any particular form of supplementation. In Pearce and Cronen's (1980) terms, in itself it possesses no *logical force*. The act of supplementation thus operates in two opposing ways. First, it grants a *specific potential* to the meaning of the utterance. It treats it as meaning *this* and not *that*, as requiring one form of action as opposed to another, as having a particular logical force as opposed to some other. Thus, if you come to me and say, 'Do you have a light?' I can, in the first instance, stare at you in puzzlement (thus negating what you have said as meaningful action). Or, conversely, I can react in a variety of different ways, each bestowing a different meaning on the utterance. For example, I can busily search through my pockets and answer 'no,' I can answer 'yes' and walk away, I can tell you 'I am not serving beer,' I can ask you what it is you really want, or I can even shriek and fall into a fetal position.

If I create your meaning in one of these various ways, I simultaneously act to constrain it in many others. Because your words do mean *this*, they cannot mean *that*. In this sense, although I invite you into being, I also act so as to negate your potential. From the enormous array of possibilities, I thus create direction and temporarily narrow the possibilities of your being.

ANY SUPPLEMENT (OR ACTION-AND-SUPPLEMENT) IS A CANDIDATE FOR FURTHER SUPPLEMENTATION

The social supplement, once executed, now comes to stand in the same position as the initial action or utterance. It is open to further specification, clarification, or obliteration through subsequent actions of the initial actor (or others). Its function as supplement, then, is transient and contingent on what follows. Thus, the supplement does not finally affix meaning, but serves as a temporary and defeasible functionary. At the simplest level, the supplement in its signifying capacity, comes to serve secondarily as a new form of the signified – an action that has no meaning until clarified by further supplementation. However, because the supplement is more typically viewed by the participants within the context of the initial action, it is the relationship between action and supplement (the 'sign' in semiotic terms) that becomes subject to future revision and clarification. Thus, for example, if you ask me if I have a light, and I say 'yes' and walk away, we have formed a unit that stands to be resignified by you. If you stare after me in amazement, you fail to grant to our interchange (action-and-supplement) the status of a meaningful interchange. If, however, you hurl an oath in the direction of my retreat, you affirm that the action and supplement had meaning (in this case, my supplement serving as a calloused and spiteful gesture). In the same way, you may stand puzzled at my comments on serving beer, thus negating the act-and-supplement as communication; or you may react with a laugh (granting it allusionary significance to recent light beer commercials), and thereby restore the interchange to the status of meaningful interchange.

Simultaneous with the instigation of the second-order supplement, the relationship between the interlocutors has again been expanded in its potential and again constrained. Of all possible meanings that might be made of your question and my response in terms of serving beer, your laughter constitutes us as having brought off a joke together. In this sense, your laughter grants us a particular form of potential, one that would not be furnished through, for example, a scowl or curt rejoinder. And as it invites one pattern of coordinated action, it reduces the possibility of others.

MEANINGS ARE SUBJECT TO CONTINUOUS RECONSTITUTION VIA THE EXPANDING SEA OF SUPPLEMENTATION

In light of the aforementioned considerations we find that whether meaningful communication occurs, and what is communicated among persons, is inherently undecidable. That is, 'the fact of meaning' stands as an open possibility, subject to the continuous accretion in supplementary significations. All that is fixed and settled in one instance, may be cast into ambiguity or undone in the next. Sarah and Sam may find themselves frequently laughing together, until Sam announces that Sarah's laughter is 'unnatural and forced,' just her attempt to present herself as an 'easygoing person' (in which case the definition of what had been communicated would be altered). Or Sarah announces, 'You are so superficial, Sam, that we really don't communicate' (thus negating the interchange altogether as a form of meaningful activity). At the same time, these latter moves within the ongoing sequence are subject to negation ('Sam, that's a crazy statement.'), and alteration ('You are only saying that, Sarah, because you find Bill so attractive.'). Such instances of negation and alteration may be far removed temporally from the interchange itself (e.g., consider a divorcing pair who retrospectively redefine their entire marital trajectory), and are subject to continuous change through interaction with and among others (e.g., friends, relatives, therapists, the media, etc.).

It is also this fundamentally open character of 'what is meant,' that lends itself to inquiries into the ongoing processes by which participants manage meaning within a relationship. Studies of the ways in which communities of scientists work out mutually acceptable views of 'the facts' (Latour & Woolgar, 1979), psychologists collectively hammer out a vision of the human subject (Danziger, 1990), families establish mutually acceptable views of the past (Middleton & Edwards, 1990), acquaintances structure each other's identities (Shotter, 1984), and political figures renegotiate the meaning of their public speeches (Edwards & Potter, 1992), all serve to fill out the picture of meaning in the making.

Yet, to focus on the face-to-face relationship may ultimately be delimited. For we find that whether I make sense is not under my control, nor is it ultimately under the control of the dyad in which the potential for meaning initially struggles toward realization. Rather, meaningful communication in any given situation ultimately depends on a protracted array of relationships, not only 'right here, right now,' but how it is that you and I are related to a variety of other persons, and they to still others – and ultimately, one might say, to the relational conditions of society as a whole. We are all in this way interdependently interlinked – without the capacity to mean anything, to possess an 'I' – except for the existence of a potentially assenting world of relationships.

AS LINGUISTIC RELATIONSHIPS BECOME COORDINATED (ORDERED), SO DO ONTOLOGIES AND THEIR INSTANTIATIONS DEVELOP

There is a close relationship between meaning and order. If the interchange between two individuals is random – such that any action on the part of one can serve as the prelude to any reaction of another – we would scarcely be able to say that the interchange is meaningful. It is only as our actions together come to develop order, such that the range of contingencies is constrained, that we move toward meaning. If I throw you a ball and you cast it away, I throw you another and you place it in your pocket, and I throw you another and you crush it under foot, we have generally failed by common standards to generate meaning. However, if I throw you a ball and you throw it back, and on each succeeding throw you do the same, then you have given my throw the meaning of an invitation for you to return the throw, and vice versa. Actions thus come to have meaning within relatively structured sequences. If we are to move toward meaning we must move toward mutual constraint.

The direction and form of any ordering is also critically determined by the other social orderings in which one is engaged. For example, within recent history we of the cultural West have tended to view our orderings in terms of 'purposes,' 'functions,' or 'goals.' Thus, in newly developing contexts of relationship, the ordering of relationships will typically be rationalized and directed by these understandings. We order our relationships in ways that we can index as 'functional' within these pre-existing relationships, and these orderings will tend toward recursion. If a hungry American tourist and the owner of a Kyoto noodle shop manage to coordinate their gestures so that food is sold (on the one side) and hunger is reduced (on the other), these gestures will be rapidly replicated on future visits to the shop.

To put the matter in discursive terms, participants in a relationship will tend to develop a *positive ontology*, or a series of mutually shared 'callings,' that enable interaction to proceed unproblematically. Thus, researchers in astrophysics do not shift their theoretical vocabulary from moment to moment, for to do so would mean the destruction of the group's capacity to achieve what they term productive research results. The effective functioning of the group depends on maintaining a relatively stable system of discourse. In other terms, the positive ontology becomes the culture's array of sedimented or commonsense understandings. It is precisely this sedimentation that enables scholars to treat the language system as a fixed structure, with logical implicature, and/or governed by rules.

AS CONSENSUS IS ESTABLISHED, SO ARE THE GROUNDS
FOR BOTH UNDERSTANDING AND MISUNDERSTANDING

In the preceding, I have laid out rudimentary grounds for understanding the communal generation of meaning. As the argument has unfolded, we find relationships tending toward ordered and recursive sequences in which meaning is transparent for the various participants. Yet, these suppositions in themselves leave us with no account of mis-meaning, that is, instances in which persons claim they do not understand, or fail to comprehend each other. Given the preceding analysis, it is clear that problems of incomprehension are not to be solved by recourse to individual subjectivities. However, the social orientation to the question 'why misunderstanding,' does engender three different but related answers. First and most simply, there are multiple contexts in which relationships are formed and local ontologies develop. Participation in one such set of coordinated activities is no necessary preparation for others. The most obvious illustration is when one visits a culture without any knowledge of the local language.

Misunderstandings are also generated within the same general culture. In these cases people employ a common language, but find the process of understanding to be fraught with difficulty. Such disharmonies may be understood in part because of the continuously unfolding nature of human relatedness. As persons move through life, the domain of relationships typically expands and the context of any given relationship typically changes. In effect, we are continuously confronted with some degree of novelty – new contexts and new challenges. Yet, our actions in such circumstances will necessarily represent some simulacre of the past; we borrow, reformulate, and patch together various pieces of preceding relationships in order to achieve local coordination of the moment. Figuratively put, in each new action one becomes a metaphor of one's past identity – a translocation of the self from a previous (or literal) context, a reformation of self but for different purpose. In this sense, every cultural implement for engendering meaning (words, gestures, pictures, etc.) is subject to multiple recontextualization. Each term in the language becomes polysymous, multiply meaningful. This places us in the following condition: Each move within a coordinated sequence is simultaneously a move in other possible sequences. Each action is thus a possible invitation to a multiplicity of intelligible sequences; each meaning is potentially some other, and the potential for misunderstanding permanently and pervasively at hand.

There is a third major source of misunderstanding within a given culture, and to me the most interesting. The Russian literary theorist Mikael Bakhtin recognized two major tendencies in the linguistic patterns of a culture, the one *centripetal* (or moving toward a centralization or unification) and the other *centrifugal* (decentering and unsettling the existing unity). Thus, forces toward stabilization were forever competing with opposing linguistic tendencies. 'Every utterance participates in the "unitary language" ... and at the same time partakes of social and historical hetero-glossia' (Bakhtin, 1981, p. 272). In the present context we may frame this oppositional dynamic in terms of the necessary discursive domain established by and at the margins of the positive ontology. That is, as the positive ontology is constituted, so does it generate the grounds for the negative – or oppositional – ontology. The existence of the *negative ontology* has significant implications for subsequent patterns of relationship. For the nuclear group confronts the lingering possibility of negation – that their premises may be replaced by their opposition – and thus the possibility of relational extermination. As communities sustain themselves by virtue of concepts such as God, democracy, equality, and so on, they must be forever watchful of negating discourses (e.g., atheism, fascism, racism). This antagonistic posture would not exist save for the initial articulation of the positive ontology. Or to put it otherwise, the development of meaning within a community establishes the grounds for a domain of countermeaning that forever poses a threat to meaning itself.

Of course, there is ample reason within a dominant culture for such continued suspicion of the unspoken. The negative ontology always stands open to development and enrichment. For any marginalized or mistreated subculture, the negative ontology is ready-made as a language for coordinating new forms of community – or more precisely, countercommunities. If there is a 'necessity for war,' a peace movement is invited; if there are prohibitions against abortion, there is an opportunity for a language of 'choice'; and if there is a celebration of free expression, the way is paved for a critique of 'political correctness.' Further, as communities coalesce around the opposing argots, as they elaborate, enrich, and adorn the opposing discourses, the ground is prepared for nothing less than *systematic misunderstanding*. Each community is now dependent on a positive ontology, the very sustenance of which is dependent on maintaining its opposition. The communities seek each other's destruction, but simultaneously must ensure a continued existence. 'To understand,' that is, to coordinate one's actions with those of the opposition, would be to lose one's sense of the real and the right. Discussions seeking 'mutual understanding' will often lurch toward failure, for participants will ensure that the other is not understood – otherwise both sides of the essential antimony would give way.

By weaving together and extending various lines of recent inquiry, I have tried to fashion the rudiments of a communal theory of meaning. The formulation envisions the generation of meaning as a constantly shifting, dynamic social process. 'Successful' communication may be achieved under local circumstances through coordinated and interdependent actions of the participants. However, each localized coordination is dependent on the vicissitudes of broader social processes in which it is embedded – and thus vulnerable to reconstitution as a failed project. My sense of understanding you is not thus my possession, but ours, and ours only by virtue of the cultural processes in which we are embedded.

REFERENCES .

Bakhtin, M. (1981). *The dialogic imagination*. Austin: University of Texas Press.

Danziger, K. (1990). *Constructing the subject: Historical origins of psychological research*. Cambridge, England: Cambridge University Press.

Edwards, D., & Potter, J. (1992). *Discursive psychology*. London: Sage.

Garfinkel, H. (1967). *Studies in ethnomethodology*. Englewood Cliffs, NJ: Prentice-Hall.

Latour, B. & Woolgar, S. (1979). *Laboratory life: The social construction of scientific facts*. Thousand Oaks, CA: Sage.

Middleton, D. & Edwards, D. (1990). *Collective remembering*. London: Sage.

Pearce, W.B. & Cronen, V. (1980). *Communication, action and meaning*. New York: Praeger.

Shotter, J. (1984). *Social accountability and selfhood*. Oxford, England: Blackwell.

profusions of practice

Part five

Social constructionism and pragmatism are closely linked. Constructionist dialogues replace traditional issues of truth and objectivity with concerns of practice. It is not whether an account is true in some absolute or god's eye view that matters so much as the results for our lives that follow from taking avowals of truth seriously. There can be many truths, depending on community tradition, but as the constructionist asks, what happens to us – for good or ill – as we honor one as opposed to another account? This concern with practical outcomes also fuels an investment in developing new practices. Constructionism invites us to see language as an action in the world, but scarcely the only action of significance. It invites us to move beyond creating, criticizing, and reconstructing our discourses of the real and the good, to generating practices that directly advance our visions.

This emphasis on new practices does not simultaneously cast out all previous practices – for example, in education, organizations, therapy, families, and so on. All existing practices are born of traditions that have internal validity for their participants. However, constructionist ideas do contain the seeds for a new range of practices. They draw our attention to limits on existing practices, and the possibility of augmenting our resources of relationship. Specifically, constructionist ideas place an emphasis on the power of relationship over individual minds, multiple worlds over singular realities, collaborative interdependence over individual heroism, and dialogue over monologue. In the present context we select innovative offerings from three significant areas: therapy, education, and change practices in organizations and communities. We select these areas because they have been sites of flourishing expansion. However, the interested reader might also wish to explore how constructionist ideas play out in social work (Chambon, Irving, & Epstein, 1999), religion (Hermans, et al., 2002), organizational management (Anderson et al., 2001), evaluation (Guba and Lincoln, 1989), counseling (Sexton & Griffin, 1997), grief management (Neimeyer, 2001), gerontology (www.healthandage.com/html/res/gergen/contenu/newsletter.htm), pain management (Frank, 1995), and feminist psychology (M. Gergen, 2001).

THERAPEUTIC PRACTICE

Constructionist ideas have had a global impact on the practice of psychotherapy. One finds their influence in wide-ranging schools of practice – narrative therapy (McLeod, 1997), family therapy (Hoffman, 2002), brief therapy (de Shazer, 1994), constructivist therapy, and postmodern therapy (Anderson, 1997) among them. These various therapies all share in one major constructionist vision: we live in worlds of human meaning, and these meanings are inextricably bound to our actions. At this point such an assumption may seem innocuous enough, but it is important to realize the way this proposal contrasts with three traditional assumptions. First, from early Freudian thinking to recent developments in cognitive therapy, therapists have assumed that the aberrant actions of their clients are driven or determined by forces or mechanisms *beyond conscious awareness* or control. Second, there is a strong emphasis in most existing therapies on *accurate* knowledge of the world – 'living in the real world,' as we might say. These assumptions also contribute to a third assumption, namely that the therapist possesses *privileged knowledge*. It is the therapist, by traditional accounts, who can help the otherwise unwitting client to understand and overcome the forces beyond awareness, and to know reality for what it is. As you can see, not only does constructionist oriented therapy challenge the idea of unconscious forces and 'one true reality', but as well the presumption that the therapist is the expert on such matters. Rather, constructionist oriented therapists typically work collaboratively with clients in helping them to reshape the meaning of their worlds. Their expertise lies, not in 'knowing that' the client has one form of 'mental disease' or another, but in 'knowing how' to work with clients in a transformative way.

In the present volume we feature an offering from perhaps the most widely practiced form of therapy in a constructionist mold, namely narrative therapy. Narrative therapists draw sustenance in particular from the constructionist emphasis on language, and particularly the way in which the understanding of ourselves is cast in narrative structures or 'life stories.' (See Reading 12). Therapy, in this instance, is not bent on 'curing a disease,' but is directed toward re-storying, or hammering out a new and more viable way of articulating self and world. For the narrative therapist, for example, an adolescent girl whose meager eating habits are becoming life threatening does not suffer from 'a disease' called 'anorexia.' Rather, the girl lives within a potentially dangerous narrative about herself, one that may for example, be a reflection of the broad cultural value placed on having a trim body. The therapist's task is to help such an individual challenge this dominant narrative, and to realize an alternative that can be lived, without such danger.

Perhaps the classic account of narrative therapy is contained in Michael White and David Epston's volume, *Narrative Means to Therapeutic Ends*. We include here an excerpt (Reading 24) that is especially interesting in its refinement of narrative practice. It is one thing to recognize the importance of stories, but how does the therapist help to open a space for alternatives? Here White paves the way by outlining a practice of *externalization*. In externalization the therapist offers another way of talking about 'the problem.' Rather than viewing it as 'inside the person' – a basic part of their make-up – the client is invited to talk about it as external – as 'out there.' Rather than exploring 'my depression,' for example, one might talk about 'when depression pays me a visit.' Externalization represents an effective beginning to another story, in which one is not defined by the ailment ('my problem and I are one'), but stands independent of it and thus capable of resistance.

PEDAGOGICAL PRACTICE

The challenge of human transformation is scarcely limited to the domain of human suffering. Perhaps society's chief investment in transformation is located in our schools. It is precisely because of its broad effects on the culture that constructionist scholars are particularly concerned with educational practices. In part, the concerns are critical. For one, contemporary curricula are typically wedded to traditional beliefs in a singular truth ('the correct answer'), a singular vocabulary of reason ('correct thinking'), and an individualist ideology ('every student for him/herself') – all thrown into question by the constructionist dialogues. In addition, constructionists are concerned with the ways in which the diverse voices and logics making up the culture are suppressed or obliterated by standardized school curricula, evaluation systems hold students alone responsible for their poor performance, schooling suppresses challenges to the status quo, and school curricula are cut away from the local community needs (for a review, see Gergen, 2001).

Yet, constructionist discussions have also moved beyond critique to face the challenge of creating alternative practices. If realities, logics and values issue from relationships then what kinds of curricula, pedagogical practices, and policies would follow? Although there is much to be said on this subject, we include here an introduction to the possibilities, as offered by educational doyen, Jerome Bruner (Reading 25). Although once a leading figure in a movement stressing individual cognition, Bruner has become increasingly impressed with the ways in which individual thought is culturally embedded. Private meanings are not essentially private, but are constituted within cultural relationships. The present offering is taken from his recent work, *The Culture of Education*, which includes a line of argument that gives clarity to the relationship between cultural meaning and educational process. The interested reader is encouraged, as well, to see Bruffee's *Collaborative Learning* and Rogoff, Turkanis, and Bartlett's *Learning Together*.

ORGANIZATIONAL AND COMMUNITY CHANGE PRACTICES

As schooling is completed, most people enter the world of work and community life. A common complaint of people who work in organization is that of stasis – 'We are stuck in our structures,' 'We have great aspirations but just can't seem to mobilize,' 'The world changes and we sit still,' 'The spark is gone; I am just plain bored.' The challenge of organizational change is central to organizational theorists, schools of management, communication theorists, and the entire profession of organizational development. It is precisely this challenge to which constructionist ideas are ideally suited. For the constructionist, both stability and change in organizations can be understood in terms of the meanings created by people together. In this sense, organizational participants do have control over their condition; working *together* they have the capacity to generate new meanings and thus the grounds for new action. The challenge of change, then, is the challenge of generating new conversations.

In Reading 26 we introduce a constructionist change practice that is sweeping rapidly through the profession of organizational development and around the globe. The practice of *appreciative inquiry* is lodged in the assumption that when we begin to explore people's positive experiences in an organization, the conversations begin to change. And when we use these stories of value to create visions of a desired future, powerful forces of change are unleashed. As outlined by David Cooperrider and Diana Whitney, it is useful to break such inquiry into specific stages, each with its own function. At the outset, organizational participants are asked to share with each other personal narratives, stories typically oriented toward what has worked well or has been the most energizing in the past. As these stories are shared, optimistic relations develop among participants. In this context, participants are invited to envision the future of the organization. What are their dreams, and how can these be put into practice? From these discussions, plans are developed and set in motion. Transformation takes place in an atmosphere of excitement and mutual caring.

Appreciative inquiry attempts to create change without conflict. Yet, from a constructionist perspective, conflict within and between groups is virtually inevitable. As people come together in different relationships, in different conditions of life, so are they likely to generate diverse realities, logics, and values. Such diversity can rapidly lead to a sense of competition or antagonism, 'us' (our kind, the right kind) vs. 'them' (the inferior, the threatening, the evil). Such divisions can take place in families and communities, as well as organizations large and small, and on the national and global sphere. When intensified the result can be murder, terrorism, or war. Yet, by viewing antagonisms through a constructionist lens, we are also open to new vistas of practice. We begin to see the possibility for multiple realities and values, each legitimate and desirable within its own interpretive community. And, rather than seeking ways of determining which way is 'the right way,' we are drawn into searching for forms of dialogue out of which meanings can be transformed.

Reading 27 by members of the Public Conversations Project (*www.publicconversations.org*) represents a dramatic and effective practice of transformative dialogue. The practice is particularly noteworthy because it moves beyond traditional assumptions of debate, in which there is a winner and loser. Rather, by shifting the focus to dialogue, the group offers opportunities for hostile and alienated groups to come together in new ways. The dialogic practice differs from many because it does not aim to change the beliefs of the participants. The hope is to open new vistas of understanding − both of the other and oneself. For example, there is no attempt to change the views of either pro-life or pro-choice advocates described in this reading; however, by engaging in new forms of conversation their antipathies are softened. In our view, many components of these carefully crafted exchanges can be adapted to our everyday life.

REFERENCES

Anderson, H. (1997). *Conversation, language and possibilities, a postmodern approach to psychotherapy*. New York: Basic Books.

Anderson, H. , et al. (2001). *The appreciative organization*. Cleveland: Taos Institute Publications.

Bruffee, K. (1992). *Collaborative learning*, Baltimore, MD: Johns Hopkins University Press.

Bruner, J. (2000). *The culture of education*. Cambridge: Harvard University Press.

Chambon, A.S., Irving, A. and Epstein, L. (Eds) (1999) *Reading Foucault for social work*. New York: Cambridge University Press.

de Shazer, S. (1994) *Words were originally magic*. New York: Norton.

Frank, A. (1995). *The wounded storyteller*. Chicago: University of Chicago Press.

Gergen, K.J. (2001). *Social construction in context*. London: Sage.

Gergen, M. (2001). *Feminist reconstructions in psychology: Narrative, gender & performance*. Thousand Oaks, CA: Sage.

Guba, E. G., & Lincoln, Y. S. (1989). *Fourth generation evaluation*. Thousand Oaks, CA: Sage.

Hermans, et al., (Eds) (2002). *Social constructionism and theology*. Leiden, The Netherlands, Boston, USA & Cologne, Germany: Brill.

Hoffman, L. (2002). *Family therapy: An intimate history*. New York: Norton.

McLeod, J. (1997). *Narrative and psychotherapy*. London: Sage.

Neimeyer, R. (Ed.) (2001). *Meaning, reconstruction and the expression of loss*. Washington, D.C.: American Psychological Association Press.

Rogoff, B., Turkanis, C. & Bartlett, L. (Eds). *Learning together: Children and adults in a school community*. New York, London: Oxford University Press.

Sexton, T. L., & Griffin, B. L. (1997). *Constructivist thinking in counseling practice, research, and training*. New York, London: Teachers College Press at Columbia University.

White, M. and Epston, D. (1990). *Narrative means to therapeutic ends*. New York: Norton.

24

narrative therapy and externalizing the problem

michael white

'Externalizing' is an approach to therapy that encourages persons to objectify and, at times, to personify the problems that they experience as oppressive. In this process, the problem becomes a separate entity and thus external to the person or relationship that was ascribed as the problem. Those problems that are considered to be inherent, as well as those relatively fixed qualities that are attributed to persons and to relationships, are rendered less fixed and less restricting.

I began my first systematic attempts at encouraging persons to externalize their problems approximately ten years ago. These attempts took place predominantly within the context of work with families that presented for therapy with problems identified in children.

The externalization of the child's problem clearly had great appeal for these families. Although the problem was usually defined as internal to the child, all family members were affected and often felt overwhelmed, dispirited and defeated. In various ways, they took the ongoing existence of the problem and their failed attempts to solve it as a reflection on themselves, each other, and/or their relationships. The continuing survival of the problem and the failure of corrective measures served to confirm, for family members, the presence of various negative personal and relationship qualities or attributes. Thus, when the members of these families detailed the problems for which they were seeking therapy, it was not at all unusual for them to present what I call a 'problem-saturated description' of family life.

In helping these family members separate themselves and their relationships from the problem, externalization opened up possibilities for them to describe themselves, each other, and their relationships from a new, nonproblem-saturated perspective; it enabled the development of an alternative story of family life, one that was more attractive to family members. From this new perspective, persons were able to locate 'facts' about their lives and relationships that could not be even dimly perceived in the problem-saturated account of family life: 'facts' that contradicted this problem-saturated account; facts that provided the nuclei for the generation of new stories. And, in the process, the child's problem was invariably resolved.

The very positive responses to these early systematic attempts at encouraging families to externalize their problems led me to extend this practice to a wide range of presenting problems. Throughout my subsequent explorations of this approach, I have found the externalization of the problem to be helpful to persons in their struggle with problems. Consequently, I have concluded that, among other things, this practice:

1. Decreases unproductive conflict between persons, including those disputes over who is responsible for the problem;
2. Undermines the sense of failure that has developed for many persons in response to the continuing existence of the problem despite their attempts to resolve it;
3. Paves the way for persons to cooperate with each other, to unite in a struggle against the problems, and to escape its influence in their lives and relationships;
4. Opens up new possibilities for persons to take action to retrieve their lives and relationships from the problem and its influence;
5. Frees persons to take a lighter, more effective, and less stressed approach to 'deadly serious' problems; and
6. Presents options for dialogue, rather than monologue, about the problem.

Within the context of the practices associated with the externalizing of problems, neither the person nor the relationship between persons is the problem. Rather, the problem becomes the problem, and then the person's relationship with the problem becomes the problem.

Not only do the stories that persons have about their lives determine the meaning that they ascribe to experience, but these stories also determine which aspects of lived experience are selected out for the ascription of meaning. As Bruner (1986) argues, it is not possible for narratives to encompass the full richness of our lived experience:

> ...life experience is richer than discourse. Narrative structures organize and give meaning to experience, but there are always feelings and lived experience not fully encompassed by the dominant story. (p. 143)

Since the stories that persons have about their lives determine both the ascription of meaning to experience and the selection of those aspects of experience that are to be given expression, these stories are constitutive or shaping of persons' lives. The lives and relationships of persons evolve as they live through or perform these stories.

Through the lens of the text analogy, various assumptions can be made about persons' experience of problems. Here I make the general assumption that, when persons experience problems for which they seek therapy, (a) the narratives in which they are storying their experience and/or in which they are having their experience storied by others do not sufficiently represent their lived experience, and (b), in these circumstance, there will be significant and vital aspects of their lived experience that contradict these dominant narratives.

The externalizing of the problem enables persons to separate from the dominant stories that have been the shaping of their lives and relationships. In so doing, persons are able to identify previously neglected but vital aspects of lived experience – aspects that could not have been predicted from a reading of the dominant story. Thus, following Goffman (1961), I have referred to these aspects of experience as 'unique outcomes' (White, 1987, 1988).

As unique outcomes are identified, persons can be encouraged to engage in performances of new meaning in relation to these. Success with this requires that the unique outcome be plotted into an alternative story about the person's life. I have referred to this alternative story as a 'unique account' and have developed an approach to questioning that encourages persons to locate, generate, or resurrect alternative stories that will 'make sense' of the unique outcomes. Other questions inspire persons to investigate what these new developments might reflect about personal and relationship attributes and qualities. In the process of entertaining and responding to these questions, persons derive new and 'unique redescriptions' of themselves and of their relationships (White, 1988). Unique rediscription questions can also assist persons in the revision of their relationships with themselves (e.g., 'In what way do you think these discoveries might affect your attitude towards yourself?'), in the revision of their relationship with others (e.g., 'How might this discovery affect your relationship with…?'), and in the revision of their relationship with problems (e.g., 'In refusing to cooperate with the problem in this way, are you supporting it or undermining it?').

RELATIVE INFLUENCE QUESTIONING

A general interviewing process that I have referred to as 'relative influence questioning' (White, 1986) is particularly effective in assisting persons to externalize the problem. This process of questioning is initiated at the outset of the first interview, so that persons are immediately engaged in the activity of separating their lives and relationships from the problem.

Relative influence questioning is comprised of two sets of questions. The first set encourages persons to map the influence of the problem in their lives and relationships. The second set encourages persons to map their own influence in the 'life' of the problem. By inviting persons to review the effects of the problem in their lives and relationships, relative influence questions assist them to become aware of and to describe their relationship with the problem. This takes them out of a fixed and static world, a world of problems that are intrinsic to persons and relationships, and into a world of experience, a world of flux. In this world, persons find new possibilities for affirmative action, new opportunities to act flexibly.

To illustrate the practice of 'mapping the influence of the problem,' I have selected the problem of encopresis. I believe that this is appropriate, as many of these practices originated in my work with families where children had histories of persistent and unremitting soiling.

Nick, aged six years, was brought to see me by his parents, Sue and Ron.* Nick had a very long history of encopresis, which had resisted all attempts to resolve it, including those instituted by various therapists. Rarely did a day go by without an 'accident' or 'incident,' which usually meant the 'full works' in his underwear.

To make matters worse, Nick had befriended the 'poo.' The poo had become his playmate. He would 'streak' it down walls, smear it in drawers, roll it into balls and flick it behind cupboards and wardrobes, and had even taken to plastering it under the kitchen table. In addition, it was not uncommon for Ron and Sue to find soiled clothes that had been hidden in different locations around the house, and to discover poo pushed into various corners and squeezed into the shower and sink drains. The poo had even developed the habit of accompanying Nick in the bath.

In response to my questions about the influence of the poo in the lives and relationships of family members, we discovered that:

1. The poo was making a mess of Nick's life by isolating him from other children and by interfering with his school work. By coating his life, the poo was taking the shine off his future and was making it impossible for him and others to see what he was really like as a person. For example, this coating of poo dulled the picture of him as a person, making it difficult for other people to see what an interesting and intelligent person he was.
2. The poo was driving Sue into misery, forcing her to question her capacity to be a good parent and her general capability as a person. It was overwhelming her to the extent that she felt quite desperate and on the verge of 'giving up.' She believed her future as a parent to be clouded with despair.
3. The ongoing intransigence of the poo was deeply embarrassing to Ron. This embarrassment had the effect of isolating him from friends and relatives. It wasn't the sort of problem that he could feel comfortable talking about to workmates. Also, the family lived in a relatively distant and small farming community, and visits of friends and relatives usually required that they stay overnight. These overnight stays had become a tradition. As Nick's 'accidents' and 'incidents' were so likely to feature in any such stay, Ron felt constrained in the pursuit of this tradition. Ron had always regarded himself as an open person, and it was difficult for him to share his thoughts and feelings with others and at the same time keep the 'terrible' secret.
4. The poo was affecting all the relationships in the family in various ways. For example, it was wedged between Nick and his parents. The relationship between him and Sue had become somewhat stressed, and much of the fun had been driven out of it. And the relationship between Nick and Ron had suffered considerably under the reign of tyranny perpetrated by the poo. Also since their frustrations with Nick's problems always took center stage in their discussions, the poo had been highly influential in the relationship between Sue and Ron, making it difficult for them to focus their attention on each other.

---

*To preserve confidentiality, all names are fictitious.

Mapping the Influence of Persons

Once a description of the problem's sphere of influence has been derived by mapping its effect in persons' lives and relationships, a second set of questions can be introduced. This set features those questions that invite persons to map their influence and the influence of their relationships in the 'life' of the problem. These questions bring forth information that contradicts the problem-saturated description of family life and assist persons in identifying their competence and resourcefulness in the face of adversity.

When mapping the influence of family members in the life of what we came to call 'Sneaky Poo,' we discovered that:

1. Although Sneaky Poo always tried to trick Nick into being his playmate, Nick could recall a number of occasions during which he had not allowed Sneaky Poo to 'outsmart' him. These were occasions during which Nick could have cooperated by 'smearing,' 'streaking,' or 'plastering,' but declined to do so. He had not allowed himself to be tricked into this.
2. There was a recent occasion during which Sneaky Poo could have driven Sue into a heightened sense of misery, but she resisted and turned on the stereo instead. Also, on this occasion she refused to question her competence as a parent and as a person.
3. Ron could not recall an occasion during which he had not allowed the embarrassment caused by Sneaky Poo to isolate him from others. However, after Sneaky Poo's requirements of him were identified, he did seem interested in the idea of defying these requirements. In response to my curiosity about how he might protest against Sneaky Poo's requirements of him, he said that he might try disclosing the 'terrible' secret to a workmate. (This intention is a unique outcome in that it could not have been predicted by a reading of the problem-saturated story of a family life.)
4. Some difficulty was experienced in the identification of the influence of family relationships in the life of Sneaky Poo. However, after some discussion, it was established that there was an aspect to Sue's relationship with Nick that she thought she could still enjoy, that Ron was still making some attempts to persevere in his relationship with Nick, and that Nick had an idea that Sneaky Poo had not destroyed all of the love in his relationship with his parents.

After identifying Nick's Sue's, and Ron's influence in the life of Sneaky Poo, I introduced questions that encouraged them to perform meaning in relation to these examples, so that they might 're-author' their lives and relationships.

How had they managed to be effective against the problem in this way? How did this reflect on them as people and on their relationships? What personal and relationship attributes were they relying on in these achievements? Did this success give them any ideas about further steps that they might take to reclaim their lives from the problem? What difference would knowing what they now knew about themselves make to their future relationship with the problem?

In response to these questions, Nick thought that he was ready to stop Sneaky Poo from outsmarting him so much, and decided that he would not be tricked into being its playmate anymore. Sue had some new ideas for refusing to let Sneaky Poo push her into misery, and Ron thought that he just might be ready to take a risk and follow up with his idea of telling a workmate of his struggle with Sneaky Poo.

I met with this family again two weeks later. In that time Nick had only one minor accident – this described as light 'smudging'. Sneaky Poo had tried to win him back after nine days, but Nick had not given in. He had taught Sneaky Poo a lesson – he would not let it mess up his life anymore. He described how he had refused to be tricked into playing with Sneaky Poo and believed that his life was no longer coated with it, that he was now shining through. He was talkative, happier, felt stronger, and was more physically active. Sneaky Poo had been a tricky character, and Nick had done very well to get his life back for himself.

Sue and Ron had also 'gotten serious' in their decision not to cooperate with the requirements of Sneaky Poo. Sue had started to 'treat herself' more often, particularly on those occasions during which Sneaky Poo was giving her a hard time, and 'had put her foot down,' showing that it couldn't take her so lightly anymore.

Ron had taken a risk and had protested Sneaky Poo's isolation of him. He had talked to a couple of his workmates about the problem. They had listened respectfully, offering a few comments. An hour later, one of them had returned and had disclosed that he had been experiencing a similar problem with a son. There ensued a very significant conversation and a strengthening bond of friendship. And without that coating on Nick's life, Ron had discovered that 'Nick was good to talk to'.

I encouraged Nick, Sue, and Ron to reflect on and speculate about what this success said about the qualities that they possessed as people and about the attributes of their relationships. I also encouraged them to review what these facts suggested about their current relationship with Sneaky Poo. In this discussion, family members identified further measures that they could take to decline Sneaky Poo's invitations to support it.

We met on a third occasion three weeks later, and I discovered that all had proceeded to take further steps to outrun Sneaky Poo, steps to ensure that it would be put in its proper place. Nick had made some new friends and had been catching up on his school work, and the family had visited overnight with several friends and relatives. Sue was making good her escape from guilt. This had been facilitated, to an extent, by the fact that she and Ron had been talking more to other parents about the trials and tribulations of parenting. In so doing they had learned that they were not the only parents who had doubts about their parenting skills.

We then did some contingency planning, just in case Sneaky Poo tried to make a comeback and to outstreak Nick again. I saw this family again one month later for a review. At the six-month follow-up, Nick was doing very well. Only on one or two occasions had there been a slight smudging on his pants. He was more confident and doing even better with friends and at school. Everyone felt happy with his progress.

REFERENCES

Bruner, J. (1986). *Actual Minds, Possible Worlds*. Cambridge, MA: Harvard University Press.

Goffman, E. (1961). *Asylums: Essays in the Social Situation of Mental Patients and Other Inmates*. New York: Doubleday.

White, M. (1986). 'Negative Explanation, Restraint and Double Description. A Template for Family Therapy' *Family Process*, 25(2)

White, M. (1987). Family Therapy and Schizophrenia. Addressing the 'in the corner lifestyle'. *Dulwich Centre Newsletter*. Spring.

White, M. (1988). The Process of Questioning. A Therapy of Literary Merit? *Dulwich Centre Newsletter*, Spring.

25

the culture of education

jerome bruner

The 'reality' that we impute to the 'worlds' we inhabit is a constructed one. To paraphrase Nelson Goodman, 'reality is made, not found.' Reality construction is the product of meaning making shaped by traditions and by a culture's tool-kit of ways of thought. In this sense, education must be conceived as aiding young humans in learning to use the tools of meaning making and reality construction, to better adapt to the world in which they find themselves and to help in the process of changing it as required. In this sense, it can even be conceived as akin to helping people become better architects and better builders.

The interactional tenet. Passing on knowledge and skill, like any human exchange, involves a subcommunity in interaction. At the minimum, it involves a 'teacher' and a 'learner' – or if not a teacher in flesh and blood, then a vicarious one like a book, or film, or display, or a 'responsive' computer.

It is principally through interacting with others that children find out what the culture is about and how it conceives of the world. Unlike any other species, human beings deliberately teach each other in settings outside the ones in which the knowledge being taught will be used. Nowhere else in the animal kingdom is such deliberate 'teaching' found – save scrappily among higher primates. To be sure, many indigenous cultures do not practice as deliberate or decontextualized a form of teaching as we do. But 'telling' and 'showing' are as humanly universal as speaking.

It is customary to say that this specialization rests upon the gift of language. But perhaps more to the point, it also rests upon our astonishingly well developed talent for 'intersubjectivity' – the human ability to understand the minds of others, whether through language, gesture, or other means. It is not just words that make this possible, but our capacity to grasp the role of the settings in which words, acts, and gestures occur. We are the intersubjective species par excellence. It is this, that permits us to 'negotiate' meanings when words go astray.

Our Western pedagogical tradition hardly does justice to the importance of intersubjectivity in transmitting culture. Indeed, it often clings to a preference for a degree of explicitness that seems to ignore it. So teaching is fitted into a mold in which a single, presumably omniscient teacher explicitly tells or shows, presumably unknowing learners, something they presumably know nothing about. Even when we tamper with this model, as with 'question periods' and the like, we still remain loyal to its unspoken precepts. I believe that one of the most important gifts that a cultural psychology can give to education is a reformulation of this impoverished conception. For only a very small part of educating takes place on such a one-way street – and it is probably one of the least successful parts.

So back to the innocent but fundamental question: how best to conceive of a sub-community that specializes in learning among its members? One obvious answer would be that it is a place where, among other things, learners help each other learn, each according to their abilities. And this, of course, need not exclude the presence of somebody serving in the role of teacher. It simply implies that the teacher does not play that role as a monopoly, that learners 'scaffold' for each other as well. The antithesis is the 'transmission' model first described, often further exaggerated by an emphasis on transmitting 'subject matter'. But in most matters of achieving mastery, we also want learners to gain good judgment, to becomes self-reliant, to work well with each other. And such competencies do not flourish under a one-way 'transmission' regimen. Indeed, the very institutionalization of schooling may get in the way of creating a sub-community of learners who bootstrap each other.

Consider the more 'mutual' community for a moment. Typically, it models ways of doing or knowing, provides opportunity for emulation, offers running commentary, provides, 'scaffolding' for novices, and even provides a good context for teaching deliberately. It even makes possible that form of job-related division of labor one finds in effective work groups: some serving pro tem as 'memories' for the others, or as record keepers of 'where things have got up to now,' or as encouragers or cautioners. The point is for those in the group to help each other get the lay of the land and the hang of the job.

One of the most radical proposals to have emerged from the cultural-psychological approach to education is that the classroom be reconceived as just such a subcommunity of mutual learners, with the teacher orchestrating the proceedings. Note that, contrary to traditional critics, such subcommunities do not reduce the teachers's role nor his or her 'authority.' Rather, the teacher takes on the additional function of encouraging others to share it. Just as the omniscient narrator has disappeared from modern fiction, so will the omniscient teacher disappear from the classroom of the future.

There is obviously no single formula that follows from the cultural-psychological approach to interactive, intersubjective pedagogy. For one thing, the practices adopted will vary with subject: poetry and mathematics doubtless require different approaches. Its sole precept is that where human beings are concerned, learning (whatever else it may be) is an interactive process in which people learn from each other, and not just by showing and telling. It is surely in the nature of human cultures to form such communities of mutual learners. Even if we are the only species that 'teaches deliberately' and 'out of the context of use,' this does not mean that we should convert this evolutionary step into a fetish.

The externalization tenet. A French cultural psychologist, Ignace Meyerson first enunciated an idea that today, a quarter-century after his death, now seems both obvious and brimming with educational implications. Briefly, his view was that the main function of all collective cultural activity is to produce 'works' – *oeuvres*, as he called them, works that, as it were, achieve an existence of their own. In the grand sense, these include the arts and sciences of a culture, institutional structures such as its laws and its markets, even its 'history' conceived as a canonical version of the past. But there are minor oeuvres as well: those 'works' of smaller groupings that give pride, identity, and a sense of continuity to those who participate, however obliquely, in their making. These may be 'inspirational' – for example, our school soccer team won the country championship six years age, or our famous Bronx High School of Science has 'produced' three Nobel Laureates. Oeuvres are often touchingly local, modest, yet equally identity-bestowing, such as this remark by a 10-year-old student: 'Look at *this* thing we're working on if you want to see how *we* handle oil spills.'

The benefits of 'externalizing' such joint products into oeuvres have too long been overlooked. First on the list, obviously, is that collective oeuvres produce and sustain group solidarity. They help *make* a community, and communities of mutual learners are no exception. But just as important, they promote a sense of the division of labor that goes into producing a product: Todd is our real computer wonk, Jeff's terrific at making graphics, Alice and David are our 'word geniuses,' Maddalena is fantastic at explaining things that puzzle some of the rest of us. One group we will examine in later discussions even devised a way to highlight these 'group works' by instituting a weekly session to hear and discuss a report on the class's performance for the week. The report, presented by a 'class ethnographer' (usually one of the teaching assistants), highlights *overall* rather than individual progress; it produces 'metacognition' on the class's oeuvre and usually leads to lively discussion.

Works and works-in-progress create *shared* and *negotiable* ways of thinking in a group. The French historians of the so-called *Annales* school, who were strongly influenced by Meyerson's ideas, refer to these shared and negotiable forms of thought as *mentalités*, styles of thinking that characterize different groups in different periods living under various circumstances. The class's approach to its 'weekly ethnography' produces just such a *mentalité*.

I can see one other benefit from externalizing mental work into a more palpable oeuvre, one that we psychologists have tended to ignore. Externalization produces a *record* of our mental efforts, one that is 'outside us' rather than vaguely 'in memory.' It is somewhat like producing a draft, a rough sketch, a 'mock-up.' 'It' takes over our attention as something that, in its own right, needs a transitional paragraph, or a less frontal perspective there, or a better 'introduction.' 'It' relieves us in some measure from the always difficult task of 'thinking about our own thoughts' while often accomplishing the same end. 'It' embodies our thoughts and intentions in a form more accessible to reflective efforts. The process of thought and its product become interwoven, like Picasso's countless sketches and drawings in reconceiving Velásquez's *Las Meninas*.

There is a Latin motto, *scientia dependit in mores*, knowledge works its way into habits. It might easily be retranslated as 'thinking works its way into its products.'

All viable cultures, Ignace Meyerson noted, make provisions for conserving and passing on their 'works.' Laws get written down, codified, and embodied in the procedure of courts. Law schools train people in the ways of a 'profession' so that the *corpus juris* can be assured for the future. These 'hard copy' externalizations are typically supported as well by myth-like ones: the indomitable Lord Mansfield bringing the skepticism of Montaigne and Montesquieu into English law, the equally indomitable Mr. Chief Justice Holmes injecting a new, Darwinian 'realism' into American jurisprudence, and even John Mortimer's fictional Rumpole struggling commonsensically against the legal pedants. What finally emerges is subtle mix of starchy procedures and their informal human explication.

Obviously, a school's classroom is no match for the law in tradition-making. Yet it can have long-lasting influence. We carry with us habits of thought and taste fostered in some nearly forgotten classroom by a certain teacher. I can remember one who made us relish as a class 'less obvious' interpretations of historical happenings. We lost our embarrassment about offering our 'wilder' ideas. She helped us invent a tradition. I still relish it. Can schools and classrooms be designed to foster such tradition-inventing? Denmark is experimenting with keeping the same group of children and teachers together through all the primary grades – an idea that goes back to Steiner. Does that turn 'work' into 'works' with a life of their own? Modern mobility is, of course, the enemy of all such aspirations. Yet the creation and conservation of culture in shared works is a matter worth reflecting upon. Nor are we without good examples in our own time. Sarah Lightfoot has documented how certain public high schools create a sense of their enduring meaning, and Michael Cole's 'computer networking' seems to yield the interesting by-product of widely separated groups of children finding a wider, more enduring, and palpable world through contact with each other by e-mail.

Externalizing, in a word, rescues cognitive activity from implicitness, making it more public, negotiable, and 'solidary'. At the same time, it makes it more accessible to subsequent reflection and metacognition. Probably the greatest milestone in the history of externalization was literacy, putting thought and memory, 'out there' on clay tablets or paper. Computers and e-mail may represent another step forward. But there are doubtless myriad ways in which jointly negotiated thought can be communally externalized as oeuvres – and many ways in which they can be put to use in schools.

26

appreciative inquiry

david l. cooperrider and diana whitney

Appreciative Inquiry (AI) is about the co-evolutionary search for the best in people, their organizations, and the relevant world around them. In its broadest focus, it involves systematic discovery of what gives 'life' to a living system when it is most alive, most effective, and most constructively capable in economic, ecological, and human terms. AI involves, in a central way, the art and practice of asking questions that strengthen a system's capacity to apprehend, anticipate, and heighten positive potential. It centrally involves the mobilization of inquiry through the crafting of the 'unconditional positive question,' often involving hundreds or sometimes thousands of people. In AI, the arduous task of intervention gives way to the speed of imagination and innovation; instead of negation, criticism, and spiraling diagnosis, there is discovery, dream, and design. AI seeks, fundamentally, to build a constructive union between a whole people and the massive entirety of what people talk about as past and present capacities: achievements, assets, unexplored potentials, innovations, strengths, elevated thoughts, opportunities, benchmarks, high point moments, lived values, traditions, strategic competencies, stories, expressions of wisdom, insights into the deeper corporate spirit or soul, and visions of valued and possible futures. Taking all of these together as a gestalt, AI, deliberately in everything it does, seeks to work from accounts of this 'positive change core' – and it assumes that every living system has many untapped and rich and inspiring accounts of the positive. Link the energy of this core directly to any change agenda and changes never thought possible are suddenly and democratically mobilized.

The positive core of organizational life, we submit, is one of the greatest and largely unrecognized resources in the field of change management today. At present, we are clearly in our infancy when it comes to tools for working with it, talking about it, and designing our systems in synergistic alignment with it. But one thing is evident and clear as we reflect on the most important things we have learned with AI: human systems grow in the direction of what they persistently ask questions about and this propensity is strongest and most sustainable when the means and ends of inquiry are positively correlated. The single most prolific thing a group can do if its aims are to liberate the human spirit and consciously construct a better future is to make the positive change core the common and explicit property of all.

Let's Illustrate: The Appreciative Inquiry. '4-D' Cycle

You have just received the following unsettling phone call:

My name is Rita Simmel. I am President of a New York consulting partnership. Our firm specializes in dealing with difficult conflict in organizations: labor-management issues, gender conflict, issues of diversity. We have been retained by a Fortune 500 corporation for the past several years. The contract is around sexual harassment, an issue that is deeper and more severe than virtually any corporation realizes. The issues are about power, the glass ceiling, and many things. As you know, millions of dollars are being expended on the issues. Our firm has specialized in this area for some years and now I'm beginning to ask myself the Hippocratic oath. Are we really helping? Here is the bottom line with our client. We have been working on the issues for two years, and by every measure – numbers of complaints, lawsuits, evaluations from sexual harassment training programs, word of mouth – the problem continues in its growth. Furthermore people are now voting with their feet. They are not coming to the workshops. Those that do seem to leave with doubts: our post-workshop interviews show people feel less able to communicate with those of the opposite gender, they report feeling more distance and less trust, and the glass ceiling remains. So here is my question. How would you take an appreciative inquiry approach to sexual harassment?

This was a tough one. We requested time to think about it, asking if we could talk again in a day or two? We can do the same for you right now (give you a bit of time) as we invite you to think about things you might seriously propose in the callback.

Before going further with the story let's pause and look at a typical flow for AI, a cycle that can be as rapid and informal as in a conversation with a friend or colleague, or as formal as an organization-wide analysis involving every stake-holder, including customers, suppliers, partners, and the like.

Figure 26.1 shows four key stages in AI: *Discovery* – mobilizing a whole system inquiry into the positive change core; *Dream* – creating a clear results-oriented vision in relation to discovered potential and in relation to questions of higher purpose, i.e., 'What is the world calling us to become?'; *Design* – creating possibility propositions of the ideal organization, an organization design which people feel is capable of magnifying or eclipsing the positive core and realizing the articulated new dream; and *Destiny* – strengthening the affirmative capability of the whole system enabling it to build hope and momentum around a deep purpose and creating processes for learning, adjustment, and improvisation, like a jazz group over time (Barrett, 1998).

At the core of the cycle, is Affirmative Topic Choice. It is the most important part of any AI. If, in fact, knowledge and organizational destiny are as intricately interwoven as we think, then isn't it possible that the seeds of change are implicit in the very first questions we ask? AI theory says 'yes' and takes the idea quite seriously: It says that the way we know people, groups, and organizations is fateful. It further asserts the time is overdue to recognize that symbols and conversations, emerging from all our analytic modes, are among the world's paramount resources.

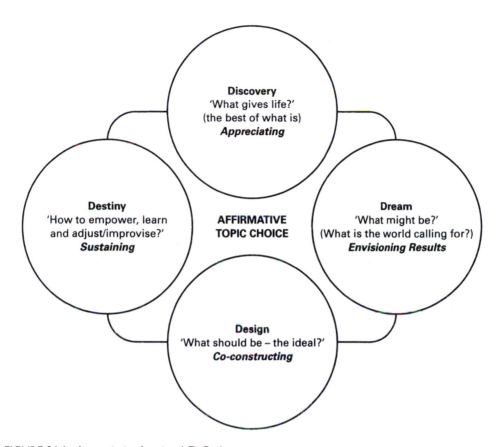

FIGURE 26.1 Appreciative Inquiry 4-D Cycle

BASIC PRINCIPLES OF APPRECIATIVE INQUIRY

To address this question in anything other than Pollyannaish terms, we need to at least comment on the generative-theoretical work that has inspired and given strength to much of AI in practice. Here are five principles and scholarly streams we consider as central to AI's theory-base of change.

1. The Constructionist Principle: Simply stated – human knowledge and organizational destiny are interwoven. To be effective as executives, leaders, change agents, etc., we must be adept in the art of understanding, reading, and analyzing organizations as living, human constructions. Knowing (organizations) stands at the center of any and virtually every attempt at change. Thus, the way we know is fateful.

At first blush this statement appears simple and obvious enough. We are, as leaders and change agents, constantly involved in knowing/inquiring/reading the people and world around us – doing strategic planning analysis, environmental scans, needs analysis, assessments and audits, surveys, focus groups, performance appraisals, and so on. Certainly success hinges on such modes of knowing. And this is precisely where things get more interesting because throughout the academy a revolution is afoot, alive with tremendous ferment and implication, in regard to modernist views of knowledge. In particular, what is confronted is the Western conception of objective, individualistic, historic knowledge – 'a conception that has insinuated itself into virtually all aspects of modern institutional life.' (Gergen, 1985, p. 272). At stake are questions that pertain to the deepest dimensions of our being and humanity: how we know what we know, whose voices and interpretations matter, whether the world is governed by external laws independent of human choices and consciousness, and where is knowledge to be located (in the individual 'mind', or out there 'externally' in nature or impersonal structures)? At stake are issues that are profoundly fundamental, not just for the future of social science but for the trajectory of all our lives.

In our view, the finest work in this area, indeed a huge extension of the most radical ideas in Lewinian thought, can be found in Ken Gergen's Toward Transformation in Social Knowledge (1982) and Realities and Relationships: Soundings In Social Construction (1994). What Gergen does, in both of these, is synthesize the essential whole of the post modern ferment and crucially takes it beyond disenchantment with the old and offers alternative conceptions of knowledge, fresh discourses on human functioning, new vistas for human science, and exciting directions for approaching change. Constructionism is an approach to human science and practice which replaces the individual with the relationship as the locus of knowledge, and thus is built around a keen appreciation of the power of language and discourse of all types (from words to metaphors to narrative forms, etc.) to create our sense of reality – our sense of the true, the good, the possible.

Philosophically it involves a decisive shift in western intellectual tradition from *cogito ergo sum,* to *communicamus ergo sum* and in practice constructionism replaces absolutist claims or the final word with the never ending collaborative quest to understand and construct options for better living. The purpose of inquiry, which is talked about as totally inseparable and intertwined with action, is the creation of 'generative theory,' not so much mappings or explanations of yesterday's world, but anticipatory articulations of tomorrow's possibilities. Constructionism, because of its emphasis on the communal basis of knowledge and its radical questioning of everything that is taken-for-granted as 'objective' or seemingly immutable, invites us to find ways to increase the generative capacity of knowledge. However there are warnings: 'few are prepared', says Gergen (1985, p. 271) 'for such a wrenching, conceptual dislocation. However, for the innovative, adventurous and resilient, the horizons are exciting indeed.' This is precisely the call to which AI has responded. Principle number two takes it deeper.

2. The Principle of Simultaneity: Here it is recognized that inquiry and change are not truly separate moments, but are simultaneous. Inquiry is intervention. The seeds of change – that is, the things people think and talk about, the things people discover and learn, and the things that inform dialogue and inspire images of the future – are implicit in the very first questions we ask. The questions we ask set the stage for what we 'find,' what we 'discover' (the data) becomes the linguistic material, the stories, out of which the future is conceived, conversed about, and constructed.

One of the most impactful things a change agent or practitioner does is to articulate questions. Instinctively, intuitively and tacitly we all know that research of any kind can, in a flash, profoundly alter the way we see ourselves, view reality, and conduct our lives. Consider the economic poll, or the questions that led to the discovery of the atom bomb, or the surveys that, once leaked, created a riot at a unionized automobile plant in London. If we accept the proposition that patterns of social-organizational action are not fixed by nature in any direct biological or physical way, that human systems are made and imagined in relational settings by human beings (socially constructed), then attention turns to the source of our ideas, our discourses, our researches – that is, our questions. Alternations in linguistic practices – including the linguistic practice of crafting questions – hold profound implications for changes in social practice.

One great myth that continues to dampen the potential here is the understanding that first we do an analysis, and then we decide on change. Not so, says the constructionist view. Even the most innocent question evokes change – even if reactions are simply changes in awareness, dialogue, feelings of boredom, or even laughter. When we consider the possibilities in these terms, that inquiry and change are a simultaneous moment, we begin reflecting anew. It is not so much 'Is my question leading to right or wrong answers?' but rather 'What impact is my question having on our lives together ... is it helping to generate conversations about the good, the better, the possible ... Is it strengthening our relationships?'

3. The Poetic Principle: A metaphor here is that human organizations are a lot more like an open book than, say, a machine. An organization's story is constantly being co-authored. Moreover, pasts, presents, or futures are endless sources of learning, inspiration, or interpretation – precisely like, for example, the endless interpretive possibilities in a good piece of poetry or a biblical text. The important implication is that we can study virtually any topic related to human experience in any human system or organization. We can inquire into the nature of alienation or joy, enthusiasm or low morale, efficiency or excess, in any human organization. There is not a single topic related to organizational life that we could not study in any organization.

What constructionism does is remind us that it is not the 'world out there' dictating or driving our topics of inquiry but again the topics are themselves social artifacts, products of social processes (cultural habits, typifying discourses, rhetoric, professional ways, power relations). It is in this vein that AI says: Let us make sure we are not just reproducing the same worlds over and over again because of the simple and boring repetition of our questions (not 'one more' morale survey in which everybody can predict the results ahead of time). AI also says with a sense of excitement and potential, that there can be great gains made in a better linking of the means and ends of inquiry. Options begin to multiply. For example, informally, in many talks with great leaders in the NGO world (Save the Children, World Vision), we have begun to appreciate the profound joy that CEO's feel as 'servant leaders' – and the role this positive effect potentially plays in creating healthy organizations. But then one questions: Is there a book on the Harvard Business book-list, or anywhere for that matter, titled Executive Joy? And even if there isn't, does this mean that joy has nothing to do with good leadership, or healthy human systems? Why aren't we including this topic in our change efforts? What might happen if we did?

What the poetic principle invites is re-consideration of aims and focus of any inquiry in the domain of change management. It is becoming clearer that our topics, like windsocks, continue to blow steadily onward in the direction of our conventional gaze. As we shall soon explore, seeing the world as a problem has become 'very much a way of organizational life.'

4. The Anticipatory Principle: The infinite human resource we have for generating constructive organizational change is our collective imagination and discourse about the future. One of the basic theorems of the anticipatory view of organizational life is that it is the image of the future, which in fact guides what might be called the current behavior of any organism or organization. Much like a movie projector on a screen, human systems are forever projecting ahead of themselves a horizon of expectation (in their talk in the hallways, in the metaphors and language they use) that brings the future powerfully into the present as a mobilizing agent. To inquire in ways that serve to refashion anticipatory reality – especially the artful creation of positive imagery on a collective basis – may be the most prolific thing any inquiry can do.

Our positive images of the future lead our positive actions – this is the increasingly energizing basis and presupposition of Appreciative Inquiry.

5. The Positive Principle: This last principle is not so abstract. It grows out of years of experience with appreciative inquiry. Put most simply, it has been our experience that building and sustaining momentum for change requires large amounts of positive affect and social bonding – things like hope, excitement, inspiration, caring, camaraderie, sense of urgent purpose, and sheer joy in creating something meaningful together. What we have found is that the more positive the question we ask in our work, the more long lasting and successful the change effort. It does not help, we have found, to begin our inquiries from the standpoint of the world as a problem to be solved. We are more effective the longer we can retain the spirit of inquiry of the everlasting beginner. The major thing we do that makes the difference is to craft and seed, in better and more catalytic ways, the unconditional positive question.

Although the positive has not been paraded as a central concept in most approaches to organization analysis and change, it is clear we need no longer be shy about bringing this language more carefully and prominently into our work. And personally speaking, it is so much healthier. We love letting go of 'fixing' the world. We love doing interviews, hundreds of them, into moments of organizational life. And we are, quite frankly, more effective the more we are able to learn, to admire, to be surprised, to be inspired alongside the people with whom we are working. Perhaps it is not just organizations – we too become what we study. So suggested, over and over again, is the life-promoting impact of inquiry into the good, the better, and the possible. A theory of affirmative basis of human action and organizing is emerging from many quarters – social constructionism, image theory, conscious evolution and the like. And the whole thing is beginning, we believe, to make a number of our change-management traditions look obsolete.

APPRECIATIVE INQUIRY AND POWER IN ORGANIZATIONS

We could have easily called this section 'Eulogy for Problem Solving'. In our view, the problem solving paradigm, while once perhaps quite effective, is simply out of sync with the realities of today's virtual worlds. Problem solving approaches to change are

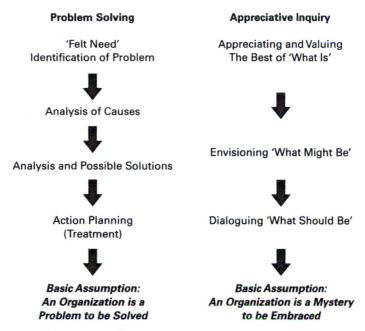

Problem Solving	Appreciative Inquiry
'Felt Need' Identification of Problem	Appreciating and Valuing The Best of 'What Is'
Analysis of Causes	
Analysis and Possible Solutions	Envisioning 'What Might Be'
Action Planning (Treatment)	Dialoguing 'What Should Be'
Basic Assumption: An Organization is a Problem to be Solved	*Basic Assumption: An Organization is a Mystery to be Embraced*

FIGURE 26.2   Problem Solving through Appreciative Inquiry

painfully slow (always asking people to look backward to yesterday's causes); they rarely result in new vision (by definition we can describe something as a problem because we already, perhaps implicitly, assume an ideal, so we are not searching to expansive new knowledge of better ideals but searching how to close 'gaps'); and in human terms problem approaches are notorious for generating defensiveness (it is not my problem but yours). But our real concern, from a social constructionist perspective, has to do with relations of power and control. It is the most speculative part of this chapter; and hopefully, it better illuminates the potentials advocated by AI. In particular is the more conscious linking of language, including the language of our own profession, to change. Words do create worlds – even in unintended ways.

There was an unforgettable moment in a conference in Chicago on AI for inner city change agents, mostly community mobilizers from the Saul Alinsky school of thought, Rules for Radicals. After two days a participant challenges: 'This is naïve ... Have you ever worked in the depths of the inner city, like the Cabrini Green public housing projects? You're asking me to go in and "appreciate" it ... Just yesterday I'm there and the impoverished children are playing soccer, not with a ball, no money for that, but with a dead rat. Tell me about appreciative inquiry in the housing projects!'

It was a powerful question. It was one that made us go deeper theoretically. At one level we were arguing typical approaches to problem diagnosis, including the Alinsky confrontation methods, would work, but at about half the speed of AI. But then as we explored the subject of the cultural consequences of deficit discourse we began seeing a disconcerting relationship between the society-wide escalation of deficit-based change methods and the erosion of people power. The analysis, from here, could proceed from virtually any professional discipline – the diagnostic vocabularies of social work, medicine, organization development, management, law, accounting, community development, editing.

After talking this over with the people in the inner city Chicago conference – and tracing the vocabularies of human deficit not only to the rise of the professions but also to the rise of bureaucracy, skeptical science, original sin theological accounts, the cynical media – the Alinsky-trained activist sat down with a gasp. He said: 'In the name of entertainment, my people are being fed negative views of human violence – and they are surrounded by endless description of their negative "needs" their "problem lives". Even in my methods, the same. And what do I see? I see people asleep in front of their TVs. Unable to move, like sleeping dogs. Yes, they have voice in the housing project assessments. But it is a certain kind of voice ... it is visionless voice. They get to confirm the deficit analysis; all the reports are the same. "Yes," they say, "the reports are true."' What is hitting me right now is how radical the AI message might be. Marx could have said it better: Perhaps the vocabularies of human deficit are the opiates of the masses.

Elsewhere we have cautioned, in our own discipline, that it is not so much the problem solving methodologies per se that are of central concern, but the growing sense that we all, throughout the culture, have taken the tools a step further. It is not so much that organizations have problems, they are problems. (See Figure 26.2.) Somewhere a shift of this kind has taken place. Once accepted as fundamental truth about organizations, virtually everything in change-management becomes infused with a deficit consciousness.

CONCLUSION

To be sure, Appreciative Inquiry (AI) begins an adventure. The urge for and call to adventure have been sounded by many people and many organizations, and it will take many more to fully explore the vast vistas that are now appearing on the horizon.

As said at the outset, we believe we are infants when it comes to our understanding of appreciative processes of knowing and social construction. Yet we are increasingly clear the world is ready to leap beyond methodologies of deficit based changes and enter a domain that is life-centric. Organizations, says AI theory, are centers of human relatedness, first and foremost. And relationships thrive where there is an appreciative eye – when people see the best in one another, when they share their dreams and ultimate concerns in affirming ways, and when they are connected in full voice to create not just new worlds, but better worlds. The velocity and largely informal spread of the appreciative learnings suggests, we believe, a growing sense of disenchantment with exhausted theories of change, especially those wedded to vocabularies of human deficit; and a corresponding urge to work with people, groups, and organizations in more constructive, positive, life-affirming, even spiritual ways. AI, we hope it is being said, is more than a simple 4-D cycle of discovery, dream, design, and destiny. What is being introduced is something deeper at the core. Perhaps our inquiry must become the positive revolution we want to see in the world.

REFERENCES

Barrett, F. (1998). 'Creativity and Improvisation in Jazz and Organizations: Implications for Organizational Learning'. *Organization Science*, 9, 605–22.

Gergen, K. J. (1982). *Toward transformation in social knowledge*. London: Sage.

Gergen, K. J. (1985). The social constructionist movement in psychology. *American Psychologist*, 40, 266–75.

Gergen, K. J. (1994). *Realities and relationships*. Cambridge, MA: Harvard University Press.

27

from stuck debate to new conversation

carol becker, laura chasin, richard chasin,
margaret herzig and sallyann roth

When democracy works well, an emerging political problem stimulates broad and open public discussion. Concerned individuals and groups analyze the dilemma and a wide range of advocates submit carefully argued positions for public deliberation. Political leaders propose policy solutions. Ultimately, a majority of the people, or their representatives, construct a resolution that is acceptable or at least tolerable to everyone.

Many public controversies are resolved through some sequence of problem definition, analysis, advocacy, argument, discussion, compromise, and resolution. However, political disputes do not always follow such a course. Some controversies become defined by opposing views that cluster around two seemingly irreconcilable poles. In these instances, democratic procedures often become perversely counter-productive. Analysis becomes a slave to dogma; advocacy gets laced with vituperation; argument degenerates into diatribe; and discussions deteriorate into shouting matches. Thus every aspect of the public debate is hamstrung by polemics. Compromise is broadly seen as surrender and a widely acceptable resolution becomes hard to imagine. Once disputes become this divisive, the time-honored practices of democracy seem only to intensify and entrench the conflict.

The Public Conversations Project seeks to understand such deadlocks, and more important, to discover and experiment with forms of public discussion that might release hot controversies from polarized public debate so that democratic resolution can become possible. We have been especially interested in what happens to people when they engage in or witness conversations on polarized public issues. How do they speak and listen? What parts of themselves do they open or shut down?

THE DOMINANT DISCOURSE IN POLARIZED PUBLIC DEBATE

Polarized public conversations can be described as conforming to a 'dominant discourse.' The dominant discourse is the most generally available and accepted way of discussing the issue in a public context. For example, the dominant discourse about the American Revolutionary War defined the war as one of colonial liberation. It is not usually described in the United States as a conspiracy of tax dodgers led by a multi-millionaire from Virginia.

Dominant discourses strongly influence which ideas, experiences, and observations are regarded as normal or eccentric, relevant or irrelevant. On a subject that has been hotly polarized for a long time, the dominant discourse often delineates the issue in a win-lose bi-polar way; it draws a line between two simple answers to a complex dilemma and induces people to take a stand on one side of that line or the other. (For example, you are either a royalist or a revolutionary.) Most people who care deeply about the issue yield to this induction.

Being aligned with one group offers benefits. It gives one a socially validated place to stand while speaking and it offers the unswerving support of like-minded people. It also exacts costs. It portrays opponents as a single-minded and malevolent gang. In the face of such frightening and unified adversaries, one's own group must be unified, strong, and certain. To be loyal to that group, one must suppress many uncertainties, morally complicated personal experiences, inner value conflicts, and differences between oneself and one's allies. Complexity and authenticity are sacrificed to the demands of presenting a unified front to the opponent. A dominant discourse of antagonism is self-perpetuating. Win-lose exchanges create losers who feel they must retaliate to regain lost respect, integrity, and security, and winners who fear to lose disputed territory won at great cost.

The dominant discourse on polarized issues is fostered and sustained by a number of forces, most obviously, the media. The drama of polarized debate seems to capture the public's interest more than stories of subtle shifts in understanding on complicated issues. As simplified and dramatic conflicts about a controversial issue become more and more accepted by the public and the media, more complicated viewpoints seem less and less to the point, as if they are not about the issue at all.

Polarized public debates exact costs not only from those who directly participate in them, but also from those who do not. Those who are conflicted or uncertain may come to believe that their views are unwelcome in public discussions. Those who are aware of discordance between some of their personal beliefs and the political position espoused by 'like-minded' others may choose to place themselves safely on the sidelines. They may worry that if they speak about their reluctance to become politically active on one side of the battle line they will be viewed as soft, muddled, unprincipled, or even as traitors. They may stop conversing even with themselves, assuming that if there is no societal validation for their views or the experiences that have shaped their views, then their views and experiences must be worthless, dangerous, or aberrant. The political process is deprived of their voices and their ideas and democracy suffers.

DIALOGUE AS AN ALTERNATIVE TO POLARIZED DEBATE

Dialogue, as we use the term, involves an exchange of perspectives, experiences, and beliefs in which people speak and listen openly and respectfully. In political debates, people speak from a position of certainty, defending their own beliefs, challenging and attacking the other side, and attempting to persuade others to their point of view. They generally speak not as individuals, but as representatives of a position defined by the dominant discourse. In dialogue, participants speak as unique individuals about their own beliefs and experiences, reveal their uncertainties as well as certainties, and try to understand one another. As people in dialogue listen openly and respectfully to each other, their relationship shifts from one of opposition to one of interest – and sometimes to one of compassion and even empathic connection. The limitations of the dominant discourse are often acknowledged and possibilities for moving beyond it may be considered. Differences among participants become less frightening and may even begin to look more like potential social resources than insurmountable social problems. Old patterns of retaliation lose their appeal as the experience of dialogue leaves people feeling listened to and respected rather than beaten and embittered, or victorious and braced for backlash.

BRINGING CLINICAL SKILLS TO WORK ON DIALOGUE

Why did a group of family therapists enter the arena of divisive public issues? We were not certain at the outset that we had anything at all to offer in the realm of 'public conversations.' Our hopefulness was grounded in our observations of similarities between polarized public conversations and 'stuck' family conversations. In conflicted couples and families, each person overgeneralizes and builds a case about the other person. That case is supported by selective perception of confirming data and inattention to exceptions, ambiguity and alternative ideas. In conversations replete with blaming and counter-attack, one hears self-fulfilling prophecies that fuel the futile and seemingly endless conflict.

In our consulting rooms we see families and couples move from impasse to dialogue – from closed to more open conversations. We see that relationships characterized by anger and fear, and relationships of domination and subordination, can be transformed and that people with different experiences and ideas can find ways of being together that do not require either self-silencing or shouting. We hoped to use our clinical skills to create conditions in which partisans trapped in frozen patterns of speaking could shape new ways of talking and listening, in which they could participate fully as complex individuals.

We chose the abortion controversy as the focus of our early efforts in dialogue facilitation. We wondered what would happen if we offered partisans with strong views on abortion an opportunity to experience their differences in a safe atmosphere, one where inner conflicts and ethically perplexing personal experiences would be welcome and urges to convert the other side to the 'correct' way of thinking would be set aside. If we offered them the same sense of safety and respect that we offer our clients, could they speak about the issue and their differences in a way that differed from the predictable accounts favored by the dominant discourse? If so, what previously silent voices might be heard? How would differences and similarities within and across groups be encountered? Through dialogue, could full participation in a group that welcomed diversity come to be valued as much as, or more than, the security of belonging to one 'like-minded' side or the other? If, in such a group, conversation was released from the dams of political correctness, could the free flow of genuine exploration deposit fertile soil for the growth of new ideas and relationships?

OUTLINE OF THE MODEL

The project team has worked together intensively on this project since 1989. Our goal has been to develop and disseminate models that are relatively easy to use so that people who have facilitation skills can conduct dialogue sessions on public issues without having to go through the demanding process of developing models themselves. The model that we have most fully tested is for a single dialogue session among strangers who have different views on abortion.

In our initial telephone call with participants, we take whatever time is needed to describe our process and goals, to answer questions, and to respond to any reservations that a potential participant may express. In the letter, which includes a copy of our dialogue-debate table (see Table 27.1), we reiterate our goals and outline some of the agreements we propose to foster a safe atmosphere during the dialogue. We also give participants some questions to ponder and explicitly request that they bring to the dialogue session 'the part of you that listens thoughtfully and respectfully to others, not the part that is prone to persuade, defend or attack.'

When participants arrive, we share with them a light buffet dinner during which they get acquainted with each other and with us. Each person takes a couple of minutes to say something about him or her self. Participants are asked not to include information that would indicate where they stand on the issue. After dinner, but before going to the interview room, participants sign video releases that they can rescind later.

We begin the session by proposing that participants make agreements with each other to maintain confidentiality; to use respectful language (e.g., 'prolife' and 'prochoice' not 'anti-choice' and 'anti-abortion'); to let each person finish speaking (i.e., no interrupting); and to allow each other to decline to answer any question without needing to explain (i.e., participants have the 'right to pass'). The facilitators outline the schedule for the evening and remind participants that they 'have an opportunity here to have a different conversation, one in which you will be able to share your thoughts and feelings and what you struggle with ... This is a time to speak as unique individuals and be with people with different views and ask questions about which you are genuinely curious.' Participants are also reminded to set aside the urge to persuade.

During the first 45 minutes of the session, the facilitators ask three questions of the participants. The first two questions are answered in 'go-rounds,' that is, each participant answers the same question in turn. The third is answered 'popcorn-style,' i.e., the speaking sequence is determined by readiness to speak, not by seating arrangement.

TABLE 27.1 Distinguishing debate from dialogue*

Debate	Dialogue
Pre-meeting communication between sponsors and participants is minimal and largely irrelevant to what follows.	Pre-meeting contacts and preparation of participants are essential elements of the full process.
Participants tend to be leaders known for propounding a carefully crafted position. The personas displayed in the debate are usually already familiar to the public. The behavior of the participants tends to conform to stereotypes.	Those chosen to participate are not necessarily outspoken 'leaders.' Whoever they are, they speak as individuals whose own unique experiences differ in some respect from others on their 'side.' Their behavior is likely to vary in some degree and along some dimensions from stereotypic images others may hold of them.
The atmosphere is threatening; attacks and interruptions are expected by participants and are usually permitted by moderators.	The atmosphere is one of safety; facilitators propose, get agreement on, and enforce clear ground rules to enhance safety and promote respectful exchange.
Participants speak as representatives of groups.	Participants speak as individuals, from their own unique experience.
Participants speak to their own constituents and, perhaps, to the undecided middle.	Participants speak to each other.
Differences within the 'sides' are denied or minimized	Differences among participants on the same 'side' are revealed, as individual and personal foundations of beliefs and values are explored.
Participants express unswerving commitment to a point of view, approach, or idea.	Participants express uncertainties, as well as deeply held beliefs.
Participants listen in order to refute the other side's data and to expose faulty logic in their arguments. Questions are asked from a position of certainty. These questions are often rhetorical challenges or disguised statements.	Participants listen to understand and gain insight into the beliefs and concerns of the others. Questions are asked from a position of curiosity.
Statements are predictable and offer little new information.	New information surfaces.
Success requires simple impassioned statements.	Success requires exploration of the complexities of the issue being discussed.
Debates operate within the constraints of the dominant public discourse. (The discourse defines the problem and the options for resolution. It assumes that fundamental needs and values are already clearly understood).	Participants are encouraged to question the dominant public discourse, that is, to express fundamental needs that may or may not be reflected in the discourse and to explore various options for problem definition and resolution. Participants may discover inadequacies in the usual language and concepts used in the public debate.

*This table contrasts debate as commonly seen on television with the kind of dialogue we aim to promote in dialogue sessions conducted by the Public Conversations Project. © The Public Conversations Project of the Family Institute of Cambridge, 51 Kondazian Street, Watertown, MA 02172.

After the participants have responded to our opening questions, we invite them to ask questions of each other. Before they start, we suggest that these questions be ones that arise from their genuine curiosity about each other, and not be rhetorical questions or statements in disguise. We remind them that this is not a time to persuade, and we suggest that they speak about themselves and ask questions about each other (not about 'they' and 'them' outside of the room).

About twenty minutes before the session is scheduled to end, we ask: 'What do you think you have done or not done to make this conversation go as it has?' and 'Do you have any parting thoughts that you'd like to share?' At the end, we ask participants if they would like to alter the agreements they made about confidentiality and about allowing us to keep the video of the session for research purposes. We also ask permission to call them for feedback.

A few weeks after the session, we call participants to elicit feedback as a guide to improving the model, to ask about their further thoughts, and to learn what they have taken or might yet take from the session into their lives. Follow-up calls usually last about 45 minutes. Most are taped and transcribed.

GUIDING OBJECTIVES

The principles guiding our work are closely tied to each other and interwoven in each step in the model. In this paper we will somewhat artificially tease out four general objectives and indicate what principles they reflect and what methods they guide. The four objectives are: (1) preparing participants for a journey into the new; (2) creating a safe context; (3) avoiding the old debate; and (4) fostering the co-creation of a new conversation.

PREPARING PARTICIPANTS FOR A JOURNEY INTO THE NEW

In our initial phone call with participants, in the letter of invitation, and in our orienting remarks at the beginning of the session, we clearly distinguish between *dialogue*, as we understand it, and *debate* as typically seen on television (see Table 27.1). We aim to leave no room for misunderstanding about the nature of the event, as we want people to participate with informed consent. We want those who feel unwilling to set aside the urge to persuade, or who are uninterested in respectful exploratory exchanges with the 'other side,' to self-select out of the process. (Only four people, two on each 'side,' have declined participation for such reasons).

There is a second reason for our fully presenting our thinking to participants. Although our structured process is totally voluntary, participants can experience it as so unnatural and anxiety provoking that they may seek refuge in the familiar. To help participants resist this retreat, we highlight the differences between the usual discourse on abortion and a new dialogue among individuals to prepare them for the challenges of their voyage into the new.

We prepare them in many ways. We outline our expectations for their session, spell out specific agreements we will propose to ensure their safety throughout the session, and indicate what they might ponder in getting ready for it. We also hold before them the image of an achievable alternative to divisive debate when we mention that past participants have been able to participate with integrity and respectful curiosity, and speak about their own views and experiences with authenticity.

The careful and patient way we convey this information to participants models the respectfulness and attentiveness that will be expected of them in the dialogue. Our early interactions with participants give them reason to believe that we will diligently assist them in maintaining their agreements and consistently support the part of them that is open to listening respectfully, speaking in new ways, and learning something new about others and about themselves.

CREATING A SAFE CONTEXT

People are unlikely to risk openness with adversaries unless they are assured of safety. If we ask participants to come rhetorically disarmed then we must provide protection. We believe that the extensive care with which we prepare participants for the event contributes to their sense of safety. The more they know about it the safer they feel. What they learn about our approach also helps. They discover immediately that we provide explicit expectations and a definite structure for the session; they need not worry about encountering adversaries in a free-for-all setting. They learn that we ask for specific agreements that effectively reduce any fears they might have of public exposure, rude interruptions, hurtful insults, and pressure to speak against their will.

Another way in which we foster safety is through role clarity regarding process and content. As facilitators, we provide a structure and facilitate a process; we do not contribute on the level of content. We ask for and earn the participants' trust that we will dedicate our energy to their safety as they explore experience and meaning with themselves and each other.

The participants' feeling of safety is also supported by the respectful way in which we involve them in our process of learning. We approach them not as 'subjects,' but as co-investigators. We present ourselves not as all-knowing experts prepared to judge them but as explorers interested in their guidance. In follow-up calls we ask participants about every phase of the process. We ask what helped and what hindered their journey? If participants report uncomfortable moments, we ask if they have ideas as to how we might have helped them at that moment, or reduced their discomfort? Follow-up calls represent opportunities for us not only to learn, but to demonstrate our continued interest in participants' safety, integrity and well-being.

AVOIDING THE OLD DEBATE

Several features of our model constitute interventions designed to prevent the old conversation and make room for a new one. When we ask people not to reveal where they stand on the issue during dinner, we prevent participants from sizing each other up through the lenses of friend or foe. This allows them to meet as unique individuals. They sometimes make guesses about who will be on which side, and find that they are not always correct. This gives them an opportunity to notice their own stereotyping process at work.

When participants enter the dialogue room they are assigned seats next to rather than opposite people with different views. This breaks up the usual face-off of opposing sides and leads to a sequence of responses in the opening go-rounds that highlights variety and interrupts tendencies to group people into 'camps.'

The agreements and guidelines that we propose avoid fruitless and destructive patterns of interaction. The pass rule frees people to make inquiries and it protects everyone from being cornered. The go-round structure and the agreement about not interrupting prevent reactivity and help listeners to set aside habits of preparing responses while others are speaking. Guidelines about speaking personally, avoiding rhetorical questions, and leaving 'they' and 'them' out of the room, block polemics, grandstanding and blaming.

In parting comments and follow-up calls, participants sometimes comment on the liberating effect of these constraints. One man said, 'Taking the superheat out of it at least allows you to hear the other point of view better ... [It] provides an opportunity to be a little more of who you are and a little less guarded.' Another man said that the safety offered through the ground rules allowed him to share his uncertainties. He said, 'If I were debating this issue I wouldn't have told you half these things.' One woman commented at the end of her session that it was 'a personal victory' that she did not feel a need to make a closing comment 'meant to persuade.' Another said that she is usually vulnerable to 'group think' but in this case 'she really felt everything she said.' A few people have said that they noticed themselves biting their tongues. One man, in his closing remarks during the session, said that he didn't feel totally honest setting aside strong language. However, in his follow-up call, he described the tone of the exchange as 'admirable' and he commended the facilitators for 'keeping the thing on track' without making anyone feel 'hamstrung or crowded.' When he was asked about his parting comment during the session, he said that it had been good for him to shape his comments with our guidelines in mind. 'Let's face it,' he said, 'arguments are a dime a dozen. This was unique.'

FOSTERING CO-CREATION OF A NEW CONVERSATION

We begin the process of encouraging a new conversation when we propose and reiterate the 'alternative frame,' i.e., when we set goals and offer guidelines for a conversation that differs fundamentally from debate. We establish a tone that is heartfelt, curious, open and respectful. We set a slow pace. By the time the floor is turned over to participants, they clearly understand how we view the old 'stuck' conversation and what elements we expect may emerge in a new one: curiosity, complexity, personal narrative, and sharing of uncertainties as well as certainties. The opening questions are carefully worded and sequenced to encourage these elements. They are designed with the recognition that chronic political conflict is generally not amenable to resolution through discussions of facts; it is generally rooted in deeply personal experiences and values.

The first question is: *We would like you to say something about your own life experiences in relation to the issue of abortion. For example, something about your personal history with the issue, how you got interested in it, what your involvement has been?* This question grounds the discussion in rich personal narratives and reveals connections between strongly held beliefs and subjective experiences. For some participants, it leads to reflections on the beliefs that were 'in the air' in their families. For some it elicits poignant stories about abortions, adoptions, tragedies, triumphs and complicated turns of events in the lives of individuals and families. Interest is high and curiosity is stirred; no story is predictable.

> *Prolife Woman:* As a sophomore, my closest friend took it upon herself to be president of the prolife group on campus … [She] was physically handicapped with cerebral palsy and she was very concerned about the value our society places on handicapped individuals. She died, for reasons we still don't understand to this day, and I couldn't bear to see all that she worked so hard for go by the wayside…. At this point, I had come to what I term a prolife feminist position.

> *Prochoice Man:* Well, I was catapulted into this many decades ago because my sister had an abortion and it turned out that the baby's father was my father. And that's a hard place to begin to think about all this stuff. When I was married, my wife had three miscarriages before our son was born and I have seen what it does to a woman, even in terms of that being something she has no control over…. I cannot advise people about [abortion]. I have to see what their particular feeling is.

The second question, *What's at the heart of the matter for you as an individual?* gives people an opportunity to say what they need to say about their convictions but it locates the core of the issue in the heartfelt, the unique and the personal. Throughout the session, our language draws participants' attention to what they care most about.

> *Prochoice Woman:* I think the moral maturity of women is what's really at stake for me. Anything that legislates or removes choice from an individual woman removes respect for her as a mature, moral person who is capable of making decisions that are right for her in the context of her life and her relationships.

> *Prolife Woman:* The fact that a child is wanted or not wanted by someone else – it would frighten me to think that the importance of my life is contingent upon the fact that someone wants me. I am special in myself and it doesn't matter to me whether someone wants me. My life certainly shouldn't depend on it at any stage.

We pose the third question as follows: *Many people have within their general approach to abortion some gray areas, some dilemmas about their own beliefs, or even some conflicts within themselves. Sometimes these gray areas are revealed when people consider hard cases – circumstances in which a prolife person might want to allow an abortion, or situations in which a prochoice person might not want to permit an abortion. Or, in a very different way, sometimes an individual feels that his or her own views on abortion come into conflict with other important values and beliefs. We have found it to be productive and helpful when people share whatever dilemmas, struggles, and conflicts they have within their prevailing view. We invite you to mention any pockets of uncertainty or lesser certainty, any concerns, value conflicts, or mixed feelings you may have and wish to share.* This question brings forth differentiation among the views of those with similar positions and suggests bridges between those on different sides. It encourage participants to grapple with the complexity of their own views.

> *Prolife Man:* I guess the way I look at it, if you terminate that life ... there's an evil there. If it's a case of an unwanted pregnancy, there's an evil there. If it's a byproduct of rape or incest, if you have a severely impaired baby in the process, all of those things are evils. And where the uncertainty comes in for me is [in a situation like] a 13 year old girl has just been raped by her uncle and it's basically going to destroy her life.... And I can't just sit there and say, on my high moral horse, 'it's the ultimate universal wrong to kill an unborn child.' Because I know that there are other bad things in the world and you've got to balance them.

> *Prochoice Woman:* The sanctity of life is precious to me ... and I don't think God takes it lightly that we make a decision about choosing to end a life, for whatever reason it may be. I would like us not to make abortion something we can do without having to think about it.... I don't think there is a right answer. Sometimes there is a less bad answer than another.

> *Prolife Woman:* One time I was discussing this issue with a friend and he said, 'Obviously you never grew up an unwanted child.' And he was right, they wanted me. I think of the children that suffer and think to myself, would it have been better if they had been aborted? Then I think, well, they have life. But it's really hard to watch children in pain and sometimes it's hard to be prolife, but I'm so prolife. So that's something I really struggle with.

> *Prochoice Woman:* After I had my baby I realized that I would never have an abortion, personally. That changed my personal view of abortion.... It bothers me that there hasn't been much dialogue within the prochoice community about how far along abortions should be allowed. To me an end point would be 5 or 6 months. That, to me, is the point where we are talking about a baby, not a fetus.

Some prolife participants have said that their moral position about abortion conflicts with their political belief in a pluralistic society founded on the idea that different values can co-exist. A prochoice woman said that thoughts about the damage done to children by drugs and alcohol before they are born are what evoke in her compassion for the fetus. This is when she entertains the idea that the fetus may have rights. A feminist prolife woman explained her belief that legal abortions allow women to be used by men who do not have to take responsibility for their actions; abortion becomes a substitute for finding solutions to the social problems of our time. She said that a woman's choice is not a genuine choice until it is made in the context of equally viable alternatives. She indicated that she is ambivalent about prohibiting abortions in a society without adequate supports for women facing unplanned pregnancies.

During the time in which we call for questions of curiosity, we have witnessed many meaningful and interesting exchanges. A prochoice leader asked a prolife leader if he could think of any reasons for keeping abortion legal. He said that he could: women would not die from illegal abortions. A Jewish prochoice woman asked a Catholic prolife woman active in Operation Rescue to describe her views about the relationship between abortion and the soul. The prolife woman disclosed a complex belief system about what happens to the soul of an aborted baby.

Hearing about beliefs in a more complex manner that can be conveyed through slogans, hearing about ambiguities usually suppressed, and finding and revealing one's own silenced complexities and dilemmas can be both humbling and empowering. At the end of one session, one woman said, 'None of us knows the truth. But together we can come closer to the truth. We can be safe, liberated and accepted. We can continue struggling, even though we may never have it right.' Sometimes the experience of listening and speaking in a new way in the dialogue group contains lessons for participants' personal relationships. One woman said, 'I'm afraid I really don't make room for others' views if they are different from mine. I don't make room for my husband's views. I don't like that about myself. I want to change that.' Another woman commented that it is hard to share personal experiences with people who hold opposing ideological positions, 'but this is, in my mind how human community is formed and deepens. We do not change the world by staying on two sides of the fence and yelling at each other.'

DIALOGUE IN DEMOCRACY

Each of us joined the project with somewhat different perspectives and experiences pertaining to the abortion debate, but all of us have come to appreciate how much our thinking had been constrained by the dominant discourse on abortion and the stereotypes it fosters. Witnessing and facilitating these conversations has been a source of humility and excitement. It has deepened our commitment to the project's objectives. Our experiences have reinforced our belief that the rhetoric of the abortion controversy has belittled valid concerns, denigrated positive social values, and obscured rich and complex meanings. We are increasingly certain that dialogue is essential to the democratic society, to keep it alive in spirit and practice as well as in law, to keep it responsive to its diverse participants, and inclusive of all who live their lives within it. We count among our own ways of participating in democracy our work on this project and we are delighted to have the opportunity to share this work with our colleagues.

reading culture

part six

Wwe are everywhere and at all times constructing meaning. Most of the preceding chapters focus on making meaning through language. However, the focus on language is limited. Language is typically entwined with actions, objects, structures and patterns of interchange – in what Wittgenstein (1963) calls 'forms of life.' Thus, in our choice of clothing or food, magazines or television programs, toothpaste or watches, we are also generating meaningful cultural forms – either sustaining the old or creating the new, and often doing both simultaneously. Although everyday objects and practices may seem unremarkable in many respects ('just normal life'), the consequences of the commonplace can be enormous – both for good and ill. There is an increasing public consciousness of this fact – represented, for example, in the realization that otherwise trivial practices of consumption can deplete the ozone layer, destroy species of wildlife, pollute the air and water, and contribute to worker exploitation in Third World countries. Scholars now extend this critical consciousness in rich and significant directions, and it is to this work that the present section is devoted.

Congenial with the constructionist investments in liberation and cultural reconstruction, scholars from across the disciplines are turning reflexive attention to our common cultural practices. They focus on everything from small details to powerful movements, sometimes helping us see the subtle symbolic dimensions of the commonplace or enabling us to appreciate how various objects or actions sustain a tradition. At other times such scholarship attempts to create reflexive resistances to the taken-for-granted. In a constructionist vein, we may view these reflections on cultural life as *readings*; they are not accurate probings but provocative ways of interpreting our ways of life. We do not find here maps or pictures of the way things are, but lenses of understanding. In this sense, the works invite collective dialogue from which new futures can be created.

The range and richness of inquiry into cultural life defies convenient summary. A sense of the landscape may be gained by exploring such works as *Media, Culture and Society* (Collins et al., 1986), *Rethinking Popular Culture* (Mukerji and Schudson, 1991), *An Introduction to Theories of Popular Culture* (Strinati, 1995), *Channels of Discourse, Reassembled* (Allen, 1992), *Exploring Media Culture* (Real, 1996), and *Cultural Studies* (Grossberg, Nelson, and Treichler, 1992). In the present volume, we sample from both classic and contemporary contributions. We begin with a selection from Roland Barthes, a major figure in the development of French literary theory. Although Barthes' produced over 20 volumes of writing during his career, his small work, *Mythologies*, essentially established the genre of 'cultural reading.' In this work, Barthes explores the layers of cultural meaning embedded in such commonplaces as margarine, soap-powders, steak and chips, and striptease. Here we share an excerpt from his illuminating analysis of wrestling (Reading 27), an analysis that adds layers of significant meaning to what might otherwise seem a degraded form of popular entertainment.

With Ariel Dorfman's work (Reading 28), we move from France to Chile, where a far different intellectual climate prevails. While France has long enjoyed the status of a major world power, many Chilean intellectuals like Dorfman join other Latin American scholars in seeing their cultures threatened by the world powers. At times these threats can be direct – both economically and militarily. However, the most insidious threats are what they see as subtle infiltrations of the commonplace – products, media, tourism and the like. As reasoned, when another culture's objects and meanings enter into one's own, they may erode long-standing values and ways of life. Many Latin American scholars in particular, place a high value on the communally oriented traditions, and believe that a prosperous future depends on linking these traditions to a socialist economic system. Thus, with the infiltration of capitalist/individualist artifacts and meanings from the dominant powers, both their traditions and their dreams for the future are undermined. Dorfman's book, *How to Read Donald Duck*, with Armand Mattelart, was written as an angry response to cultural invasion. The work, which became an instant classic – subsequently translated into eleven languages – allowed the world to see that even the most innocent media, in this case children's comics, are saturated with ideology. The present offering reflects Dorfman's passion and insight.

While critique is a dominant theme for cultural analysts, many find patterns worthy of praise. Typically these are patterns disparaged or suppressed by the dominant culture; they often stand as creative forms of resistance to the dominant culture. In effect, the analyst provides a lens enabling the reader to find value in otherwise devalued forms of resistance. Perhaps the classic offering of this kind is Dick Hebdige's 1979 volume, *Subculture: The Meaning of Style*. In this work Hebdige first offered a way of understanding the development of new sub-cultures. Where many analysts have worried about the homogenization of culture resulting from mass media, Hebdige was struck with the creative resistance of young people to the dominant culture. In his analysis of punk culture, he generates a certain admiration for the seemingly anti-cultural youth movements. The reader will readily appreciate the implications of Hebdige's insights (Reading 30) as they may apply today to Goths, Nerds, and Punks. Whether such an orientation extends to neo-Nazi or skinhead movements is an interesting topic for debate.

Our final offering in this section also moves us past simple critique to confront us with difficult issues of cultural difference. Here Lama Abu Odeh (Reading 31), a feminist scholar from Jordan, takes up the issue of the veil. The veiling of the face is a tradition embraced by Muslim women, but largely condemned by Western feminists. For feminists, the veil is often seen as a form of patriarchal control. It sustains the dominance of the male over the female, and suppresses the potential for female autonomy, development, and self-expression. However, while Abu Odeh is party to such culture critique, she is also immersed in Muslim culture. Through a sensitive interpretation of her home culture, she is able to enrich our understanding of the veil. In effect, she provides us with multiple cultural readings, and in doing so mutes the comfortable distinctions between good and evil.

REFERENCES

Allen, R. C. (1992). *Channels of discourse, reassembled*. Chapel Hill, NC: University of North Carolina Press.

Collins, R., et al. (1986). *Media, culture and society: A critical reader*. Thousand Oaks, CA, London: Sage.

Grossberg, L., Nelson, C., and Treichler, P. (1992). *Cultural Studies*. New York: Routledge.

Hebdige, D. (1979). *Subculture: The Meaning of Style*. London: Routledge.

Mukerji, C., and Schudson, M. (1991). *Rethinking popular culture: Contemporary perspectives in cultural studies*. Berkeley: Univ. of CA Press.

Real, M. R. (1996). *Exploring media culture*. Thousand Oaks, CA, London: Sage.

Strinati, D. (1995). *An introduction to theories of popular culture*. New York: Routledge.

Wittgenstein, L. (1963). *Philosophical investigations (Translated by G. E. M. Anscombe)*. London: Blackwell.

28

the world of wrestling

roland barthes

The grandiloquent truth of gestures on life's great occasions.

Baudelaire

The virtue of all-in wrestling is that it is the spectacle of excess. Here we find a grandiloquence which must have been that of ancient theatres. And in fact wrestling is an open-air spectacle, for what makes the circus or the arena what they are is not the sky (a romantic value suited rather to fashionable occasions), it is the drenching and vertical quality of the flood of light. Even hidden in the most squalid Parisian halls, wrestling partakes of the nature of the great solar spectacles, Greek drama and bull-fights: in both, a light without shadow generates an emotion without reserve.

There are people who think that wrestling is an ignoble sport. Wrestling is not a sport, it is a spectacle, and it is no more ignoble to attend a wrestled performance of Suffering than a performance of the sorrows of Arnolphe or Andromaque.* Of course, there exists a false wrestling, in which the participants unnecessarily go to great lengths to make a show of a fair fight; this is of no interest. True wrestling, wrongly called amateur wrestling, is performed in second-rate halls, where the public spontaneously attunes itself to the spectacular nature of the contest, like the audience at a suburban cinema. Then these same people wax indignant because wrestling is a stage-managed sport (which ought, by the way, to mitigate its ignominy). The public is completely uninterested in knowing whether the contest is rigged or not, and rightly so; it

*In Molière's *L'École des Femmes* and Racine's *Andromaque*.

abandons itself to the primary virtue of the spectacle, which is to abolish all motives and all consequences: what matters is not what it thinks but what it sees.

This function of grandiloquence is indeed the same as that of ancient theatre, whose principle, language and props (masks and buskins) concurred in the exaggeratedly visible explanation of a Necessity. The gesture of the vanquished wrestler signifying to the world a defeat which, far from disguising, he emphasizes and holds like a pause in music, corresponds to the mask of antiquity meant to signify the tragic mode of the spectacle. In wrestling, as on the stage in antiquity, one is not ashamed of one's suffering, one knows how to cry, one has a liking for tears.

Each sign in wrestling is therefore endowed with an absolute clarity, since one must always understand everything on the spot. As soon as the adversaries are in the ring, the public is overwhelmed with the obviousness of the roles. As in the theatre, each physical type expresses to excess the part which has been assigned to the contestant. Thauvin, a fifty-year-old with an obese and sagging body, whose type of asexual hideousness always inspires feminine nicknames, displays in his flesh the characters of baseness, for his part is to represent what, in the classical concept of the *salaud*, the 'bastard' (the key-concept of any wrestling-match), appears as organically repugnant. The nausea voluntarily provoked by Thauvin shows therefore a very extended use of signs: not only is ugliness used here in order to signify baseness, but in addition ugliness is wholly gathered into a particularly repulsive quality of matter: the pallid collapse of dead flesh (the public calls Thauvin *la barbaque*, 'stinking meat'), so that the passionate condemnation of the crowd no longer stems from its judgement, but instead from the very depth of its humours. It will thereafter let itself be frenetically embroiled in an idea of Thauvin which will conform entirely with this physical origin: his actions will perfectly correspond to the essential viscosity of his personage.

The physique of the wrestlers therefore constitutes a basic sign, which like a seed contains the whole fight. But this seed proliferates, for it is at every turn during the fight, in each new situation, that the body of the wrestler casts to the public the magical entertainment of a temperament which finds its natural expression in a gesture. ... Sometimes the wrestler triumphs with a repulsive sneer while kneeling on the good sportsman; sometimes he gives the crowd a conceited smile which forebodes an early revenge; sometimes, pinned to the ground, he hits the floor ostentatiously to make evident to all, the intolerable nature of his situation; and sometimes he erects a complicated set of signs meant to make the public understand that he legitimately personifies the ever-entertaining image of the grumbler, endlessly confabulating about his displeasure.

We are therefore dealing with a real Human Comedy, where the most socially-inspired nuances of passion (conceit, rightfulness, refined cruelty, a sense of 'paying one's debts') always felicitously find the clearest sign which can receive them, express them and triumphantly carry them to the confines of the hall. It is obvious that at such a pitch, it no longer matters whether the passion is genuine or not. What the public wants is the image of passion, not passion itself. There is no more a problem of truth in wrestling than in the theatre. In both, what is expected is the intelligible representation of moral situations which are usually private....

What is thus displayed for the public is the great spectacle of Suffering, Defeat, and Justice. Wrestling presents man's suffering with all the amplification of tragic masks. The wrestler who suffers in a hold which is reputedly cruel (an arm-lock, a twisted leg) offers an excessive portrayal of Suffering; like a primitive Pietà, he exhibits for all to see his face, exaggeratedly contorted by an intolerable affliction. It is obvious, of course, that in wrestling reserve would be out of place, since it is opposed to the voluntary ostentation of the spectacle, to this Exhibition of Suffering which is the very aim of the fight. This is why all the actions which produce suffering are particularly spectacular, like the gesture of a conjuror who holds out his cards clearly to the public. Suffering which appeared without intelligible cause would not be understood; a concealed action that was actually cruel would transgress the unwritten rules of wrestling and would have no more sociological efficacy than a mad or parasitic gesture. On the contrary suffering appears as inflicted with emphasis and conviction, for everyone must not only see that the man suffers, but also and above all understand why he suffers.

29

the lone ranger, barbar and other innocent heroes

ariel dorfman

These essays were originally written for someone whose name and face I cannot remember. She was a slum dweller, a woman whom I only met twice, years ago, in Chile.

Even then, I didn't notice anything special about her. Misery has a way of leveling individual nuances. In recollection, therefore, she turns into a blurred picture. She was very poor, and lived in one of the numerous shantytowns that mushroom around all big cities in Latin America. They brim with migrant workers and their families. She, like them, had built a small shack out of any stray sort of material that life had washed within her reach. I vaguely recall that she had children, and there must have been many of them. The rest is conjecture, almost a sociological construct, valid for her as for so many other women living in those subhuman conditions. Filth, disease, hunger, and a husband who was unemployed, alcoholic, or plagued by worse demons. Or maybe no husband at all. I just don't remember.

But what she said to me on the two separate occasions when we talked still rings clear. An intellectual, I suppose, remembers words better than people.

She came up to me and asked quite frankly if it was true that I thought people shouldn't read photo novels? Photo novels are just like comics, but instead of using drawings, they convey their romantic love stories through photographs peopled by handsome actors. When she asked me the question, I was digging a ditch. I had come to that shanty town with my students in order to help after a severe thunderstorm had left everything a sea of mud. They had been talking to the slum dwellers and had informed this particular woman of my crusade against the industrial products of fiction. Comics, soap operas, westerns, radio and TV sitcoms, love songs, films of violence – you name it – I had it under scrutiny.

So I stopped digging and answered her. It was true. I thought that photo novels were a hazard to her health and her future.

She did not seem to feel any special need for purification. 'Don't do that to us, *compañerito*,' she said in a familiar, almost tender way. 'Don't take my dreams away from me.'

We were unable – and now I suspect I understand the reasons – to convince each other. She wanted, she needed, to dream. I wanted to dissect those dreams, the ones that had nourished my childhood and adolescence, that continued to infect so many of my adults habits and simply would not disappear. I wanted to discover the underlying principles of the buried behavioral models which simmered inside me. But there were other, more significant, reasons for what I was doing. I believed that these models and illusions clashed head-on with the immediate needs of their consumers. This was especially so in a land like Chile, which imported most of these forms of entertainment or simply imitated them in bastardized local versions. We imported our weapons, our machinery, our banking techniques, our freeways, our technology. We also imported much of our popular culture. But this was of little importance to the woman in front of me. She required those illusions in order to survive. She had to make up somehow for what was missing in her life, and she didn't mind – or care – if she was being manipulated. So what sort of conversation could we hold, if I couldn't offer her any concrete alternative or substitute for those myths? Between the nakedness of her urgent, practical needs and my own psychological and intellectual needs there was not much room, or chance, for a fruitful dialogue.

Some months later, as will happen from time to time, history stepped into our lives, and that dialogue became possible – indeed, imperative: In September 1970, Salvador Allende was elected president of Chile.

Her attitude, and mine, were about to be modified.

A few years went by – that would make it 1972 or the beginning of 1973 – and I returned to that same part of town for some sort of inauguration. It might have been a neighborhood clinic or an alphabetization center. (There were many buildings and events in those days.) By chance, I ran into that woman again. I didn't recognize her at first, but she remembered me. She came up to me, just like that, and announced that I was right, that she didn't read 'trash' anymore. Then she added a phrase which still haunts me. 'Now, *compañero*, we are dreaming reality.'

She had experienced, in those years, something truly different. She had outdistanced her old self, and was no longer entertained by those images which had been her own true love. She could now oppose her experience of liberation, and that of her community, to the fraudulent visions of the media, run and owned by the same people who ran and owned Chile's economy and political system. She no longer perceived those media experiences as real, as eternal, as natural.

Of course, what had happened to her was happening to everybody. When a people attempt to liquidate centuries' worth of economic and social injustice, when they begin to gain a sense of their dignity as a nation, what is really at stake, what really inspires them, is an alternate vision of humanity, a different way of feeling and thinking and projecting and loving and keeping faith. And a different future. Allende's government nationalized our natural resources and minerals, reallocated the land to those who tilled it, allowed workers to participate in the management of their own factories, and democratized most of society's institutions. But that was not enough. Simultaneously we had to democratize and control a territory more difficult to split up and expropriate, a territory called communication.

That woman from the slums was being shoved, poked, awakened. And while she was in that turbulent, searching stage, what she needed was a parallel interpretation at all levels of what her situation, of what the world, was. Not just a political explanation of why things were one way and how they might be transformed, but channels for expressing the joys, the doubts, the anxieties that come when people who were previously powerless begin to have some say in their existence. What she needed was a new language.

The Chilean people and its intellectuals tried to produce that new language, or at least fragments, intimations of it. We had always proclaimed that here was one task the dispossessed could not postpone. They had to take control of the production of their own ideas and gain access to the means and methods which would help them communicate with one another. The task could not be postponed, and yet it was, time and again. Without effective outlets, resources, industries, what else could be done but patiently fabricate with the scantest of means an extended, almost subterranean network of cultural visions?

Allende's victory gave this enterprise a real grounding, and a vaster dimension. At least, what had previously been declared by generations of politicians and intellectuals to be urgent and unavoidable could now be put into practice. The economic transformations had placed in the hands of the government and the workers the industrial tools and human resources necessary to attempt a profound alteration of mass culture's fictional outgrowths. There were printing presses, record companies, television and radio programs available. For the first time, it was within our means to conceive and explore far-reaching creative alternatives to existing mass-market fictions. I was personally involved in producing new comic books, in inexpensive paperback literature sold on news stands, a series of TV programs, a magazine for adolescents.

The problems the people involved in this undertaking had to solve were gigantic. How to subtly use and change publications, programs, and formats which already had a following; how to create new messages without making them into propaganda; how to find new ways of distribution and getting feedback; how to stimulate contributions from a generally passive audience. And how to do all this without losing money.

Among all these pressing matters, one in particular attracted me. In order to change a structure, it became necessary to understand it, to examine the manner in which these prevailing fantasies functioned. Why did these widespread myths enjoy such an immense success among the very people whose daily practices should have called them into question?

These essays were conceived as one of many responses to that need. So, during their first incarnation, they were born for eminently practical reasons. The purpose of investigations such as these, and books like *How to Read Donald Duck* (which I co-authored with the Belgian sociologist Matelart), was to expose the mechanisms behind those industrialized works of fiction, strip them of their mystery, or lay bare their secret structures. To do so, we felt, would assist in the elaboration of another sort of communications system which would reject authoritarian and competitive models and provoke doubts, questions, dialogue, real participation, and, eventually, a breakthrough in popular art.

But the essays transcended their utilitarian ends. If this were not so, it wouldn't make much sense to present them ten years later to foreign readers. I believe that those irreverent views still retain their relevance. Once you have penetrated the invisible network of everyday domination which lurks behind the genres and characters analyzed here (children's mass literature of assorted varieties, superheroes, the infantilization of knowledge in magazines such as *Reader's Digest*), you are left with something far more valuable than a mere guidebook on how to read popular culture. What unfolds before us is a veritable black-and-blueprint of the ways in which men and women repress themselves in contemporary society, the way they transform reality's unsettling questions into docile, comforting, bland answers.

It is this inadvertent process of self-censorship that is meant to be revealed by a book like this one. And such a process does not happen only in Chile. On the contrary, if people in the so-called Third World are expected to swallow these deformed versions of reality (along with heavier goods and foreign technology), it is because those messages have been produced by the 'developed' countries in the first place and injected into their populace in hardly more sophisticated forms. The same methods which the cultural industry uses to narrate, observe, transmit problems in Europe and especially in the U.S. are those which, with minor modifications and at times adaptations, are imported into our miserable and twisted zones.

Their point of view is supposed to be accepted as the universally valid means of human measurement, definition, and perspective, the only one by which we can see ourselves in the global mirror. I'll go deeper into this subject as the book progresses, but it is worth noting here that this imposition is possible, among other reasons, because within their own borders the industrial nations have already colonized their own conflicting social strata – their minorities, their women, their working classes, their immigrants, their unruly and rebellious elements. The Third World of humanity is just a filthy, undesirable, oversized, underdeveloped brother to the fourth, fifth, sixth, and infinite contradictory worlds which teem within the frontiers of the 'advanced' nations.

Among all these subordinate worlds there is one, however, which might be more important than all the rest, which might be the only universal world, and which constitutes the axis of all processes of domination: namely, the world of children. No matter whether a country is oozing with opulence or on the path to pauperdom, the new generation is always required to accept the status quo of their parents, comfortably, devoutly, and without interruption, at the same time learning to judge and preinterpret every rupture and rift in reality with the same indisputable assumptions used by their forefathers.

Since those communities, classes, races, continents, and individuals who don't fit the official mold tend to be viewed as 'children,' as incomplete beings who haven't yet reached the age of maturity, it is children's literature, or the infantilization of mass market adult literature, which forms the basis for the entire process of cultural domination....

In the first few frames of the episode 'Safe Kids,' we are presented with a meeting of the Founding Fathers of Duckland Club. 'It is the duty of all fathers to watch over their children,' says an antiquated female mastodon from the podium. One of the audience members is Donald Duck, who admits that if his nephews were in trouble, 'I would resort to my extraordinary strength and skill to save them.' He soon gets the chance to put his knowledge and foresight into practice. They are about to travel to South America ('full of danger'). Apparently we are in the presence of a protective, paternalistic attitude except, the adult world – Donald in particular – is satirized from the first scene on. The grown-ups are ridiculous, squinting, archaic, grotesque, and mock-solemn; they smile idiotically, adopt rigid postures, and are gathered for an absurd purpose. They are caricatures of parents. In the multitude we see dogs, hogs, and human beings all mixed together. And Donald is the worst of all. His showing off, trite observations, and know-it-all answers are made even more ironic by his pathetic, scrawny figure (his feet don't even touch the floor), his imbecilic expression, and his one-track mind.

Sure enough, the following frames bear out this critical intent. On board a boat, his nephews calmly contemplate the dock as it moves away from them. Donald (boasting that he'll save the kids if they get into trouble) promptly loses his balance and falls overboard, and it is the youngsters who must save him. This situation is repeated to excess. Donald is awkward, unsteady, cowardly; he constantly makes mistakes, doesn't plan ahead, is egotistical and disorderly. His nephews must constantly rescue him from the most unlikely predicaments. His is a topsy-turvy world, a fact that is emphasized by four or five frames in which Donald is drawn with his feet up in the air (falling down, floating upside down, etc.). The adult is worthless, in spite of his grandiloquence and external gestures.

Although we should bear in mind that this is a comic genre, and that one of the functions of laughter is to shift the weight of society onto those beings who don't know how to fulfill properly their obligations, there is unquestionably more to it than that. In Disney's world, children represent goodness and intelligence, and they are joined by quite a number of other small beings who are more mature than their elders and who emerge triumphant from various adventures: the chipmunks Chip 'n' Dale, the Little Bad Wolf, Dumbo, the fairy Tinkerbell, the mice Gus and Jacques, Jiminy Cricket, the Three Little Pigs, Thumper the rabbit, and Scamp the dog. In other words, he allows his readers to immerse themselves in the dream of all who are on the outside looking in – namely, to criticize those in power and expose them as eccentric, outlandish, dim-witted failures.

However, it is necessary to ask from what vantage point is the critique of Donald Duck and his foolish escapades directed, according to what standards and which norms? First of all, there are, of course, Donald's own indisputable and unfulfilled intentions: to establish an order that protects the defenseless from harm. But, more to the point, Donald is judged by the responsible actions of his nephews. They embody all the things that he should be. They are rational, provident, generous, wise, prudent, courageous – in a word, paternal.

What has happened is that Donald Duck, in his adult form, is really a child; and the little ducks, in their children's form, are really adults. The child (or the adult) reading this narrative takes to task a Donald Duck who embodies all the characteristics that are supposed to be infantile; and he aligns himself with the nephews, who symbolize the sacred virtues of maturity. To give but one example: Huey, Dewey, and Louie base their knowledge of reality on their 'Junior Woodchucks Manual,' where their entire universe (including, naturally, South America) is found to be defined and prescribed.

There is nothing new under the sun. Everything has already been written down; everything is already known.

All you have to do to make threats and dilemmas go away is to consult a dictionary of the established and the proven. Even chance, the great protagonist-adventurer of these cartoons, is subordinate to order and reason. If Donald would only subscribe to these categories, he would no longer be laughable, and there wouldn't be any discord in the world.

Once the child identifies with other children who are really adults, he participates in his own self-domination, thereby circumscribing his freedom not only to become another person, but also to invent another kind of world. In this way his natural rebellious energies – which should normally be used to question the established order and risk imagining one that is different – are neutralized. It is as if all the characters (and the reader) were trapped in a 'nineteenth century orphanage' where no one ever engendered them. Without an escape via biological growth, without the capacity to exercise moral repudiation, without an artistic language to shatter their drab existence, they will live forever on the tyrannical merry-go-round of dominant-versus-dominated, competing to join the club of the fortunate, the rich, and the adult. The instability of this world, where anyone can be displaced at any moment and once again have to begin his mad dash against the others, is not, however, total. For while this delirious pace is maintained, great care is taken not to raise doubts about the foundations of society or its basic tenets – there will always be one voice or one position that offers a wise word to point us in the right direction; for if there weren't, we would be in the anguished terrain of art.

People can be questioned; values are eternal.

In order to prove that this is the message, it will be useful to analyze another Donald Duck episode. Donald and his nephews are sweating it out on rich Uncle Scrooge McDuck's farm. As usual, Donald complains. If he had a million dollars he wouldn't have to feed the pigs, milk the cows, or plow the soil. But Huey, Dewey, and Louie understand that that kind of whining is for little kids. 'Unca Donald is hollering his head off about work, as usual,' one of them announces. 'I know! He's too young to understand things – that boy!' They, on the other hand, are different. They appreciate the meaning and value of work (as Uncle Scrooge himself later recognizes when he plans to raise their salary ten cents a week). 'If you're gonna wear a light wool jacket, you've gotta *work* to get the wool,' says one of the nephews. Another, gleefully running among the hens, adds, 'If you like poached eggs on toast, you've got to *work* to get the eggs.'

Donald, however, does not want to recognize that behind money there is effort. It would be easier, he says, as he stomps on a plant, to go to the store and buy 'one of these doggoned cucumbers, or whatever they are.' But you would need 'a million bucks' for that. As he explains to his lucky cousin Gladstone Gander a little while later, after abandoning his chores, it's a question of luck. He tries to convince the lucky goose that he desires such a sum for the two of them. Gladstone does not act immediately, because in recent days his good luck has led him to a diamond ring and gold nugget. But he finally gives in, and naturally a couple of million promptly drops into those two lazy barnyard birds' hats.

As a result of this miraculous catch, the readers will have the opportunity to judge who is right – Donald or his nephews. They will also receive a lesson on the origin of Wealth (of Nations) on the side, because all those bills actually belong to Uncle Scrooge. A tornado emptied the enormous silo where the tightwad hoarded his septillions in order to confuse thieves, and they have been scattered 'all over the place.' The old curmudgeon doesn't bat an eyelash. He must certainly have read Adam Smith, and Voltaire's *Candide*, for that matter. 'Who cares?' he says. 'As long as I stay here and worry about my string beans and pumpkins. I'll get it all back.' In other words, '*Il faut cultiver son jardin.*' The children also stay put when Donald suggests a round-the-world trip. Frugal, honest, loyal – their concern for the weak serves to exalt them in our eyes. 'The pigs and chickens need us.' Perhaps they are murmuring, '*Il faut cultiver le jardin des autres*' (You must cultivate the gardens of others, too).

Donald, in turn, is tired of being exploited, so he and Gladstone leave on a tour of the world. Disney tends never to introduce unpleasant things such as hunger, lack of shelter, cold, or disease into his world. (Just try to get these things past the turn-stiles at Disneyland sometime!) So there's always been something fishy about Donald's habitual compulsions. His search for money owes more to hysteria and overindulgence than to basic brute necessity. His needs are as false as his eternal unemployment.

In this particular cartoon, tourism and leisure seem to be the prevalent preoccupations. Not just the duck and the goose, but all those who held out their hands have received their million and gone on vacation, fleeing their immediate circumstances.

Which means that there's no one left to pump gas, no one to cook at the diner, no one to drive the bus to some other place. Donald and Gladstone can't even buy a pair of boots to go for a walk! This should not come as a surprise, since workers have never appeared in the Disney universe.

However, in this case it is fundamental to the moral of the story for the workers' very absence – not generally a matter of concern in the mass media – to be brought to our attention. And Donald must be afflicted with something more than bogus necessities. For once, he must be reduced to a true state of misery and destitution. Because his discovery of his own hunger and the value of work will bring him back, as Uncle Scrooge predicted, to the farm. It seems that McDuck has the only food in a world suddenly become rich, where the pressures to produce something no longer exist. The ex-millionaire is able to recuperate his fortunate by charging billions for eggs, ham, wool, and cabbage. 'Everything went back to normal,' the narrator informs us.

Readers and nephews (with their adult voice) have good-naturedly learned how to criticize anyone who absurdly suggests that you can live without working, as the irres-ponsible Mr. Duck dreamed he could do. They have also learned something else. Donald can start with a million and end up with zero, while McDuck can start with zero and regain all his vast wealth. The old geezer has rewritten the Horatio Alger story in just one episode. The fact that he loses and recovers his fortune in the face of adversaries or thieves, as usually happens in other adventures where he is reduced to penury, once again legitimizes its origins. Behind all that money there is clearly sweat, cunning, calculation, and perseverance. Now. And in the past, too. Such resplendent success sanitizes the past and places years of suffering and setbacks in a self-justifying perspective. Thus, our world, redeemed and sanctified, has been left exactly as it was when we were born. According to this theory, the amount of money each person possesses is equal to the amount of work and cunning he has put into it. There's no reason to think that it took years of appropriating other people's labor to build up that wealth, because it has just been reconstituted in its entirety right before our astonished eyes.

So we are faced with a conflict in which at the very start both competitors have been deceptively and crookedly defined. McDuck is a false capitalist, because he possesses only the abstract, external signs of wealth and not the concrete means to produce it – the means of production. Of course, on top of that, his loss appears unjust because it has been transferred into the hands of someone who hasn't got the slightest intention of working for it. McDuck would, however, be singing (or quacking) a different tune if instead of going after his dollars, they were going after his factories, banks, and land; and even more so if such demands came from the mouths of the laborers, workers, peasants, technicians, and employees who, unlike Donald, have wasted their bodies and minds so such wealth could exist. But, of course, such people are inaudible in the world of Disney.

Donald is their false representative. Donald doesn't claim McDuck's money because its accumulation was made possible solely through the efforts of him and his fellow creatures, nor does he argue that he was forced to sell himself in the marketplace because he was born into a world in which the unjust division of capital had already taken place. He aspires to a million dollars because he's a compulsive freeloader. His industrious and impartial nephews, on the other hand, keep quiet and go along with everything. They never even ask for a percentage of the profits. They keep on working for Uncle Scrooge, participating in the immaculate reincarnation of his estate, without requesting any compensation other than the inherent virtue work confers on them. This deceptive division within the world of McDuck's subordinates (those who don't work are disqualified at the outset because of their own laziness and gluttony, and those who do work have declared themselves happy with their lot) guarantees that an authentic critique on the origin of McDuck's wealth will never be forthcoming.

Furthermore, such a vindication of that cool million's return can be pulled off because the reader's natural resentment toward its initial inequitable distribution is simultaneously deflected into other channels. McDuck poses no threat to anybody, because his money has made him vulnerable and pathetic, without granting him, as we've pointed out, either the power or the means for productive investment. The relationship between the miser and his mountains of gold is completely puerile. At the same time that he jumps into his piles of coins with such playful sensuality, he's also getting a bath of innocence, since it's perfectly clear to the reader that this old man remains paralyzed in a preadult stage.

The result? The socioeconomic status quo has been reinforced, without making McDuck, from the point of view of his behavior and personality, a model for young people, just as Donald could never be such a model. The (class?) struggle between the two, each struck in his own belligerent, deformed extreme, each recognizable but impossible to identify with, seems like a ridiculous and infantile quarrel from the three nephews' point of view.

They will grow up, industrious, obedient readers of encyclopedic manuals, equidistant from the excesses of their elders, taking care not to repeat the mistakes of the 'grown-ups'. The little ducks present to their readers – children of all ages – the possibility of realizing the most dogged, undying dream of the twentieth century, the dream which led to the founding of the USA, the dream of working and being your own boss at the same time.

30

style in revolt: revolting style

dick hebdige

Nothing was holy to us. Our movement was neither mystical, communistic nor anarchistic. All of these movements had some sort of programme, but ours was completely nihilistic. We spat on everything, including ourselves. Our symbol was nothingness, a vacuum, a void. (George Grosz on Dada)

We're so pretty, oh so pretty . . . vac-unt. (The Sex Pistols)

Although it was often directly offensive (T-shirts covered in swear words) and threatening (terrorist/guerilla outfits) punk style was defined principally through the violence of its 'cut ups'. Like Duchamp's 'ready mades' – manufactured objects which qualified as art because he chose to call them such, the most unremarkable and inappropriate items – a pin, a plastic clothes peg, a television component, a razor blade, a tampon – could be brought within the province of punk (un)fashion. Anything within or without reason could be turned into part of what Vivien Westwood called 'confrontation dressing' so long as the rupture between 'natural' and constructed context was clearly visible (i.e. the rule would seem to be: if the cap doesn't fit, wear it).

Objects borrowed from the most sordid of contexts found a place in the punks' ensembles: lavatory chains were draped in graceful arcs across chests encased in plastic bin-liners. Safety pins were taken out of their domestic 'utility' context and worn as gruesome ornaments through the cheek, ear or lip. 'Cheap' trashy fabrics (PVC, plastic, lurex, etc.) in vulgar designs (e.g. mock leopard skin) and 'nasty' colours, long discarded by the quality end of the fashion industry as obsolete kitsch, were salvaged by the punks and turned into garments (fly boy drainpipes, 'common' miniskirts) which offered self-conscious commentaries on the notions of modernity and taste. Conventional ideas of prettiness were jettisoned along with the traditional feminine lore of cosmetics. Contrary to the advice of every woman's magazine, make-up for both boys and girls was worn to be seen. Faces became abstract portraits: sharply observed and meticulously executed studies in alienation. Hair was obviously dyed (hay yellow, jet black, or bright orange with tufts of green or bleached in question marks), and T-shirts and trousers told the story of their own construction with multiple zips and outside seams clearly displayed. Similarly, fragments of school uniform (white bri-nylon shirts, school ties) were symbolically defiled (the shirts covered in graffiti, or fake blood; the ties left undone) and juxtaposed against leather drains or shocking pink mohair tops. The perverse and the abnormal were valued intrinsically. In particular, the illicit iconography of sexual fetishism was used to predictable effect. Rapist masks and rubber wear, leather bodices and fishnet stockings, implausibly pointed stiletto heeled shoes, the whole paraphernalia of bondage – the belts, straps and chains – were exhumed from the boudoir, closet and the pornographic film and placed on the street where they retained their forbidden connotations. Some young punks even donned the dirty raincoat – that most prosaic symbol of sexual 'kinkiness' – and hence expressed their deviance in suitably proletarian terms.

Of course, punk did more than upset the wardrobe. It undermined every relevant discourse. Thus dancing, usually an involving and expressive medium in British rock and mainstream pop cultures, was turned into a dumbshow of blank robotics. Punk dances bore absolutely no relation to the desultory frugs and clinches intrinsic to the respectable working-class ritual of Saturday night at the Top Rank or Mecca. Indeed, overt displays of heterosexual interest were generally regarded with contempt and suspicion and conventional courtship patterns found no place on the floor in dances like the pogo, the pose and the robot. Though the pose did allow for a minimum sociability (i.e. it could involve two people) the 'couple' were generally of the same sex and physical contact was ruled out of court as the relationship depicted in the dance was a 'professional' one. One participant would strike a suitable cliché fashion pose while the other would fall into a classic 'Bailey' crouch to snap an imaginary picture. The pogo forebade even this much interaction, though admittedly there was always a good deal of masculine jostling in front of the stage. In fact the pogo was a caricature – a *reductio ad absurdum* of all the solo dance styles associated with rock music. The same abbreviated gestures – leaping into the air, hands clenched to the sides, to head an imaginary ball – were repeated without variation in time to the strict mechanical rhythms of the music. In contrast to the hippies' languid, free-form dancing, and the 'idiot dancing' of the heavy metal rockers, the pogo made improvisation redundant: the only variations were imposed by changes in the tempo of the music – fast numbers being 'interpreted' with manic abandon in the form of frantic on-the-spots, while the slower ones were pogoed with a detachment bordering on the catatonic.

The robot, a refinement witnessed only at the most exclusive punk gatherings, was both more 'expressive' and less 'spontaneous' within the very narrow range such terms acquired in punk usage. It consisted of barely perceptible twitches of the head and hands or more extravagant lurches (Frankenstein's first steps?) which were abruptly halted at random points. The resulting pose was held for several moments, even minutes, and the whole sequence was as suddenly, as unaccountably, resumed and re-enacted. Some zealous punks carried things one step further and choreographed whole evenings, turning themselves for a matter of hours, like Gilbert and George, into automata, living sculptures.

The music was similarly distinguished from mainstream rock and pop. It was uniformly basic and direct in its appeal, whether through intention or lack of expertise. If the latter, then the punks certainly made a virtue of necessity ('We want to be amateurs' – Johnny Rotten). Typically, a barrage of guitars with the volume and treble turned to maximum accompanied by the occasional saxophone would pursue relentless (un)melodic lines against a turbulent background of cacophonous drumming and screamed vocals. Johnny Rotten succinctly defined punk's position on harmonics: 'We're into chaos not music'.

The names of the groups (the Unwanted, the Rejects, the Sex Pistols, the Clash, the Worst, etc. and the titles of the songs: 'Belsen was a Gas', 'If You Don't Want to Fuck Me, fuck off', 'I Wanna be Sick on You', reflected the tendency towards willful desecration and the voluntary assumption of outcast status which characterized the whole punk movement. Such tactics were, to adapt Levi-Strauss's famous phrase, 'things to whiten mother's hair with'. In the early days at least, these 'garage bands' could dispense with musical pretensions and substitute, in the traditional romantic terminology, 'passion' for 'technique', the language of the common man for the arcane posturings of the existing élite, the now familiar armoury of frontal attacks for the bourgeois notion of entertainment or the classical concept of 'high art'.

It was in the performance arena that punk groups posed the clearest threat to law and order. Certainly, they succeeded in subverting the conventions of concert and nightclub entertainment. Most significantly, they attempted both physically and in terms of lyrics and life-style to move closer to their audiences. This in itself is by no means unique: the boundary between artist and audience has often stood as a metaphor in revolutionary aesthetics (Brecht, the surrealists, Dada, Marcuse, etc.) for that larger and more intransigent barrier which separates art and the dream from reality and life under capitalism. The stages of those venues secure enough to host 'new wave' acts were regularly invaded by hordes of punks, and if the management refused to tolerate such blatant disregard for ballroom etiquette, then the groups and their followers could be drawn closer together in a communion of spittle and mutual abuse. At the Rainbow Theatre in May 1977 as the Clash played 'White Riot', chairs were ripped out and thrown at the stage. Meanwhile, every performance, however apocalyptic, offered palpable evidence that things could change, indeed were changing: that performance itself was a possibility no authentic punk should discount. Examples abounded in the music press of 'ordinary fans' (Siouxsie of Siouxsie and the Banshees, Sid Vicious of the Sex Pistols, Mark P of *Sniffin Glue*, Jordan of the Ants) who had made the symbolic crossing from the dance floor to the stage. Even the humbler positions in the rock hierarchy could provide an attractive alternative to the drudgery of manual labour, office work or a youth on the dole.

If these 'success stories' were, as we have seen, subject to a certain amount of 'skewed' interpretation in the press, then there were innovations in other areas which made opposition to dominant definitions possible. Most notably, there was an attempt, the first by a predominantly working-class youth culture, to provide an alternative critical space within the subculture itself to counteract the hostile or at least ideologically inflected coverage which punk was receiving in the media. The existence of an alternative punk press demonstrated that it was not only clothes or music that could be immediately and cheaply produced from the limited resources at hand. The fanzines (*Sniffin Glue, Ripped and Torn*, etc.) were journals edited by an individual or a group, consisting of reviews, editorials and interviews with prominent punks, produced on a small scale as cheaply as possible, stapled together and distributed through a small number of sympathetic retail outlets.

The language in which the various manifestoes were framed was determinedly 'working class' (i.e. it was liberally peppered with swear words) and typing errors and grammatical mistakes, misspellings and jumbled pagination were left uncorrected in the final proof. Those corrections and crossings out that were made before publication were left to be deciphered by the reader. The overwhelming impression was one of urgency and immediacy, of a paper produced in indecent haste, of memos from the front line.

This inevitably made for a strident buttonholing type of prose which, like the music it described, was difficult to 'take in' in any quantity. Occasionally a wittier, more abstract item might creep in. For instance, *Sniffin Glue*, the first fanzine and the one which achieved the highest circulation, contained perhaps the single most inspired item of propaganda produced by the subculture – the definitive statement of punk's do-it-yourself philosophy – a diagram showing three finger positions on the neck of a guitar over the caption: 'Here's one chord, here's two more, now form your own band'.

Even the graphics and typography used on record covers and fanzines were homologous with punk's subterranean and anarchic style. The two typographic models were graffiti which was translated into a flowing 'spray can' script, and the ransom note in which individual letters cut up from a variety of sources (newspapers, etc.) in different type faces were pasted together to form an anonymous message. The Sex Pistols' 'God Save the Queen' sleeve (later turned into T-shirts, posters, etc.) for instance, incorporated both styles: the roughly assembled legend was pasted across the Queen's eyes and mouth which were further disfigured by those black bars used in pulp detective magazines to conceal identity (i.e. they connote crime or scandal). Finally, the process of ironic self-abasement which characterized the subculture was extended to the name 'punk' itself which, with its derisory connotations of 'mean and petty villainy', 'rotten', 'worthless', etc. was generally preferred by hardcore members of the subculture to the more neutral 'new wave'.

STYLE AS HOMOLOGY

The punk subculture, then, signified chaos at every level, but this was only possible because the style itself was so thoroughly ordered. The chaos cohered as a meaningful whole. We can now attempt to solve this paradox by referring to another concept originally employed by Levi-Strauss: homology.

Paul Willis (1978) first applied the term 'homology' to subculture in his study of hippies and motor-bike boys using it to describe the symbolic fit between the values and lifestyles of a group, its subjective experience and the musical forms it uses to express or reinforce its focal concerns. In *Profane Culture*, Willis shows how, contrary to the popular myth which presents subcultures as lawless forms, the internal structure of any particular subculture is characterized by an extreme orderliness: each part is organically related to other parts and it is through the fit between them that the subcultural member makes sense of the world. For instance, it was the homology between an alternative value system ('Tune in, turn on, drop out'), hallucogenic drugs and acid rock which made the hippy culture cohere as a 'whole way of life' for individual hippies. In *Resistance Through Rituals*, Hall *et al.* crossed the concepts of homology and *bricolage* to provide a systematic explanation of why a particular subcultural style should appeal to a particular group of people. The authors asked the question: 'What specifically does a subcultural style signify to the members of the subculture themselves?'

The answer was that the appropriated objects reassembled in the distinctive subcultural ensembles were 'made to reflect, express and resonate ... aspects of group life' (Hall *et al.*, 1976b). The objects chosen were, either intrinsically or in their adapted forms, homologous with the focal concerns, activities, group structure and collective self-image of the subculture. They were 'objects in which (the subcultural members) could see their central values held and reflected' (Hall *et al.*, 1976).

The skinheads were cited to exemplify this principle. The boots, braces and cropped hair were only considered appropriate and hence meaningful because they communicated the desired qualities: 'hardness, masculinity and working-classness'. In this way 'The symbolic objects – dress, appearance, language, ritual occasions, styles of interaction, music – were made to form a *unity* with the group's relations, situation, experience' (Hall *et al.*, 1976).

The punks would certainly seem to bear out this thesis. The subculture was nothing if not consistent. There was a homological relation between the trashy cut-up clothes and spiky hair, the pogo and amphetamines, the spitting, the vomiting, the format of the fanzines, the insurrectionary poses and the 'soulless', frantically driven music. The punks wore clothes which were the sartorial equivalent of swear words, and they swore as they dressed – with calculated effect, lacing obscenities into record notes and publicity releases, interviews and love songs. Clothed in chaos, they produced Noise in the calmly orchestrated Crisis of everyday life in the late 1970s – a noise which made (no)sense in exactly the same way and to exactly the same extent as a piece of *avant-garde* music. If we were to write an epitaph for the punk subculture, we could do no better than repeat Poly Styrene's famous dictum: 'Oh Bondage, Up Yours!', or somewhat more concisely: the forbidden is permitted, but by the same token, nothing, not even these forbidden signifiers (bondage, safety pins, chains, hair-dye, etc.) is sacred and fixed.

This absence of permanently sacred signifiers (icons) creates problems for the semiotician. How can we discern any positive values reflected in objects which were chosen only to be discarded? For instance, we can say that the early punk ensembles gestured towards the signified's 'modernity' and 'working-classness'. The safety pins and bin liners signified a relative material poverty which was either directly experienced and exaggerated or sympathetically assumed, and which in turn was made to stand for the spiritual paucity of everyday life. In other words, the safety pins, etc, 'enacted' that transition from real to symbolic scarcity which Paul Piccone (1969) has described as the movement from 'empty stomachs' to 'empty spirits – and therefore an empty life notwithstanding [the] chrome and the plastic ... of the life style of bourgeois society'.

We could go further and say that even if the poverty was being parodied, the wit was undeniably barbed; that beneath the clownish make-up there lurked the unaccepted and disfigured face of capitalism; that beyond the horror circus antics, a divided and unequal society was being eloquently condemned. However, if we were to go further still and describe punk music as the 'sound of the Westway', or the pogo as the 'high-rise leap', or to talk of bondage as reflecting the narrow options of working-class youth, we would be treading on less certain ground. Such readings are both too literal and too conjectural. They are extrapolations from the subculture's own prodigious rhetoric, and rhetoric is not self-explanatory: it may say what it means but it does not necessarily 'mean' what it 'says'. In other words, it is opaque: its categories are part of its publicity.

To reconstruct the true text of the punk subculture, to trace the source of its subversive practices, we must first isolate the 'generative set' responsible for the subculture's exotic displays. Certain semiotic facts are undeniable. The punk subculture, like every other youth culture, was constituted in a series of spectacular transformations of a whole range of commodities, values, common-sense attitudes, etc. It was through these adapted forms that certain sections of predominantly working-class youth were able to restate their opposition to dominant values and institutions. However, when we attempt to close in on specific items, we immediately encounter problems. What, for instance, was the swastika being used to signify?

We can see how the symbol was made available to the punks (via Bowie and Lou Reed's 'Berlin' phase). Moreover, it clearly reflected the punks' interest in a decadent and evil Germany – a Germany which had 'no future'. It evoked a period redolent with a powerful mythology. Conventionally, as far as the British were concerned, the swastika signified 'enemy'. None the less, in punk usage, the symbol lost its 'natural' meaning – fascism. The punks were not generally sympathetic to the parties of the extreme right. On the contrary, as I have argued the conflict with the resurrected teddy boys and the widespread support for the anti-fascist movement (e.g. the Rock against Racism campaign) seem to indicate that the punk subculture grew up partly as an antithetical response to the re-emergence of racism in the mid-70s. We must resort, then, to the most obvious of explanations – that the swastika was worn because it was guaranteed to shock. (A punk asked by *Time Out* (17–23 December 1977) why she wore a swastika, replied: 'Punks just like to be hated'.) This represented more than a simple inversion or inflection of the ordinary meanings attached to an object. The signifier (swastika) had been willfully detached from the concept (Nazism) it conventionally signified, and although it had been re-positioned (as 'Berlin') within an alternative subcultural context, its primary value and appeal derived precisely from its lack of meaning: from its potential for deceit. It was exploited as an empty effect. We are forced to the conclusion that the central value 'held and reflected' in the swastika was the communicated absence of any such identifiable values. Ultimately, the symbol was as 'dumb' as the rage it provoked. The key to punk style remains elusive. Instead of arriving at the point where we can begin to make sense of the style, we have reached the very place where meaning itself evaporates.

REFERENCES

Hall, S. *et al.* (Eds) (1976). *Resistance through rituals*. New York: Hutchinson.
Piccone, P. (1969). From youth culture to political praxis. *Radical America*, 15 November.
Willis, P. (1978). *Profane culture*. London: Routledge Kegan Paul.

31

post-colonial feminism and the veil: thinking the difference

lama abu odeh

Since the Iranian Revolution of 1979, the issue of the veil has been the topic of heated debate in Arab countries, particularly those that witnessed strong fundamentalist movements. The fact that Iranian Islamicists who took power in Iran sanctioned the veil and penalized those women who chose not to wear it was either a seductive or, alternatively, a terrifying reminder to women in other Muslim countries of what it might be like for women under Islamicist rule. In countries like Jordan, Algeria and Egypt, where fundamentalist movements have mobilized many followers including large numbers of women whose adoption of the veil signified their initiation into the movement, the question of the legal sanction of the veil has aroused intense reactions from supporters and opponents alike. In this paper I try to explore the question of the veil from the complicated perspective of an Arab feminist, who both rejects the veil as a personal choice but also recognizes its empowering and seductive effect on Arab women. My discussion will be limited to the veil as it plays itself out in an Arab context, since this is what I am most familiar with. The analysis might, or might not, be true in other non-Arab Muslim countries. Also, my 'analysis' will be more of a personal journey of exploration and reflection, than a traditional academic analysis or a strictly scientific one.

For the purpose of this paper I shall use the term 'veil' to mean the current dress adopted by Muslim women in the Arab world, as followers of the contemporary fundamentalist movements. In its most common expression, the veil entails covering the woman's hair with a scarf that is ordinarily white, leaving the face to be exposed. All of the body is usually covered with a loose dress in dark colours, with buttons from top to bottom. Women typically wear Western clothes beneath this dress, which they take-off, along with the scarf, when they are in the sole company of women. These women do not usually cover their hands with gloves, nor do they wear make-up.

FROM NON-VEIL TO VEIL

In order to make sense of the veil as a social phenomenon one needs to inspect other types of women's dress that are distinguishable from the veil. This I will do, by noting the transitional step that these women have made in their dress, historically, from non-veil to veil.

I would like first, however, to locate the women who adopt the veil in terms of class. This will be rather difficult due to the complexity of class structure in postcolonial societies. In general, these women tend to belong to the urban lower and middle classes. Professionally, they work as civil servants, schoolteachers, secretaries in private enterprise, bank employees, nurses and university students. They are usually young, in their twenties and early thirties.

In the seventies, these women walked the streets of Arab cities wearing Western attire: skirts and dresses below the knee, high heels, sleeves that covered the upper arm in the summer; their hair was usually exposed, and they wore make-up. They differed from their mothers who pretty much dressed in the same way, in that they were more fashion conscious, more liberal in the colouring of their clothing and more generous in their make-up. Their mothers usually covered their hair with a scarf when they were in public, but only in a liberal rather than a rigid way (a good proportion of their hair showed underneath the scarf in contrast to the scarf of the fundamentalist dress which showed nothing).

If one were to freeze that 'moment' in the seventies, in an attempt to understand these women's relationship to their bodies, one would find it multilayered and highly complex. In a way their bodies seemed to be a battlefield where the cultural struggles of postcolonial societies were waged. On the one hand, the Western attire which covered their bodies carried with it the 'capitalist' construction of the female body: one that is sexualized, objectified, thingified etc. ... But because capitalism never really won the day in post-colonial societies, where it managed to cohabit successfully with pre-capitalist social formations (traditionalism), these women's bodies were also simultaneously constructed 'traditionally': 'chattelized', 'propertized', terrorized as trustees of family (sexual) honour. The cohabitation in the female body of this double construction (the capitalist and the traditional) was experienced by these women as highly conflictual. The former seemed to push them to be seductive, sexy and sexual, the latter to be prudish, conservative and asexual. Whereas the former was supported by the attraction of the market (consumption of Western commodities), the latter was supported by the threat of violence (the woman is severely sanctioned, frequently by death, if she risks the family sexual honour).

It is not unusual to find the length of a girl's dress the object of family debate:

Father/brother: This dress is too short. No respectable girl would wear it. Ask your daughter (*addressing the mother*) to take it off.

Mother: Come on, let her be. Girls these days wear things like that.

Bother: Let her take it off. My friends follow girls on the streets who wear dress is that short. I won't have my sister going around dressed like that!

Girl: But it's so pretty. All my friends wear dresses that short.

Father/Brother: Maybe they do, but I won't have my daughter/sister walk in the streets with a dress like that.

The girl takes it off.

Not infrequently, Arabic newspapers carry a story structured along the following lines: 'S. M. stabbed his sister K. in a coffee shop across from the university campus. The police are investigating the crime.' A possible scenario for the crime: the woman, a university student belonging to the middle or lower classes, is having coffee with a colleague. Somebody 'tips' her brother that she is involved in sexual relations with this man. Provoked by his sister's friendly public behaviour with another man, and shamed by other people's thinking that this public behaviour has in fact led to illicit sexual contact between them, the brother kills his sister in defence of family sexual honour. The time between the 'tip' and the actual murder is usually very brief. More concerned with the public perception than with the actual fact of the sister's conduct, the brother rushes to protect the family honour, promptly and unequivocally. After trial, the brother is imprisoned for one year only. His extenuating circumstance is committing a 'crime of honour', sanctioned in most Arab penal codes.

The above two stories are pointers on a continuum. The way the girl dresses and how she behaves have heavy sexual significations. She is continuously subject to the test of 'honour' and reputation, that she never really passes once and for all. Her sense of disempowerment stems from the terror exercised over her body, death being its not infrequent extreme.

The ambivalence that these women felt about their bodies in the seventies was resolved by adopting the Islamic fundamentalist dress in the eighties. The length of her dress was no more the object of family debate, nor would she be caught having coffee with a colleague in public, thereby risking her own death. Rather than being engaged in keeping the impossible balance of the 'attractive prude' or the 'seductive asexual', these women chose to 'complete' the covering of their bodies, and 'consummate' their separation from men. I deliberately use the words 'complete' and 'consummate' because the veil was only the concealment of an already ambivalently covered body, rather than the radical transition from 'revealment' to 'concealment'. Likewise, the segregation of the veil was only the completion of an already ambivalent separation between the sexes.

THE VEIL AS EMPOWERMENT

I had earlier identified the women who adopt the veil as mostly working women or students, and young. An important part of their daily life is walking the streets and using public transport to go to work or to school and university. Public exposure of this kind has never been comfortable for women in Arab cities. Unfailingly subject to attention on the streets and on buses by virtue of being women, they are stared at, whistled at, rubbed against, pinched ... Comments by men such as, 'what nice breasts you have', or 'how beautiful. ... you must be', or something more subtle in tone such as, 'what a blessed day this is that I have seen you', are not infrequent. Ordinarily, women avoid any kind of direct verbal exchange with men when they are so approached. They either give the man a look of disapproval, or simply look ahead dismayed, and continue on their way. Whatever their reaction, they are always conscious of being looked at. Exceptionally, a woman might engage in a verbal exchange with the man, such as when he is insistent in his approaches (he continues to rub his thigh against hers on the bus despite her attempts at keeping a distance away from him). She might retort angrily, 'Keep away from me you pig; don't you have sisters of your own?'. A dramatic public scene usually ensues, whereby the man jumps to his self-defence by denying the allegation, and the men on the bus condemning such kind of behaviour as, 'unworthy of a man who has sisters, and a sign of the corruption of youth these days'. The passengers might also chide the woman for not dressing more properly implying that if she did, such kind of harassment might not have occurred. The bus driver might even gallantly ask the man to leave the bus.

A woman's willingness to raise objections to such male instrusions is notably different when she is veiled. Her sense of the 'untouchability' of her body is usually very strong in contrast to the woman who is not veiled. Whereas the latter would swallow the intrusions as inevitable and part of her daily life, trying to bypass them in all the subtle ways she can muster (by looking at the man angrily and moving away from him), the veiled woman on the other hand is more likely to confront the man with self-righteousness, 'have you no fear of Allah treating his believers in such a shameless fashion?' Public reaction is usually more sympathetic to her, the men on the bus making comments such as, 'Muslim women should not be treated like that. Young men should pray more and read the Quran.' It is also true to say that veiled women's exposure to male intrusions in the first place is considerably less than the others.

The importance of these daily experiences and their 'existential' effect on women, both veiled and non-veiled, is best understood when put in the context of Arab women's relationship to their bodies as I have tried to explore it above. Public sexual harassment seems to reinforce the non-veiled woman's ambivalence about her body making her powerless in the face of unwelcome intrusions. The problem doesn't seem to exist for veiled women, since adopting the veil was meant among other things to shield them from such sexual approaches so that when they are actually made, they are looked upon as being simply outrageous, both by the veiled women and the public.

THE VEIL AS DISEMPOWERMENT

As I wrote down the title of this section, I thought to myself that there are surely a hundred million ways in which the veil is disempowering to women. But as I searched in my mind for such examples, I discovered that those instances of disempowerment that I was thinking of reflected my own normative assumptions of how the world should be. In other words, they reflected my position as a feminist. Paradoxically enough, and feminist as I am, instances of the disempowerment of the veil did not present themselves to me as self-evident. Whereas it was obvious to me that the veil remedied the situation of sexual harrassment on the street, by discouraging men from invading veiled women's space and by empowering them to raise objections when such invasions took place, it wasn't equally obvious to me that the veil actually weakened women and disabled them from confronting an uncomfortable daily experience. Even when I activated my own normative assumptions about how the world should be, instances of disempowerment did not become any more self-evident. For instance, my normative assumptions, as an Arab feminist, are based on the premise that Arab women should be able to express themselves sexually, so that they can love, play, tease, flirt and excite. In a social context, such as the one in the Arab world, where women can incur violent sanctions if they express themselves sexually, such acts carry important normative weight to me as a feminist. In them, I see acts of subversion and liberation.

In a conversation with a veiled fundamentalist woman in her late twenties, who is single. I ask, 'But don't you have sexual needs?'

She: Sure I do.
I: What do you do with them?
She: Sure I have sexual needs, but nothing that is absolutely overwhelming and impossible to deal with. I occupy myself all the time. I read books. I love to read books on Islam. To be 'pure' as a single woman is my absolute priority. I do not let these things preoccupy my thinking. It is simply not an issue for me.

But loving, teasing, flirting and seducing was not the way these women normatively saw their sexuality. If in all these acts I saw pleasure and joy, they saw only evil. For them, a society in which the sexes interacted thus was undoubtedly corrupt. They therefore experienced the veil as normatively necessary: precisely because women should not go around seducing men (except the ones they are married to), then they should be veiled (from other men). The disempowerment of the veil that I reflected on seemed to express merely my panicked feminist self, one that saw the veil as threatening to its normative world and sexuality.

Unless I engaged in intellectual elitism by accusing these women of false consciousness and not knowing their own good, there was no way that I could point to instances of the disempowerment of the veil. What it all sounds like so far is a hopeless clash of normative visions.

In my late twenties and single myself, that was nothing my confused post-colonial feminist self could identify with.

As I wrote the above paragraph about my own normative vision of sexuality, I was fearfully conscious of my father's reaction.

Father: What is this you're writing? Women going around seducing and teasing??!!
I: ...
Father: Wipe it off. Do you want to shame me?? That's all I need!! My own daughter declaring to the world that she wants women to go around seducing and teasing! How can I show my face to the world??
I: ...
Father: So this is what you want?? This is what your feminism is all about?? Women going around whoring??
          I, desperately searching for words that might fit into his conceptual scheme and finding none, remain silent.

PREACHING TO THE UNCONVERTED

What about those who are unconverted, neither feminist nor veiled? Those whose bodies and sexuality have not been constructed by the veil discourse, nor by the feminist one? What about those whose 'moment' in the seventies has lingered, whose ambivalence about their bodies has not been 'resolved' by the adoption of the veil? What does a feminist such as myself have to offer them and how do I fare in comparison with those who preach the veil? How could what I have to offer them be empowering?

I find that my position, and that of other feminists, is not devoid of ambivalence. We obviously fare worse when it comes to empowering women on the streets. If what we have as remedy is a long agenda of changing the laws, claiming our rights to walk the streets without harassment, and raising consciousness about the 'equality' of men and women, then what we have is terribly unattractive. It is long term (when the veil as remedy is immediate), sounds hopelessly utopian and demanding of women to engage in what sounds like difficult and impossible personal/political struggle. But what is even more serious than all this, in contrast to the look of social respectability that the veil bestows on those who wear it (sort of like the respectability of a woman dressed like a nun), we seem to offer women a discourse that will make them socially conspicuous, questionable and suspect. For the ambivalent woman of the seventies, already dogged in her pursuit for good reputation, what we offer her looks not only unattractive, but almost socially suicidal.

The situation is aggravated further by the fact that most such feminists are upper- or middle-class women, with material resources that enable them to avoid, to a great extent, uncomfortable experiences on the streets (most of them drive their own cars). They also invite instinctive hostility in lower-class women by virtue of their class position.

Even more, feminist discourse sounds quite foreign. It uses concepts such as 'equality' and 'freedom', which are on the one hand indeterminate and could be easily appropriated ('equality between men and women means that men should be women's superiors because they are more qualified'), but they are also concepts that need yet to become discourse in the postcolonial context ('why should women be free when men are not free either?'). Liberalism, which postcolonial feminism seems to be based on, has yet to win the day in these societies.

Regrettably for the feminist, the importlike quality of her discourse weakens her case even further. Seen as a Western product, feminism doesn't have an obvious list of victories the postcolonial feminist can lean on. Rape, pornography and family disintegration in the West are flaunted in the face of such a feminist as she proceeds to preach her politics. Rather than seeing feminism as a political response to these social phenomena, feminism is seen as its cause. It is because Western women have become 'emancipated' that they are on the streets to be raped, morally corrupt to be playmates, and selfish about their own lives to cause the disintegration of the family. In a crude, superficial, partial, empirical way, that might be true. But before the postcolonial feminist steps in to explain the complexity of the situation in the West, she finds herself silenced by the immediate, simple, straightforward almost magical rhetoric of the veil.

But even if she is allowed to speak, she suddenly finds herself in the uncomfortable position of 'defending the West', an anomaly in itself in the postcolonial Muslim societies of the day.

SOLIDARITY WITH THE VEILED

So far I have constructed the veiled position and the feminist one as being sharply contrasted. I had indicated earlier that they seemed to me to represent a hopeless clash of normative visions. But let me step down a little bit and reshuffle the positions I have constructed. Who wants to talk about normative visions anyway? They often seem to lead nowhere.

Perhaps the feminist path and the veiled one criss-cross. Perhaps they do so to an extent that they are no longer singularly identifiable as such. To show how they might possibly do that we need to break them down and attack their coherence.

The coherence of the veiled position breaks down like this: the contemporary veil seeks to address sexual harassment on the street. It seeks to protect women on their way to work and to school. Its female subjects are socially conspicuous *a priori*: they are not women who are staying locked indoors. It has come to remedy the uncomfortable daily lives of single, young women, who are leaving the house seeking work and education. But the veil as rhetoric assumes that women should ideally be inconspicuous. They should be locked indoors out of men's way so as not to seduce them. They should not go out to work, their rightful place is in the house as wives and mothers, not as wage workers.

The veiled position thus seems to be self-deconstructing. If it seriously pursues its normative vision by inviting women to stay at home, then it loses its attractiveness and therefore its effectiveness as a tool. For it was women's conspicuousness that prompted them to adopt the veil in the first place.

Even more paradoxically, fundamentalist ideology, as the inspiration for the rhetoric of the veil, assumes that women should work only out of necessity, preferably work in professions that are considered feminine such as teaching and nursing, and once at the workplace they should minimize their contact with men to the greatest extent possible. Whether during their working hours, or during break-time, individual women and individual men should not be left alone. Men are presumed to be the leaders in any context, whether at work or at home. Women, who have adopted the veil for its empowering effect on the street as they go to work, can find themselves seriously disempowered if the veil carries its 'logic' to the workplace. Spatial and functional segregation between the sexes, as the fundamentalist ideology of the veil envisages for the workplace, could seriously affect the career prospects of veiled women. Since they live and work in a world where men are already the decision-makers, and the higher situated in the hierarchy of the workplace, minimizing contact between women and men could only possibly result in isolating women further from the positions of power and decision-making.

The ambivalence of their position as veiled women seeking work could be effectively utilized by feminists. Seeing this as a golden opportunity for joining hands with veiled women, feminists can offer their politics as remedy for the disempowerment veiled women can experience at the workplace. Liberal feminist demands such as equality in the distribution of responsibilities between men and women based on the qualifications of the individual, equality of promotion opportunities between the sexes, daycare facilities for women to nurture their children, can be offered to these women as empowering political rhetoric for them as wage workers. Such demands will undoubtedly resonate deeply in veiled women's experience at the workplace. Feminism could thus become the empowering politics of veiled women at work.

The ironic side about all this for feminists, is that all of a sudden they could find themselves joining hands with veiled women as 'comrades' in political action. The coherence of the feminist position could thus be open to question. Far from finding the beneficiaries of its rhetoric female subjects engaged in a struggle for free and equal interaction with men in a free play of sexuality, postcolonial feminism will have to adjust itself to the fact that its empowered subjects are veiled women. In other words, feminist women and veiled women are now sisters.

VEILED AND DIVIDED: THE BATTLE OVER THE BODY

I have so far talked about the veiled body as if it were monolithic. And even though I believe that the rhetoric of the veil seeks to construct a monolithic female sexuality for its followers, I do not however think that, on closer inspection, the community of the veiled reveals any such single construction. Veiled sexuality, it seems to me, reveals a multiplicity that is beyond the feminist's wildest expectations.

True, there are those who can be described as 'ideology incarnate'. Their relationship with their body replicates ideology so well that a shift in this construction looks almost hopeless. They are the leaders, the preachers, the passionate believers, the puritans. They are the ones whose public veiled self takes over, even when they are in the private quarters of women. Their bodies seem to adopt the daily rituals of the veil, where they come to look, for the more colour-loving aesthetic eye, rather bland, insipid and otherworldly. It is the body of the virtuous.

But there are also those in the community of the veiled who are tentative and wavering. Once secure in the company of women, they reveal bodies that are more colourful, lively and sexual. One is surprised at the shift their bodies make when they take the veil off. The bland face becomes colourful with creative make-up. The loose dress of the veil, once taken off, reveals underneath fashionable clothing, making a more individual and personal statement than the collective public one of the veil. Their sexuality appears to be more forthcoming, assertive and joyful. Once together, their interaction with each other is not devoid of seductiveness and flirtation. Their private bodies are almost unrelated to their public ones.

And there are also those whose private more colourful bodies, shyly but daringly, push to become more public. They wear make-up with the veil. They are more creative, fashion-conscious in public, constantly attempting to subvert the blandness of the veil. They invent a million ways to tie the scarf on their heads, which itself becomes more varied in colours than the more standard white. The loose dress of the veil suddenly becomes slightly tighter, more colourful, more daring in emulating Western fashions, even if it doesn't explicitly reveal more parts of the female body. One also notices them on the streets conversing with men, strolling with them, subverting the segregation that the veil imposes on the sexes.

And there are those who wear the veil, but retain a fiercely ambivalent relationship with it, so that wearing it is a conscious decision that is made almost every day. It is not uncommon to find them wearing it some days and taking it off others. 'Wearing the veil, I find sometimes encourages me to binge on food since my whole body is covered in public, and I tend to lose touch with it. I feel I need to take it off sometimes. I need the public voyeur's gaze to control myself.'

And, there are those who use their bodies and dress as a statement of opposition. They differentiate themselves in their environment by wearing the veil, and using it as a statement on female subordination in nonfundamentalist (pseudo-secular, pseudo-religious) Arab households in which they find themselves. Wearing the veil allows them to have a singular and individual voice: 'You are all not wearing the veil, but I AM. I am powerful enough to do it, and this is how I carve myself a space that you cannot reach. I disapprove of what you are, who you are, and what you think!'

Of course, a veiled woman is not necessarily either this or that. She could shift from one position to the other. At times colourful, other times bland, seductive and prudish, public and private. A veiled woman's subjectivity appears to be much more complicated than the simple word of the veil can possibly convey.

For the feminist, such multiplicity of veiled sexuality could be very exciting and promising of rich interaction and dialogue with veiled women. Her position accordingly could become more nuanced and multiple. Instead of dismissing them as the enemy, the threat, the falsely conscious, she could see them as the varied, divided, seemingly united, female community trying to survive in an environment that is hostile to them as much as it is to her. It is a multiplicity that invites conversation between the 'same', rather than the apartness of the 'other'.

THE FEMINIST RESITUATES HERSELF

In the section below, I shall refer to the 'rhetoric of the veil'. What I mean by it is the fundamentalist construction of the veil, as it is circulated ideologically. A woman who decides to wear the veil is usually subjected to a certain ideological indoctrination (by a fundamentalist preacher), about how every Muslim woman needs to cover her body so as not to seduce men, and how in doing this she obeys the word of Allah.

Otherwise, she would face his wrath on the day of judgement. I have already tentatively referred to it in the section entitled 'Solidarity with the veiled'. It is in relation to, and at the same time by means of, this 'official' rhetoric that the different women I have just described construct their position of ambivalence or subversion.

In my construction so far, I have largely ignored the question of power. What I mean by power in this context is the power attached to a particular discourse as the only possible representation of 'reality' to the exclusion of others. This is a particularly important issue for the postcolonial feminist who is interested in understanding and possibly impacting the female community of the veiled. The excitement over the multiplicity and richness of such a community for the postcolonial feminist might be immediately dampened by the ideological power of the veil over that community. This will still be the case, despite the variety and richness of veiled women's lives that could be read as subverting the rhetoric of the veil.

It is interesting to note that since the veiled women of the contemporary fundamentalist movements have adopted the veil as a political act (they were not born into it), the rhetoric of the veil has a strong hold over them, since it provided the rationale for their act. In articulating their lives and their relationship with their bodies, they can only engage in such rhetoric. This seems to have the effect, at the end of the day, of reifying the 'reality' of their daily lives, by disabling them from seeing the subversions and variations that exist or could exist to disrupt the ideology of the veil.

This seriously complicates the position of the feminist. In order to have a hearing with these women, she needs to 'hook up' with their conceptual system (rhetoric). But she also needs to do it in a way that subverts it and allows conceptual openings in it, through which veiled women can start to see their lives differently. This is a slippery road since she will always risk being overwhelmed by the 'logic' of the rhetoric, and thereby end up being rendered ineffective and immobilized by it. She will also find herself in the uncomfortable position of having to say things that she 'doesn't really mean' in order to have a hearing in the first place. Conscious of having to keep the balance of being both inside and outside the system, the feminist risks being pushed one side or the other.

The feminist:	I like the way you wear your scarf. It's creative and most unusual.
Veiled woman:	Thank you. I get bored with the way I look if I wear it the same every day.
The feminist:	I thought the whole point was to wear it the same every day so that you don't attract attention to your body.
Veiled woman:	It's just that I think that people need to look beautiful to others. That doesn't mean they have to seduce them. Allah is beautiful and he likes beauty.
The feminist:	I agree with you. I think women can look beautiful without having to appear as if they are out to seduce men. I believe that women can look both proper and beautiful. In my opinion, you can do that either wearing the veil or even Western clothes. I, personally, feel more comfortable wearing the latter. The veil appears to me rather exaggerated.
Veiled woman:	Except that Allah commanded us to wear the veil. But I've always believed that the important thing is how we feel inside. The important thing is that we feel pure inside, no matter what we wear, whether it is Western clothes or the veil.

constructionism in question

part seven

ocial constructionist ideas have scarcely lived a tranquil life. In fact, the controversies surrounding their entry into the scientific, scholarly and practical world have been intense and heated. Given the challenges posed by these ideas to longstanding investments in transcendent truth, purity of reason, foundational values, objectivity, and the individual as the fundamental atom of society, such resistance is scarcely surprising. To be sure, many critics of constructionism have not bothered to explore the ideas before falling into an attack mode. In particular, there is a tendency for critics to read constructionist writings in a traditional way. That is, they have understood these writings as attempts to 'tell the truth,' or provide a new foundation from which all preceding assumptions and institutions can be demolished. This misunderstanding is crucial, as *most* constructionists write with the full understanding that they too are constructing realities and moralities. They are quite aware that they have no foundations upon which to stand and that their comments are only entries into what they see as vital conversations. They do not function as fixed truths, but as invitations to new and ever-evolving dialogues and practices.

For the reader wishing further understanding of the constructionist controversies there are many works available. There is ample defense of the common traditions, as represented in Nagel's *The Last Word*, Gross and Levitt's *Higher Superstition: The Academic Left and its Quarrels with Science*, Held's *Back to Reality*, Ruse's *Mystery of Mysteries: Is Evolution a Social Construction?*, and a special issue of the journal, *Theory and Psychology* (Vol. 11, #3, 2001). Excellent defenses, amplifications, or relevant extensions of social constructionist ideas can be found in Smith's *Belief and Resistance* and Rorty's *Philosophy and the Mirror of Nature*. More conservative analyses of issues at stake can be located in Hacking's *The Social Construction of What*, and Joseph Margolis' *The Truth About Relativism*.

In this closing section we offer treatments of three pivotal critiques of constructionist endeavors. The critiques are related, inasmuch as they are aimed at what many find to be an unacceptable relativism inhering in constructionist arguments. The 'anything goes' orientation that seems to follow from constructionism is particularly vexing and is variously held to be immobilizing, incoherent, nihilistic, or immoral. In our view much of this critique is based on misunderstanding or ignorance of constructionist ideas. However, in the present volume we include two attempts to treat relativist critiques of substantial magnitude. The first is the *realist critique* of anything goes. Briefly, as the realist proposes, you cannot construct the world in any way you wish. There are realities that must inevitably be confronted, and our accounts of the world can and should be tested against these realities. Surely natural science is not just make-believe. The offering by Edwards, Ashmore and Potter (Reading 32) takes on the challenge of the realists, not only demonstrating some of the misunderstandings that inhere in realist arguments, but pointing to some of the unfortunate societal consequences of realist doctrines. Constructionists have no difficulty with locally claimed realities; these may be anticipated and honored. However, when any local reality is proclaimed The Real for all, we confront a totalitarian silencing.

The second important relativist critique may be termed *valuational*; it is set against what seems to be a moral and political emptiness in constructionist views. Constructionism seems to offer no moral or political foundation for action; it does not provide a firm basis either for opposing injustice, immorality or other evils or for building a better world. In certain respects this line of critique is ironic. As the chapters of this volume make clear constructionist writings are frequently passionate, oppositional, and idealistic. They recognize the impossibility of neutral or non-partisan accounts of the world and do their best to pursue a vision of the good. Still, the critic replies that constructionist premises themselves offer no grounds for one of these commitments over another. In Reading 33, Alexa Hepburn takes on this form of critique as it emerges in feminist circles. Many feminists are deeply skeptical of constructionism, not only because it fails to offer foundations for feminist activism, but it even raises basic questions about the reality of the distinction between men and women. Hepburn helps us to see that the feminist movement does not suffer at the hands of constructionism, and indeed a healthy and inclusive feminism will find constructionist arguments vital to its well-being. The implications of these arguments extend far beyond feminist politics.

We complete this section by engaging the world of practice. As Janis Bohan and Glenda Russell (Reading 34), point out, the culture at large is realist (or essentialist) in its orientation to life. Everyone 'knows' that rocks, furniture and death are real. To be sure, while constructionist liberation from our comfortable assumptions can be both instructive and useful, do we wish to abandon the discourse of the real and essential? Bohan and Russell work with gay and lesbian communities, and in this context, they propose that a knock-down fight between essentialist and constructionist discourses would be unfortunate. In fact, to live successfully in contemporary society requires both discourses. As they illustrate in the case of both the homosexual's self understanding, and in the molding of public policy, there are times when a realist understanding is enormously useful. Sometimes we need to claim firm identities. For other purposes, however, a constructionist discourse is most helpful. Firm identities can also operate like straight jackets, and a liberating language can be crucial to change. Again, the message of this reading is sweeping in application.

REFERENCES

Gross, B., and Levitt, N. (1994). *Higher superstition: The Academic Left and its quarrels with science.* Baltimore, MD: Johns Hopkins University Press.

Hacking, I. (1999). *The social construction of what.* Cambridge, MA: Harvard University Press.

Held, B. (1996). *Back to reality: A critique of postmodern psychotherapy.* New York: Norton.

Margolis, J. (1966). *The truth about relativism.* Cambridge, MA, London: Blackwell.

Nagel, T. (1997). *The last word.* New York: Oxford University Press.

Rorty, R. (1979). *Philosophy and the mirror of nature.* Princeton, NJ: Princeton University Press.

Ruse, R. (1999). *Mystery of mysteries: Is evolution a social construction?* Cambridge, MA: Harvard University Press.

Smith, B. H. (1997). *Belief and resistance,* Cambridge, MA: Harvard University Press.

Theory and Psychology (2001), *11*, No. 3.

32

death and furniture: arguments against relativism

derek edwards, malcolm ashmore and jonathan potter

'Death' and 'Furniture' are emblems for two very common (predictable, even) objections to relativism. When relativists talk about the social construction of reality, truth, cognition, scientific knowledge, technical capacity, social structure and so on, their realist opponents sooner or later start hitting the furniture, invoking the Holocaust, talking about rocks, guns, killings, human misery, tables and chairs. The force of these objections is to introduce a bottom line, a bedrock of reality that places limits on what may be treated as epistemologically constructed or deconstructible. There are two related kinds of moves: Furniture (tables, rocks stones, etc. – the reality that *cannot* be denied) and Death (misery, genocide, poverty, power – the reality that *should not* be denied). Our aim is to show how these 'but surely not this' gestures and arguments work, how they trade off each other, and how unconvincing they are, on examination, as refutations of relativism.

FURNITURE

No matter what the debate, whatever its content or its medium (text or talk), there is likely to be some furniture around. While we talk about things and events, principles and abstractions, cognition and reality, or read about construction and objectivity, we do so in chairs and in rooms, at desks and tables, or even out in the open, where the rocks and trees are. The appeal of these things is that they are external to the talk, available to show that it is just talk, that there is another world beyond, that there are limits to the flexibility of descriptions. Hitting the furniture also works as a non-verbal act, offering the advantage of getting outside of language; its force is that it avoids the rhetorical danger of appealing to non-verbal reality by putting it into words. But words will generally do; we can talk about tables and rocks, and invoke their external existence verbally, almost as convincingly as physically pointing to or hitting them. The Furniture argument invokes the objective world as given, as distinct from processes of representation; as directly apprehended, independent of any particular description.

THE REALIST'S DILEMMA

Of course, the hitting is not just a slapping; not only words signify. The table-thumping does its work as meaningful action, not mere behaviour. All the pointings to, demonstrations of and descriptions of brute reality are inevitably semiotically mediated and communicated. Rocks, trees and furniture are not *already* rebuttals of relativism, but become so precisely at the moment, and for the moment, of their invocation. We term this *the realist's dilemma*. The very act of producing a non-represented, unconstructed external world is inevitably representational, threatening, as soon as it is produced, to turn around upon and counter the very position it is meant to demonstrate. Furniture 'arguments' perform categorization and relevance via semiosis. Bruno Latour also notes how realists like 'to be able to thump on a table that solidly resists and proves itself not to be a dream or a social construction' (1989: 106).

The very ease with which furniture (etc.) is apprehended – its 'obvious' solidity and out-there-ness – makes it a hard case for relativist deconstruction and, therefore, a soft case for a realist defence. Furniture arguments are realism working on its chosen soft ground. However, there is a cost for realism in this strategy. For in resorting to these cases, realists appear to be setting aside, conceding even, a huge amount of more contentious stuff to relativism – language, madness, the social order, cognition, even science. And it is generally disputation about *these* sorts of things that ends in table-thumping, the point of such gestures being to bolster a realist defence of something more contestable. In the rhetorical situation we are describing, the relativists may be winning the Epistemological Wars, but are in danger of losing the final battle. The forces of relativism are gathered about the last and most well-defended castle of realism (Fortress Furniture), laying siege to it and in the process suffering a blistering bombardment – Bang! Bang! Bang! [...]

The realist thumps the table. What a loud noise! Much louder than talk. Much more gritty. Much more real. And yet we insist that this noise, being produced in *this* place, at *this* time, in the course of *this* argument, *is* an argument, *is* talk. As an argument, it takes the form of a demonstration:

> *This* (bang!) is real. *This* (bang!) is no mere social construction. Talk cannot change *that* it is or *what* it is. See how its reality constrains my hand (bang!), forcing it to stop in its tracks. Hear the inevitable result (bang!) of the collision of two solid physical objects. Need I say more?

All this is addressed of course to the relativist, the unbeliever, the heretic. And what is being asked of this unfortunate soul? Preferably, to recant (lack of response will, generously, be taken as a form of recantation). Failing this, the table-thumping argument becomes a challenge:

> Show us [the challenger and the assumed audience-of-fellow-realists] how we are wrong. Show us the contingent, could-be-otherwise, socially constructed, really-not-real character of this table – if you can!

Let us then accept the challenge. It is surprisingly easy and even reasonable to question the table's given reality. It does not take long, in looking closer, at wood grain and molecule, before you are no longer looking at a 'table'. Indeed, physicists might wish to point out that, at a certain level of analysis, there is nothing at all 'solid' there, down at the (most basic?) levels of particles, strings and the contested organization of sub-atomic space. Its solidity, then, is ineluctably a perceptual category: a matter of what tables seem to be like to us, in the scale of human perception and bodily action. Reality takes on an intrinsically human dimension, and the most that can be claimed for it is an 'experiential realism' (Lakoff, 1987).

So let us remain at the human scale. When the table is assaulted it is not the whole of it that gets thumped, but only a bit of it under the fist or hand or tips of (some of) the fingers. What exactly is warranted by this – just the bit hit? What makes it a bit of a *table*? And for whom? How does the rest of the table get included as solid and real? And how does even the part that is hit, get demonstrated as real for anybody but the hitter? And how exactly is this demonstration, here and now, supposed to stand for the table's continuing existence, then and later, and for all the other tables, walls, rocks, ad infinitum, universally and generally? A lot is being taken on trust here, however 'reasonably'.

This deconstructive nit-picking may look pedantic and unreasonable. But realism does not achieve its aim *without* all this detail. Instead, it relies upon it, but in the background, as method and assumption, stage set, props and procedures, rather than as topic. Relativists choose to topicalize it, or at least to understand it as topicalizable in this way. Realism deploys but disguises all this on-trust stuff, asks us to take the table-hitting as an existence proof for tables-as-such (and much more), while relying on the audience's cooperation in commonsensically ignoring how it is done: letting bits of tables stand for wholes (metonymy), instances stand for categories (this is a 'table'), one experience (and one person's) stand for many (and acknowledged by everybody). What we have, on closer examination, is a demonstration not so much of out-there reality, but rather of the workings of consensual common sense. For relativists, consensual common sense is an interesting topic. It can be examined for its workings, rather than wielded as a bludgeon against inquiry. [...]

Alongside Furniture, another 'hard case' for relativism is Death, our emblem for the invocation of important values and morality that, while arguably variable across cultural time and space, are often shared by realist and relativist alike, as co-members of Feyerabend's tribe of Western intellectuals' (1987: 73). Part, indeed, of the force of both Death and Furniture arguments, is their ability to appeal to *all* participants in epistemological disputes, as members of a common culture, for whom they operate as icons of a transcendent truth beyond (de)construction. One way that Death arguments differ is in the kind of politico-moral realities they invoke: the obvious and good things that relativists have no business undermining, or the obvious and bad things they have no business making moral room for (Smith, 1988: 218). The many examples of the latter include 'wife beating, bride burning, clitoridectomy.... The added piquancy of examples in which the victims are female can hardly be missed'.

But not only women victims are used; recruited also are the poor and oppressed, the dead and dying, the victims of murder, massacre and genocide.

Interestingly, we have come across few examples of the former kind, the Good kind, of invoked reality. Perhaps this is because most of our dealings (and our shared concerns and values) are with 'critical realists' of the left. Alternatively, perhaps the reason is that realism or reality (or just particular bits of it) are themselves doing duty as 'the Good that must not be undermined' in Death as well as in Furniture arguments. Thus, although *the fact that* 'the Holocaust took place' is, historically, an obvious, indeed iconic, Bad-that-should-not-be-justified, *the statement* 'the Holocaust took place,' is, rhetorically, a Good-that-should-not-be-denied.

There are two related forms of the Death argument, each of which points to relativism's alleged moral bankruptcy. One points to death, misery, tragedy, disaster, as undeniable, except by a scoundrel or a fool. This is the *ontological* version, the one linked most directly to Furniture. The other, *siren* version takes the form of the dire warning that relativism actually *produces* death and misery – that this way the Holocaust lies. The two versions are linked in a causal story: ontological denial will lead to a dropping of guards, the road to Hell, paved by the good intentions of ostrich-like relativists. This second, *siren* form of the Death argument rests on the assumption that only objectivist thought can 'bar the gate to the polis and keep the night, the jungle and the jackals at bay' (Smith, 1988: 154). Smith responds that these things happen anyway, all too obviously, despite objectivism's dominance, and that claims to have captured unvarnished reality (through having God on their side) are made on both sides of the overwhelming majority of the world's politico-moral disputes conducted exclusively by realists.

Here are two examples of Death arguments taken from reviews of relativist work which show the subtle linkages between the ontological and siren forms:

'We are creators of meanings, appropriate to the occasion, like dramatists, novelists and ordinary speakers' [Mulkay, 1985: 167].

On one level, I have no problem in accepting this; on another it seems thoroughly irresponsible. As I write this, an area of Tripoli has been laid waste by a number of aircraft currently (I hope) sitting on the ground a few miles down the road from my Ivory Tower. Some 100 people (not very many by modern standards) have been killed. They were not killed by words neither are they dead because the rest of the world decides to call them dead. Their death was brought about by the employment of a disproportionately immense amount of scientific and technical knowledge. If we can only see this knowledge as just another story, then we too deserve to fall victim to it (Craib, 1986).

As the bombs were going off and as the flesh was being ripped from the bone, I found it hard to stomach this kind of cool dispassionate sociological analysis of missile systems.... Constructivism refuses to take a stand.... [It displays] indifference to (technically embodied) features of the human condition – in this case, human suffering. (Winner, 1992).

The rhetorical effect sought in such passages is the induction of guilt. The writers being reviewed (Mulkay, 1985, and MacKenzie, 1991) are accused of an irresponsible lack of concern for the realities of death and destruction brought about by that very 'scientific and technical knowledge' that is their topic. Clearly, it is their relativist epistemology which has let them down: their stubborn refusal to recognize *any* uninterpreted reality has led them to a gross and offensive indifference. Their moral bankruptcy in choosing to talk about talk in cool and dispassionate ways rather than taking a stand, is not only personally reprehensible, it is publicly damaging. If *we* (the readership of the reviewed and the reviews) are foolish enough to be persuaded by these misguided relativists, 'then we too deserve to fall victim': a brutal nemesis, it has to be said, for writers of texts to wish upon one another. The reality we deny – and by denying, refuse to oppose – will assert itself with terrible poetic justice; it will kill us. And this apocalypse will be appropriate punishment for our lack of faith; and yet, as our lives are taken from us, lo, our faith in reality is restored! Praise the Real (and pass the ammunition)!

It is pleasant to acknowledge, however, that relativists are seldom accused of advocating evil. The crime is one of omission, not commission. They (we) are accused of moral and political quietism, of being frozen in motion, unable to speak or move or choose, of having no basis for commitment to values or goals. But this accusation trades upon the objectivist assumption (Smith, 1988) that rejecting realism is the same thing as rejecting everything that realists think is real. On a relativist analysis, as we have argued, it is the realists who are frozen in motion, because as soon as they move, they represent.

TURNING THE MORAL TABLES

The freezing is not only a matter of epistemology, either. Reality can serve as rhetoric for inaction (*be realistic ... face the facts ... come off it ... you can't walk through rocks ... you can't change reality, human nature, market forces ... it's just the way things are ... life isn't fair*). It is a familiar kind of argument against change, against action, against open-ended potentiality of any kind. Reality is given, perceived, outthere and constraining. Arguably, it is for relativists and constructionists that the good life is to be lived and made, as and in accountable social action including that of social analysis; rather than to be taken as given, ruled out as impossible or, as disengaged objective analysts, passively observed and recorded. At the very least, realism has no exclusive claim upon the pragmatics of making a better world.

Indeed, the tables are easily turned. It is difficult to see how *realists* can be so sure about moral and political issues. How does ontological realism, allied with empiricism, sit with moral conviction? What are realists doing in possession of something as irrational as conviction? Are not these the folk who say we should find out the facts, discover whether some race or gender *really is* inferior on some measure, test the hypothesis, check out whether the Holocaust *really did* happen, and so on? And yet when that sort of questioning undermines, or threatens to undermine, a specific consensual version of the world, it is suddenly considered illegitimately relativistic. As Bloor noted when discerning the sacred character of science in its resistance to scientific (a.k.a. relativistic) questioning of itself, 'some nerve has been touched' (1976: ix).

More usually, however, in scientific and academic disputes as in other kinds, it is one set of realists arguing with another. Either they already know the world non-empirically, or they have to find out. But then how do they deal with disagreement?

'I'm right and you're wrong'.
'No, *I'm* right and *you're* wrong'.
'No, no, *I'm* right and *you're* wrong.'

A more sophisticated and useful method is to start questioning the opponent's method, assumptions, or rhetoric; to use, that is, the tools of relativist-constructionist analysis. Indeed, it is hard to imagine the work of the modern academy proceeding at all in the absence of such methods. But realists use them selectively: only against *opponents*; and only *against*. Conceived exclusively as a method of criticism, Analysis (whether as sociology of knowledge, psychoanalysis, ideological or rhetorical critique) is used to *undermine* that to which it is applied. In contrast, relativists insist on the *general* applicability of Analysis. In particular, no self-serving exception can be made on one's own behalf: it has to apply reflexively to one's own position too.

The advantage of relativistic notions of reality as rhetoric is that we *can* take positions and argue. Claims for the unreality of the Holocaust are, like all preposterous claims, like all claims of any sort, examinable for how they are constructed and deployed. Realism is no more secure than relativism in making sure the good guys win, nor even of defining who the good guys are – except according to some specific realist assumptions that place such issues outside of argument. Realism is the rhetoric of no rhetoric, marshalled in favour of one particular claim against another. Realists cannot claim the political and moral high ground, nor the epistemic, if only because they disagree so much about particulars.

REFERENCES

Bloor, J. (1976). *Knowledge and social imagery.* London: Routledge Kegan Paul.

Craib, I. (1986). Review of M. Mulkay, *The word and the world* (London: Allen & Unwin, 1985), Sociology 20, 483–84.

Feyerabend, P.K. (1987). *Farewell to reason.* London: Verso.

Lakoff, G. (1987). *Women, fire and other dangerous things: What categories reveal about the mind.* Chicago: University of Chicago Press.

Latour, B. (1989). Clothing the naked truth In H. Lawson & L. Appignanesi (Eds) *Dismantling truth: reality in the postmodern world* (pp. 101–26). London: Widenfeld & Nicholson.

MacKenzie, D. (1991). *Inventing accuracy: A historical sociology of nuclear missile guidance.* Cambridge, MA: MIT Press.

Mulkay, M. (1985). *The word and the world.* London: Allen & Unwin.

Smith, B.H. (1988). *Contingencies of value: Alternative perspectives for critical theory;* Cambridge, M.A: Harvard University Press.

Winner, L. (1992). Review of D. McKenzie, *Inventing accuracy: A historical sociology of nuclear missile guidance.*(Cambridge, MA: MIT Press, 1992). Presented at the 4S/EASST joint conference, Gothenberg, August.

33

relativism and feminist psychology

alexa hepburn

It is important to stress at the outset that this paper does not represent an attack on those feminists who have explicitly criticized a relativist perspective. It is also important to acknowledge that many of the critics cited here have been an invaluable source of support and inspiration for feminist psychologists of all kinds. Moreover, given the widespread confusions highlighted above it is not surprising that these kinds of criticisms have been developed in psychology. Nevertheless, it is important to highlight some difficulties with these arguments and with the implications that are adduced from them.

Feminist critics who have argued for the incompatibility of feminism and relativism have sometimes been arguing from an explicit alternative perspective such as critical realism or psychoanalysis, and sometimes the connection between feminism and relativism is treated as intrinsically problematic. The following illustrate the sorts of concerns and criticisms raised:

Relativists' refusal to engage with questions of value has also led to a political paralysis (Wilkinson, 1997b: 186).

In other words, a motivated, partisan political orientation is proscribed [by relativism]. Theory floats disconnected from any political position, and this is a return to a disturbingly familiar liberal pluralist position (Parker and Burman, 1993: 167).

To me it's very important to say ... an incestuous act happened. And it wasn't just someone's interpretation. I mean I think it's *extremely* dangerous when women are talking about what happened – 'He hit me'; 'He beat me up'; 'He raped me'. It is very dangerous to say, 'Oh well, there's no external reality, there's only stories, nothing really happens' ... it can get to a point where nothing's real, nothing happened, nothing matters, and nobody knows – and I think that's a dangerous thing for feminists to be saying (Gilligan, in Kitzinger, 1994: 412, emphasis in original).

Increasingly, research from a [social constructionist] perspective points reflexively to its own socially constructed nature and thus loses the potential rhetorical impact of 'empirically verified facts' (Kitzinger, 1995: 156).

For feminists attempting to bring about social change, the relativism and reflexivity of constructionism, discursive and postmodern approaches pose some serious problems. If there is nothing outside the text, then there is no means to assert the existence of even the starkest material realities: war, genocide, slavery, and poverty, physical and sexual abuse (Wilkinson, 1997b: 184).

Relativists' refusal to engage with questions of value has led to political paralysis. There is no principled way in which they can intervene, choose one version over another, argue for anything (Gill, 1995: 177).

If no one set of meanings is more valid than any other, there is no basis (for example) for distinguishing between the rape victim's account of sexual coercion and the rapist's account of pleasurable seduction (Wilkinson, 1997: 185).

The fundamental claim here is that 'commitment to relativism disavows the grounds for feminist politics' (Wilkinson and Kitzinger, 1995: 6) and leads to 'depolitization' (Burman, 1990). These are important arguments, then, and – if they are correct – they make up a strong case for feminist psychologists to be circumspect in using relativist perspectives. I should stress that anti-relativist arguments are not always explicitly developed, and often appear in semi-formal and informal settings. My documentation here is meant to indicate the *type* of arguments that have been used, and their underlying *logic*. I am thus less concerned about the status of any one particular use of the argument and will not try to assign particular arguments to particular individuals.

To clarify them, and ease discussion of their merits, I will split the anti-relativist arguments into four points. These are: (1) choice between versions; (2) the problem of textual idealism; (3) the researcher's feminist commitment; (4) influencing the community. It must be stressed that these arguments are sometimes used alone and sometimes blurred together, which is part of the problem for the feminist relativist who tries to make sense of them. Let me try to spell each one out and then indicate the kinds of counter-arguments that are available.

I. CHOICE BETWEEN VERSIONS

This is the argument that relativist perspectives do not provide the basis for choice between different accounts. On a theoretical level they cannot provide the basis for choosing between moral or political perspectives. On an analytic level, they cannot provide a basis for choosing between claims made by different people (the rapist and rape victim, say).

Let me start with the way this argument has been developed on a theoretical level. When defending her claims and cases the relativist researcher will argue her case with issues of conceptual coherence, examples, evidence, rhetoric, visions of solidarity and so on. As Barbara Herrnstein Smith (1997) argues, living without epistemological guarantees does not downgrade choice; instead, it stresses its centrality and necessity.

The relativist does not believe in some separable, objective guarantees, which force a particular choice. Instead, she is likely to draw on a wide range of considerations.

At this point an objectivist/realist might respond 'but on what *basis* do we choose?' Does the absence of foundations mean there is no basis for choice? The relativist has a positive and a negative response to this. Her negative response is to point to the large body of work in philosophy, literary theory, sociology of scientific knowledge, and so on, which analyses and undermines the foundational claims of science, philosophy and social theory. That is, the negative response is to say that it is not a matter of eschewing the use of foundations; rather, she doubts that such foundations are available *for anyone*. There is nothing to reject. Her positive response is to make arguments, develop claims, marshal evidence, offer conceptions of transformation and so on. The basis for choice will be laid out in the arguments. These might be clear and effective, or cloudy and unconvincing; that is the way with arguments. They are judged on their merits. She does not, therefore, see the problem as one of choosing to live with or without foundations; rather it is a choice between wrongly imagining that knowledge can be objectively founded, and doubting that it can be and exploring the consequences of that doubt. It involves embracing the richness and political embeddedness of arguments (Billig, 1987, 1994).

None of this is an argument for 'anything goes'. Taking an anti-foundationalist position on knowledge, which rejects the sovereignty of the standard truth production machinery of data, experiments, human nature, reality or God, does not entail a belief in everything and nothing.

The anti-relativists are right, however, when they claim that relativist arguments do not *in themselves* provide the basis for choosing moral or political perspectives (see Gill, 1995). The issue is whether such positions *should* provide a basis for the choice of politics. There is no reason why feminists *must* see their political and moral views as determined by some 'scientific' analysis of society or psychology. Instead, it is perfectly coherent to argue that feminists can choose their particular politics and morality from whatever considerations seem appropriate. This might include rigorous and high-quality research, but it might *also* include features of personal biography, feelings of solidarity, visions of social transformation and outrage at inequalities and exploitation. Constructionists can, and often do, accept relativist epistemology and they can, and often do, choose feminist politics. Critics can disagree with these choices, and argue for alternative epistemologies – but that is a quite different matter from showing that constructionists who adopt a relativist epistemology cannot coherently make such choices in the first place.

Let me now move on to the issue of choice at an analytic level – the issue of choosing between the claims of research participants. This issue is of a different order and presents a variety of complexities. First, it is worth commenting on the rhetorical construction of the arguments about relativists' supposed inability properly to choose between participants' versions. Take Sue Wilkinson's suggestion quoted above that relativist researchers have no basis for distinguishing between the rape victim's account of sexual coercion and the rapist's account of pleasurable seduction. This implies that relativism involves a perverse insensitivity to the 'obvious facts' of abuse and suffering. Yet, as will be immediately apparent from studying the diversity of work in feminist psychology done under the rubric of poststructuralism, discursive psychology and deconstruction, this is almost the opposite of the case. A predominant concern for researchers using these perspectives has been social criticism, including a range of feminist issues to do with desire, exploitation, sexism and subjectivity.

The objectivist might ask at this point: how can a 'relativist' talk coherently about 'obvious facts'? The relativist's response will be to say that she makes judgements about facts, and may, like other feminists, find certain facts obvious, or even shocking. She holds beliefs about the world and its inequalities that give sense to her feminism. This does not mean, however, that such beliefs must be grounded in some separate, objective foundations. Nor does it mean that in some circumstances 'obvious facts' might not become the object of analysis themselves.

Let me return to the way the argument against relativism is constructed. Note the way Wilkinson's construction depends on an invented example that sidesteps the contingencies of the 'real world'. The problem is not that the example is invented – this is an argument, after all – it is that it is invented in such a way that it prejudges exactly what is open-ended in real-life examples, that is, the appropriate application of the categories rapist and rape victim. Relativists are not (generally) attempting to replace the various legal systems through which guilt and innocence are assigned in cases of violent sexual assault, by making their own academic prosecutions. That is not to say, however, the sexual violence is a topic beyond the purview of relativist researchers. On the contrary, a variety of studies have considered the way sexual violence is excused and justified, the way judicial judgments are bound up with assumptions about sexuality, and the way courtroom cross-examination assigns blame (e.g. Coates et al., 1994; Frohmann, 1998; Matoesian, 1993; Wood and Rennie, 1994; Wowk, 1984). These studies are not denying the awfulness of sexual assault; this is precisely the concern that motivates them. It is important to emphasize again that the general relativist scepticism concerning objectivist foundations to knowledge does not require that we abstain from making judgements, arguments and claims.

I assume that feminist researches working on topics such as sexual violence start with a variety of expectations, for example, that rape is widely underreported, that the judicial system is organized in a manner that makes it hard to get prosecutions, that judges are frequently sexist, and so on. Yet such expectations do not conflict with the epistemological uncertainties highlighted by relativists. They express the stance from which the research was created and its solidarity with other feminist critics of the wider judicial and policing systems; they do not express an epistemological position of certainty.

2. TEXTUAL IDEALISM

The argument here is that relativist perspectives have no way to encompass the real, material worldly phenomena that are central to feminism. These might be such things as incestuous acts, the experiences of rape victims, and the facts of power and patriarchy.

As with the argument about choice between versions, the way this issue has been formulated presupposes a particular realist or 'objectivist' orientation. The argument here treats the existence of particular objects as both obvious to the anti-relativist, and denied by, or inaccessible to, researchers using relativist perspectives. Arguments of this kind transform the various (more or less) subtle attempts to grapple with the practical epistemic issues that arise in relativist research and analysis into a straightforward denial of the existence of particular objects.

Take 'incest' as an example. A researcher may consider the way this category is applied as parts of different practices, and can be rhetorically worked up and undermined; but this is not a denial of the significance and awfulness of child sexual abuse. Yet while it is now easy (following the efforts of feminist researchers over the past two decades) to condemn sexual abuse, research, understanding and prevention are more complex. They will involve dealing with descriptions embedded in practices, delivered by various interested parties: children, parents, social workers, psychiatrists, social workers, outraged MPs and so on. Relativists are not persuaded that there is a simple brute reality of 'incest' or 'child sexual abuse' outside of, and separable from, those complex practices. However, to claim that such things are not simple freestanding objects is not to treat them as any less important or shocking.

Again, part of the problem here is the rhetorical construction of the objectivist complaint. Carol Gilligan's argument quoted above provides a good illustration. The constructionist is characterized as claiming that incest is *'just someone's interpretation'* (belittling? uncaring?) and as saying '*Oh well*, there's no external reality, there's only stories, *nothing really happens*' (resigned? denying?). But surely the issue is not the caring, not the strongly felt belief that child sexual abuse is awful. Rather it is to think about how topics in this area can best be researched and understood, and to recognize the complex epistemic issues that arise in doing so. Issues seem simple when they are produced in vignette-style examples which predefine the realities which we feminists agree are bad. *Actual* issues do not come predefined, and are bound up in social arenas riven with disputes, interest groups, versions and different agendas.

These anti-relativist arguments suggest that there is something simple being offered in asserting the existence of 'material realities' such as war and sexual abuse, and this simplicity is being weakened by the constructionist stress on the way these categories are assigned, built up, rhetorically used, embedded in discourses, undermined and so on. As I have emphasized, recognizing such complexity is not a perverse celebration of the limitations of truth, but the result of a body of philosophical and analytic work done across the human sciences. It is perfectly appropriate to disagree with such work, but simply legislating into existence a class of objects that come free from epistemological trouble surely cannot show its inadequacy.

My general argument here has not been that relativist perspectives are the only ones that enable critical research on topics of feminist interest (although I would elsewhere want to argue their virtues – Hepburn, 1997, 1999). Instead I have been developing the more modest, but important, argument against the way that they have been dismissed as purveyors of textual idealism. I have tried to show that scepticism about foundations does not force the feminist researcher to an idealist position that denies the existence of a range of objects.

3. THE RESEARCHER'S FEMINIST COMMITMENT

The point here is that relativist doubt about foundations of theories or claims makes it hard for the researcher to express commitment to a position or a set of values, and act on that commitment in a political arena.

I will divide the argument about commitment into two forms. The stronger form would hold that there is something about relativism that is *intrinsically* counter to being committed to some set of views. The weaker form would hold that it is *contingently* the case that relativist researchers will find it hard to commit to particular views. We can think of these as an epistemological form of argument and a psychological form. Let me take the epistemological argument first.

Commitment to some position or claim is quite different from treating that position or claim as objectively the case; that is, underwritten by some foundation. Indeed, the official rhetoric of objectivist science is that the scientist is uncommitted and disinterested, pervasively sceptical (of claims, not the apparatus through which claims are 'verified'). Scientific facts are treated as doing their work by *forcing* themselves on the scientists, who are *forced* to accept their existence (Woolgar, 1988). Nigel Gilbert and Mike Mulkay (1984) developed the terms 'empiricist repertoire' and 'contingent repertoire' to account for the way that scientists justify claims. Scientists employing the empiricist repertoire steer clear of commitment, as this contaminates their purely empiricist data-driven position. They can employ the contingent repertoire, which again sees commitment as a bad thing, in order to discount the claims of their rivals. Commitment is seen as something that is a problem as it can distort scientific development. On this analysis, commitment makes sense for a relativist who doubts the empiricist justification of science, and accepts the wide range of contingent features involved in knowledge claims. Indeed, it could be argued that commitment makes less sense for those claiming objectivist, foundational justification to their claims. Why is commitment needed in foundationalist positions? What is it doing? Nevertheless, for my current purposes I need only show the coherence of relativist commitment, not the incoherence of foundational commitment.

For relativists, no position or claim is *simply* forced by the data, by the theory, or whatever. There is *always* contingency. So, in contrast to the official objectivist story, commitment may be a *necessity* for holding positions or making claims. When a relativist takes sides in a dispute some kinds of commitment are involved: she is not claiming that she is forced to take sides by the data, say. Taking sides does not involve abandoning relativism; taking sides may be done for a wide range of arguments, judgements and allegiances. But note also that taking sides does not mean that the relativist may not dispute what the sides are and how they are constituted? Put another way, commitment is a perfectly coherent part of the relativist account of holding positions or espousing beliefs, whereas for the objectivist or realist it is a potential embarrassment. I am not arguing that all feminists have to be relativist. But I am claiming that the argument for commitment works at least as well in the reverse direction to how it is usually presented.

The psychological argument is rather different. This argument has it that the scepticism about foundations, the emphasis on the constructed basis of positions, the awareness of variability and contingency, make it hard for any particular feminist psychologist to hold on to strong commitments. This argument seems to embody a condescending and psychologically reductive view of feminists. Bronwyn Davies has recently noted that it also rests on rather weak evidence, making only 'vague reference to specific unnamed others who are incapable of commitment' (1998: 136). Again, the Gilligan argument cited above is typical in its reference to unnamed feminists who '*can* get to a point' where nothing matters. In contrast to this, Davies contends that for her, and the teachers and students she has worked with, an understanding of the inherently constructive nature of self and reality has *enabled* rather than inhibited action and commitment.

Ultimately, the psychological argument seems to depend on judgements about the evidence that objectivist feminists have significantly more commitment to feminist politics and critique than do feminists who hold constructionist positions. Like Davies, I see no evidence for this.

4. INFLUENCING THE COMMUNITY

This strand of argument holds that the complex and self-referential elements of relativist positions, combined with avowed doubt the foundation of claims, make it hard to persuade the research community of claims, let alone the broader community which might act on feminist work.

The issue of community influence is best treated in two parts: influencing the academic community, and influencing the wider community outside academia. With respect to the academic community, it is not at all clear that relativist arguments have been unpersuasive. Various positions which (commonly) involve relativist epistemological assumptions – constructionism, poststructuralism, discursive psychology – are well represented in *Feminism & Psychology*; and it is not uncommon for feminist psychologists to complain that one or other relativist perspective has *too much* influence. For example, Ros Gill suggests that: 'as Erica Burman (1991) points out, discourse analysis has become almost synonymous with critical and (sometimes) feminist research' (Gill, 1995: 168). Whether this is true or not, the major influence of this work suggests that foundationalist credentials are far from necessary to make an effective intellectual contribution.

It may be the case that many North American feminist psychologists are yet to be convinced of the virtues of constructionist perspectives. Celia Kitzinger (1997), well known for her constructionist work, argues strongly for the *strategic value* of positivist empiricism and individualism in pressing lesbian and gay issues in mainstream psychology. However, should relativists like myself conclude from this that we should readopt foundationalist perspectives to gain influence with this or any other group? Or is it more intellectually appropriate, and even effective in the long term, to develop the general case for the contribution that relativist thinking can make in feminist arenas? After all, there is a general argument currently taking place between relativists (in this case discursive psychologists) and cognitivists, and the outcome of core theoretical and analytic disputes such as this might transform the whole context of persuasion. Nevertheless, my belief (as a relativist academic) is that the most coherent position is to be committed to the perspective that I have struggled with, worked on and believe (up to now) to be the most effective, rather than simply strategically adopting other people's theories. At the very least, I would argue that the strategic case against relativism is not proven.

The second issue here is of influence in the 'broader' community. There are interesting convergences and differences here. A variety of feminist psychologists who would otherwise happily be considered anti-realist have argued for the *selective* adoption of realist narratives (Gavey, 1989; Squire, 1995; Wetherell, 1995). I would argue that there is nothing intrinsically anti-relativist about such stances. Indeed, the flexible use of realist discourses for strategic ends had been a major theme in a range of work discussing relativism and constructionism (Edwards et al., 1995; Wetherell and Potter, 1992). Reality is the heroine of many good stories. What might be more problematic would be the selective use of foundational justifications for those realist claims. Do we really want to gain social and political influence by asserting a truth-value for our claims that we elsewhere doubt? Perhaps intellectual honesty combined with criticisms of the pretensions of objectivist psychological work is the most coherent approach here too. Should we not, as feminists, value and work toward a polity that is openly forthright and epistemologically sophisticated?

The issue of persuasion is a deep one, with implications for the basis of our work as feminist *academics* (rather than feminist politicians or citizens). I have certainly not wanted to imply that the issues are simple, and that there are no potential costs for those rejecting objectivist perspectives. However, I hope to have at least indicated the case against treating the persuasion argument as necessitating a rejection of relativism.

A RELATIVIST FEMINISM

I have not argued here that objectivist feminists are wrong or incoherent, or that relativist perspectives are always superior. Rather, the main objective of this paper has been to clarify the nature and limitations of anti-relativist arguments that aim to show the incoherence or impossibility of relativist feminism. Some people will undoubtedly be left still feeling that they want to employ constructionist work, but that they don't want to subscribe to relativism. However, it is important to be clear that without the relativism of a strong constructionist position, as a researcher you are left with difficult job of arguing for, and providing evidence of, non-constructionist realities. Some may feel that this is a price worth paying in order to ground their commitment. However, as I have argued, commitment to something is different from treating it as simply objectively true, and indeed there is a tension between the notion of commitment and the objectivist story that 'truths' speak for themselves via experimentally manipulated variables. In contrast, relativists may be in a stronger – and more intellectually honest – position to deal with the many contingencies, arguments and agendas that go with doing research.

I would like to end on a positive note, by starting to trace the virtues of relativism for feminists. For centuries women have been, and still are, positioned and silenced by patriarchal ideologies that deny them the same rights as men and define them as lacking, as somehow deficient. I am committed to this belief, which expresses my solidarity with other feminist researchers – it is not something I have simply been forced to accept by my experimental findings. For most feminist researchers the ultimate goal is to assert or display the unacceptable nature of the patriarchal state of affairs. Many therefore claim that in order to gain a strong political voice we must steer clear of postmodern or relativist traps which would deny us the ability to assert the 'reality' of our own identity, language and experience. Cautioning us from her Derridean deconstructive perspective, however, Peggy Kamuf asks:

... if feminist theory lets itself be guided by questions such as what is women's language, literature, style or experience, from where does it get its faith ... if not from the same central store that supplies humanism with its faith in the universal truth of man? ... will it have done anything more than reproduce the structure of woman's exclusion in the same code which has been extended to include her? (Kamuf, 1982: 44–5).

So the 'reality' of women's 'language, literature, style or experience' is organized by the same humanist metanarrative which asks us to seek universal truths within ourselves, for example that women should be true to some fundamentally nurturing or passive nature. From a broader postmodern perspective, defining in advance what is 'femaleness' and what is 'oppression' is to engage with 'exclusionary operations and differential power relations that construct and delimit feminist invocations of 'women'' (Butler, 1993: 29). The humanist metanarrative, like all metanarratives, marginalizes other versions of femininity, feminism and humanness. The rejection of objectivist grounding therefore continues to have emancipatory potential for feminists, not a matter of static renditions. Like any other political and moral philosophy, feminism evolves to meet new findings and challenges, it expresses new solidarities, and it offers new visions of transformation.

Nevertheless, my argument in the paper does not require a particular line on the merits and demerits of the various feminist interventions from within (commonly) relativist positions such as constructionism, deconstruction, discursive psychology, poststructuralism and postmodernism. What I have been concerned to do is counter arguments that assert the principled incompatibility of relativism and feminism. Insofar as I have been successful, this clears the way for more direct engagement with the profound and substantial issues that these perspectives generate for, and within, feminism. There are issues, for example of *theory* – consider Donna Haraway's (1989) working within and around various theories when considering gender issues in primatology. There are issues, for example, of *scientific evidence* – consider Malcolm Ashmore's (1989) exploration of the various paradoxes involved in studying knowledge and evidence and its relation to theory. And there are issues, for example, of *politics* – consider Barbara Herrnstein Smith's (1988, 1997) critique of various attempts to base politics on single realities or simple axioms. A relativist position therefore clears the way for addressing the many competing versions, contingencies, arguments and agendas that go with doing feminist research.

REFERENCES

Ashmore, M. (1989) *The Reflexive Thesis: Wrighting Sociology of Scientific Knowledge*. Chicago, IL: University of Chicago Press.

Billig, M. (1987) *Arguing and Thinking: A Rhetorical Approach to Social Psychology*. Cambridge: Cambridge University Press.

Billig, M. (1994) 'Celebrating Argument within Psychology: Dialogue, Negation, and Feminist Critique', *Argumentation* 8: 49–61.

Burman, E. (1990) 'Differing with Deconstruction: A Feminist Critique', pp. 208–20 in I. Parker and J. Shotter (eds) *Deconstructing Social Psychology*. London: Routledge.

Burman, E. (1991) 'What Discourse is not', *Philosophical Psychology* 4: 325–43.

Butler, J. (1993) *Bodies that Matter*. London: Routledge.

Coates, L., Bevelas, J.B. and Gibson, J. (1994) 'Anomalous Language in Sexual Assault Trial Judgements', *Discourse & Society* 5: 189–206.

Davies, B. (1998) 'Psychology's Subject: A Commentary on the Relativism/realism Debate', pp. 133–45 in I. Parker (ed.) *Social Constructionism, Discourse and Realism*. London: Sage.

Edwards, D., Ashmore, M. and Potter, J. (1995) 'Death and Furniture: The Rhetoric, Politics, and Theology of Bottom Line Arguments against Relativism', *History of the Human Sciences* 8(2): 25–49.

Frohmann, L. (1998) 'Constituting Power in Sexual Assault Cases: Prosecutorial Strategies for Victim Management', *Social Problems* 45: 393–407.

Gavey, N. (1989) 'Feminism, Poststructuralism and Discourse Analysis: Contributions to a Feminist Psychology', *Psychology of Women Quarterly* 13: 439–76.

Gilbert, G.N. and Mulkay, M (1984) *Opening Pandora's Box: A Sociological Analysis of Scientists' Discourse*. Cambridge: Cambridge University Press.

Gill, R. (1995) 'Relativism, Reflexivity and Politics: Interrogating Discourse Analysis from a Feminist Perspective', pp. 165–86 in S. Wilkinson and C. Kitzinger (eds) *Feminism and Discourse: Psychological Perspectives*. London: Sage.

Haraway, D. (1989) *Primate Visions: Gender, Race and Nature in the World of Modern Science*. London: Routledge.

Hepburn, A. (1997) 'Teachers and Secondary School Bullying: A Postmodern Discourse Analysis', *Discourse and Society* 8: 27–49.

Hepburn, A. (1999). 'Derrida and Psychology: Deconstruction and its Ab/uses in Critical and Discursive Psychologies', *Theory and Psychology* 9(5): 641–67.

Herrnstein Smith, B. (1988) *Contingencies of Value: Alternative Perspectives for Critical Theory*. Cambridge, MA: Harvard University Press.

Herrnstein Smith, B. (1997) *Belief and Resistance: Dynamics of Contemporary Intellectual Controversy*. Cambridge, MA: Harvard University Press.

Kamuf, P. (1982) 'Replacing Feminist Criticism', *Diacritics* 12: 42–7.

Kitzinger, C. (1994) 'The Spoken Word: Listening to a Different Voice: Celia Kitzinger Interviews Carol Gilligan', *Feminism & Psychology* 4: 408–19.

Kitzinger, C. (1995) 'Social Constructionism: Implications for Lesbian and Gay Psychology', pp. 136–61 in A.R. D'Angelli and C.J. Patterson (eds) *Lesbian, Gay and Bisexual Identities over the Lifespan: Psychological Perspectives*. New York: Oxford University Press.

Kitzinger, C. (1997) 'Lesbian and Gay Psychology: A Critical Analysis', pp. 202–16 in D. Fox and I. Prilleltensky (eds) *Critical Psychology: An introduction*. London: Sage.

Matoesian, G.W. (1993) *Reproducing Rape: Domination through Talk in the Courtroom*. Oxford: Blackwell.

Parker, I. and Burman, E. (1993) 'Against Discursive Imperialism, Empiricism, and Constructionism: Thirty-two Problems with Discourse Analysis', pp. 155–72 in E. Burman and I, Parker (eds) *Discourse Analytic Research: Repertoires and Readings of Texts in Action*. London: Routledge.

Squire, C. (1995) 'Pragmatism, Extravagance and Feminist Discourse', pp. 145–64 in S. Wilkinson and C. Kitzinger (eds) *Feminism and Discourse*. London: Sage.

Wetherell, M. (1995) 'Romantic Discourse and Feminist Analysis: Interrogating Investment, Power and Desire', pp. 128–44 in S. Wilkinson and C. Kitzinger (eds) *Feminism and Discourse: Psychological Perspective*. London: Sage.

Wetherell, M. and Potter, J. (1992) *Mapping the Language of Racism: Discourse and the Legitimation of Exploitation*. Brighton: Harvester.

Wilkinson, S. (1997) 'Prioritizing the Political: Feminist Psychology', pp. 178–94 in T. Ibáñez and L. Íñiguez (eds) *Critical Social Psychology*. London: Sage.

Wilkinson, S. and Kitzinger, C., eds (1995) *Feminism and Discourse: Psychological Perspectives*. London: Sage.

Wood, L.A. and Rennie, H. (1994) 'Formulating Rape', *Discourse & Society* 5: 125–48.

Woolgar, S. (1988) *Science: The Very Idea*. Chichester: Ellis Horwood/London: Tavistock.

Wowk, M. (1984) Blame Allocation: Sex and Gender in a Murder Interrogation', *Women's Studies International Forum* 7: 75–82.

34

sexual orientation: essential and constructed

janis s. bohan & glenda m. russell

Constructionism suggests that the understandings assumed by a particular culture act to frame its members' experience and to shape their behavior. In this culture, at this time, our understanding or construction of sexual orientation is an essentialist one. That is, the dominant understanding is that sexual orientation is indeed a core, essential, fixed attribute of individual identity.

Sexual orientation may well be a socially constructed meaning imposed on experiences that could equally well accommodate myriad other meanings. However, *this particular, essentialist meaning* is the one that individuals in this culture are likely to embrace. Thus, individual identities inevitably reflect and instantiate socially constructed understandings.

Each persons's coming to her or his identity involves creating narratives about who she or he is. This is far more than a matter of making up stories, and it implies neither truth nor the absence thereof. Rather, from a constructionist perspective, creating narratives is a dynamic and reiterative process that has generative impact. Creating narratives actually shapes individual identity (e.g., Cass, 1990; Crawford, 1995; Frantz & Stewart, 1994; Hermans & Hermans-Jansen, 1995; Park, 1992; Personal Narrative Group, 1989; Sarbin, 1986; Wilkinson & Kitzinger, 1995).

The conceptual categories and the language available for narratives of individual identity necessarily consist of the languages and the categories created by our collective constructions of the notion of sexual orientation. People in this culture can thus be expected (from a weak constructionist perspective) to imbue their experience with essentialist meaning. They might also be expected (from a strong constructionist perspective) to be influenced to a large extent by the dictates of essentialist understandings of the categories provided and the attributions associated with those categories. Put directly, the understandings we have (collectively) created become scripts for our (individual) lives.

A merger of essentialist and constructionist epistemologies is philosophically impossible; we cannot both 'discover' and 'construct' reality. Here lies a fundamental challenge to psychology's approach to sexual orientation. To the degree that the very notion of sexual orientation and the categories contained within it are constructions, positivist analysis cannot yield what it intends – namely, accurate descriptions of independently existing, extralinguistic phenomena.

This last suggestion gives impetus to the constructionist challenge to the notion of validity. If there is no 'truth' to which we have recourse, the merits of a particular position must be judged by some criterion other than its validity in the usual sense. From this position, we are encouraged to examine the particular versions of reality that are widely endorsed by this culture. Thus, we might ask, 'What is the impact of holding an essentialist view of sexual orientation? Why do we define individual identity in terms of the sex of one's partner? Why these particular categories rather than some others?' And, a most important question for our purposes here, 'What are the implications of one or another understanding of sexual orientation? Who benefits, and how?' These and related queries can be subsumed within the direct and politically crucial question 'What purpose is served by one or another position? How is it used, and by whom?'

PSYCHOLOGY, CONSTRUCTIONISM, AND SEXUAL ORIENTATION

Considerable recent scholarship across a variety of disciplines has explored a constructionist perspective on sexual orientation, detailing its rationale and implications (e.g., Butler, 1990, D'Emilio, 1983, 1992; Greenberg, 1988; Kitzinger, 1987; Plummer, 1981; Rust, 1993; Weeks, 1989). In combination, these works open the way to an analysis of how individuals' lives are framed by their culture's understanding of sexual orientation and by their own self-identification as lesbian, gay, bisexual, or heterosexual.

However, this social constructionist approach to sexual orientation is not widely known outside academia, nor has it guided the psychological literature on the subject to any marked extent. Psychological theory, research, and practice that address sexual orientation – as well as the implementation of psychological understandings in the public sphere – have derived almost entirely from an essentialist approach; this is true in two senses. First, most work in the psychology of sexual orientation begins from the essentialist ontological assumption that sexual orientation is a primary, nuclear quality of self. Second, the psychology of sexual orientation is grounded in the presumption that, by conducting proper research, one can discover and describe the 'true' nature of gay/lesbian/bisexual experience. Both positions stand in contrast to the constructionist perspective, which asserts that there is no entity – sexual orientation – to be discovered, investigated, described, or explored; the very object of our curiosity is a social construct shaped by our means of knowing rather than a free-standing phenomenon that can be known directly. Thus, psychology has contributed to as well as been shaped by the cultural understanding of sexual orientation as an essential trait of individuals.

IMPLICATIONS OF ESSENTIALIST AND CONSTRUCTIONIST PERSPECTIVES

In order briefly to illustrate the implications of the contrast outlined here, we offer several situations that individually and collectively demonstrate the differences between psychological praxis from a constructionist and from an essentialist stance. These illustrations should also make clear the intransigent dilemma that underlies this discussion: there are clearly circumstances in which essentialist understandings provide a strikingly powerful instrument on behalf of those who identify as other than heterosexual, and there are instances where the reverse is true. Thus, the question is not which is 'correct' but how we tease out the outcomes of adhering (particularly without reflection) to one or the other point of view. As a means of addressing this question, let us consider several circumstances where the purposes of LGBs may be both served and impeded by each approach.

COMING OUT

In both lay and professional literature, the process of 'coming out' – coming to a gay, lesbian, or bisexual identity – is portrayed as a discovery; identifying as lesbian, gay, or bisexual involves the unearthing of something already present, even if hidden, denied, or ignored. Common images include finding one's true self or 'coming home' to the place where one always really belonged. The national support group Parents, Families, and Friends of Lesbians and Gays (PFLAG) uses the swan to represent LGB people. This symbol, taken from Anderson's fable 'The Ugly Duckling,' fits an essentialist view: LGB individuals are beautiful in their true (LGB) identity, rather than ugly in a false (heterosexual) one. Such portrayals of coming to a nonheterosexual identity represent an essentialist construal of sexual orientation. Incidentally, although the topic receives far less attention, we also hold an essentialist view of heterosexual identity. Although heterosexual individuals do not face the same struggle in coming to this identity, since the heterosexual assumption is simply embraced, we nevertheless assume that those who identify as straight are equally at home, having found (if without struggle) their true self.

This metaphor of discovery makes sense of what is otherwise often experienced as a terribly confusing and painful sense of ill fit in the world. Such coherence is widely understood as a key element to optimal mental health (Morgan, 1991). The provision of a label for oneself and one's feelings brings closure to the identity confusion that almost surely follows upon the awareness of feelings that are condemned by society (Cass, 1979) As a part of the process of coming to terms with this identity, the essentialist understanding of identity as permanent also provides a basis for a new self-narrative, for rereading the past as having contained the seeds of this identity, perhaps throughout one's lifetime. This reconstruction of identity as always having been gay or lesbian or bisexual lends a sense of continuity to one's personal history and a sense of integrity to one's current life (see, e.g., Whisman, 1996).

Further, claiming a lesbian or gay (and perhaps a bisexual) identity provides an entree to the LGB community, with all the attendant support and socialization functions the community serves; it offers other 'swans' among whom one feels at home. Like other minority communities, the LGB community takes its collectivity (at least in part) from a sense of shared identity, whether grounded in common experiences, shared oppression, or other signals of unity. A categorical identity is often central to the existence of such communities, and their members may be admitted on the basis of their claiming the appropriate identity. To deny the category of non-heterosexual identity would be to deny this basis for collective identity; to claim it is to open access to the rich resources of community.

Finally, essentialist renditions of coming out may serve a function for heterosexual people as well. First, they reinforce the perception of LGBs as 'other,' their identity defined by their deviation from the heterosexual norm. Further, when an individual claims a gay, lesbian, or bisexual identity and does so by appeal to the discovery of a core essential self, she or he contributes to the reification of discrete categories of sexual orientation. This may, in turn, lead heterosexual people to feel safer in their own identity; as long as the categories are distinct and the identity stable across time, they needn't be concerned that their own identity might somehow transform into a non-heterosexual one.

On the other hand, embracing an essentialist understanding of coming out may lead the individual to distort or disclaim elements of his or her own experience or history in order to match the newly claimed category. Thus, past relationships might be demeaned or regarded as deceitful or inauthentic, despite their having been experienced at an earlier time as good and fulfilling relationships. Personal preferences that are incompatible with the category might be expunged in the name of adhering to the socially constructed confines of the identity. For example, an individual who identifies as lesbian might feel it necessary to quell – and even disown – feelings of attraction to men. A recent highly publicized example of the failure to exorcise such unacceptable feelings is seen in the story of the lesbian sexuality expert Joann Loulan, who is involved in a relationship with a man. While some have supported Loulan's choice, many in the LGB community have ostracized her precisely because 'real' lesbians do not develop intimate relationships with men (e.g., Lipstadt, 1997; Oakley-Melvin, 1997; Quinn, 1997). The potential loss of Loulan's contributions to the community and her loss of the support of many in the community is the price exacted by the demand for rigid adherence to discrete, essentialized categories.

This same expectation for adherence to discrete categories can have direct and unfortunate consequences for individual LGBs. People who are convinced that neat categories represent the only acceptable identities may withhold information about themselves that violates this model. Where such information is important, as for example, in health care, its withholding may prove detrimental. Consider the case of an out lesbian who is afraid to tell her physician about her sexual activities with men or the man who identifies as heterosexual and dares not reveal same-sex sexual activity. Consider the case of a gay man who dares not tell his psychotherapist that he is attracted to women or the woman coming to a lesbian identity who feels compelled to conceal from her counselor her continuing involvement with men. Surely the physical or mental health care these individuals receive will be compromised by the limitations they impose on disclosure as a result of the demand to comply with precise categorical boundaries....

POLITICS AND PUBLIC POLICY

The quandary we are exploring here is also apparent in areas of politics and public policy. In recent years, political and policy efforts emanating from the LGB community and its allies have relied on essentialist renderings of sexual orientation. Psychology's essentialist position has contributed to this stand, very often undergirding successful efforts at protecting LGB rights. Very clear example of this can be taken from recent court cases such as the battle over Colorado's Amendment 2 (A2).

A2 was a popularly initiated referendum that prohibited equal protection on the basis of sexual orientation; it was passed by Colorado voters in 1992. After a lengthy court battle, the amendment was declared unconstitutional in 1996. Contributing to this decision was an *amicus curiae* brief authored by several professional mental health organizations, including the American Psychological Association. Key arguments in this brief – and, indeed, in the justices' final ruling – appealed to essentialist under-standings of sexual orientation.

As this example illustrates, an appeal to essentialism can be extremely effective, at least in the short run. However, it is also important to consider the long-range impli-cations of such arguments and the more subtle, perhaps detrimental assumptions that underlie them. The fragility of these arguments was made strikingly clear in a power-ful but little-known (at least among psychologists) flyer distributed by Colorado for Family Values (CFV), the primary impetus behind A2. This flyer explicitly referred to essentialist arguments employed by pro-LGB forces and systematically debunked them – often by an appeal to research readily available to us all.

The point here is not that one or the other position – essentialist or constructionist – is ultimately 'true;' as we have seen, according to constructionism such arguments for ultimate truth cannot be sustained by any match to a free-standing reality. Rather, the point is that invoking essentialist arguments opens the possibility for just such attacks as that issued by CFV. Forces that oppose LGB interests can easily muster information to counter the very arguments used to make a case on behalf of LGB rights. That case is, in the end, riddled with assumptions that are at best, open to question and at worst, fatal to pro-LGB positions.

It is also important to query yet another element of the essentialist position that has underpinned this political stance, namely the assertion that sexual orientation is not (ever) a matter of choice. We do not wish to argue here whether or not this is indeed the case. A great deal of literature indicates that most people do not experience sexual orientation as a matter of choice; a smaller but compelling body of work demonstrates that some people do experience it precisely that way. Rather than resolve this question, we wish to point out that this argument reflects and perpetuates and element of inter-nalized homophobia. The question we must ask is this: why would it be a problem for sexual orientation to be a choice? If lesbian, gay, and bisexual identities are truly healthy variations on human experience, why must we insist that they are not chosen in order for them to be deemed acceptable? Doesn't this argument – that sexual orien-tation is not a choice, that one can't help it – serve to reinforce the notion that it *is* a problem and that if one could choose otherwise, she or he surely should and would? In short, this argument subverts itself, rather than the homophobia that it was intended to target.

These concerns are beginning to filter into the literature dealing with psychology and sexual orientation. In an address at the American Psychological Association meeting honoring his work in the public interest, the prominent gay psychologist Gregory Herek (1997) raised just such issues. Herek urged psychologists to turn their energy to questions such as these in order to build a solid psychological foundation for addressing politics and public policy. Included among the topics he raised for ongoing discussion is the need to recognize the potential fluidity of sexual orientation and the variety of paths by which individuals come to one or another identity. In addition, the appeal to a distinction between identity and behaviour, he suggested, while useful in many ways, may reinforce the condemnation of same-sex sexual behavior by implying that such behavior is, indeed, to be condemned. Further, a focus on discrimination against and differential treatment of LGBs may foster a mentality of victimization, hampering our attempts to assume a more affirmative, proactive stance in our public policy efforts. Finally, Herek questioned LGBs embrace of the assertion that they are just like everyone else. While strategically a useful position, he maintained, this argument ignores the reality of stigma and its effects, thus obscuring the importance of questions such as how LGB individuals cope with the stress of living a stigmatized identity?

The issues raised here and those elaborated by Herek challenge truly fundamental assumptions infusing most work in the area of psychology and sexual orientation. Those assumptions have proven fruitful in their application to certain actual situations. At the same time, they pose quandaries that psychologists must address if understandings of sexual orientation and the application of those understandings are to be coherent and helpful to LGBs.

The question of how to resolve such dilemmas returns us to the initial purpose of this chapter: to lay out the two perspectives under consideration and to point out how each makes sense and at the same time raises apparently intractable questions. Given this paradoxical situation, we are led not to ask which is 'true' but what are the consequences of embracing one or the other? Who benefits? Who does not?

REFERENCES

Butler, J. (1990). *Gender trouble: Feminism and the subversion of identity*. New York: Routledge.

Cass, V. C. (1979). Homosexual identity formation: A theoretical model. *Journal of Homosexuality*, 4, 219–235.

Cass, V. C. (1990). The implications of homosexual identity formation for the Kinsey model and scale of sexual preference. In D. P. McWinther, S. A. Sanders, & J.M. Reinisch (Eds). *Homosexualityi/heterosexuality: The Kinsey scale and current research* (pp. 239–66). New York: Oxford University Press.

Crawford, M. (1995). *Talking difference*. London: Sage.

D'Emilio, J. (1983). *Sexual politics, sexual communities: The making of a homosexual minority in the United States, 1940–1970*. Chicago: University of Chicago Press.

D'Emilio, J. (1992). *Making trouble: Essays on history, politics and the university*. New York: Routledge.

Frantz, C. E., & Stewart, A. J. (1994). *Women creating lives*. Boulder, CO: Westview.

Greenberg, D.E. (1988). *The construction of homosexuality*. Chicago: University of Chicago Press.

Herek, G. (1997, August). *Sexual orientation and public policy*. Address given before American Psychological Association, Chicago.

Hermans, H. J. M., & Hermans-Jansen, E. (1995). *Self-narratives: The construction of meaning in psychotherapy*. New York: Guilford.

Kitzinger, C. (1987). *The social construction of lesbianism*. London: Sage.

Lipstadt, H. (1997, January). From lesbian to has-bian. Taking the long view of friendship and bisexuality. *In the Family*, pp. 10–12, 22.

Morgan, E. (1991). Levels of analysis and the received view-hermeneutics controversy. *Theoretical and Philosophical Psychology*, 11, 42–55.

Oakley-Melvin, D.A. (1997, February). Dyke or byke? *Icon*, pp. 6, 8–9.

Park, P. (1992). The discovery of participatory research as a new scientific paradigm: Personal and intellectual accounts. *American Sociologist*, 23, 29–42.

Personal Narrative Group (Eds) (1989). *Interpreting women's lives: Feminist theory and personal narratives*. Bloomington: University of Indiana Press.

Plummer, K. (1981). *The making of the modern homosexual*. London: Hutchinson.

Quinn, M. (1997, April 25). Sexual identity crisis sets off debate. *Denver Post*, p. 2F.

Rust, P. (1993). 'Coming out' in the age of social constructionism: Sexual identity formation among lesbian and bisexual women. *Gender and Society*, 7, 50–77.

Sarbin. T.R. (1986). *Narrative psychology: The storied lives of human conduct*. New York: Praeger.

Weeks, J. (1989). *Sex, politics, and society: The regulation of sexuality since 1800* (2nd ed.) London: Longman.

Whisman, V. (1996). *Queer by Choice: Lesbians, Gay Men and the Politics of Identity*. New York: Routledge.

Wilkinson, S. & Kitzinger, C. (Eds) (1995). *Feminism and discourse: Psychological perspectives*. London: Sage.

CPSIA information can be obtained at www.ICGtesting.com
Printed in the USA
270318BV00003B/1-52/P